CW01262042

ENGINEERS MAKING A DIFFERENCE

GATSBY

This book, and its accompanying resources, have been generously supported by the Gatsby Charitable Foundation. The Foundation was set up by Lord Sainsbury to give charitable funding to science, education and arts projects.

Imperial College London

Imperial College London and What on Earth Publishing have worked in collaboration to create this book and its associated resources. Imperial College London is one of the top ten universities in the world and has a strong focus on STEM subjects. www.imperial.ac.uk

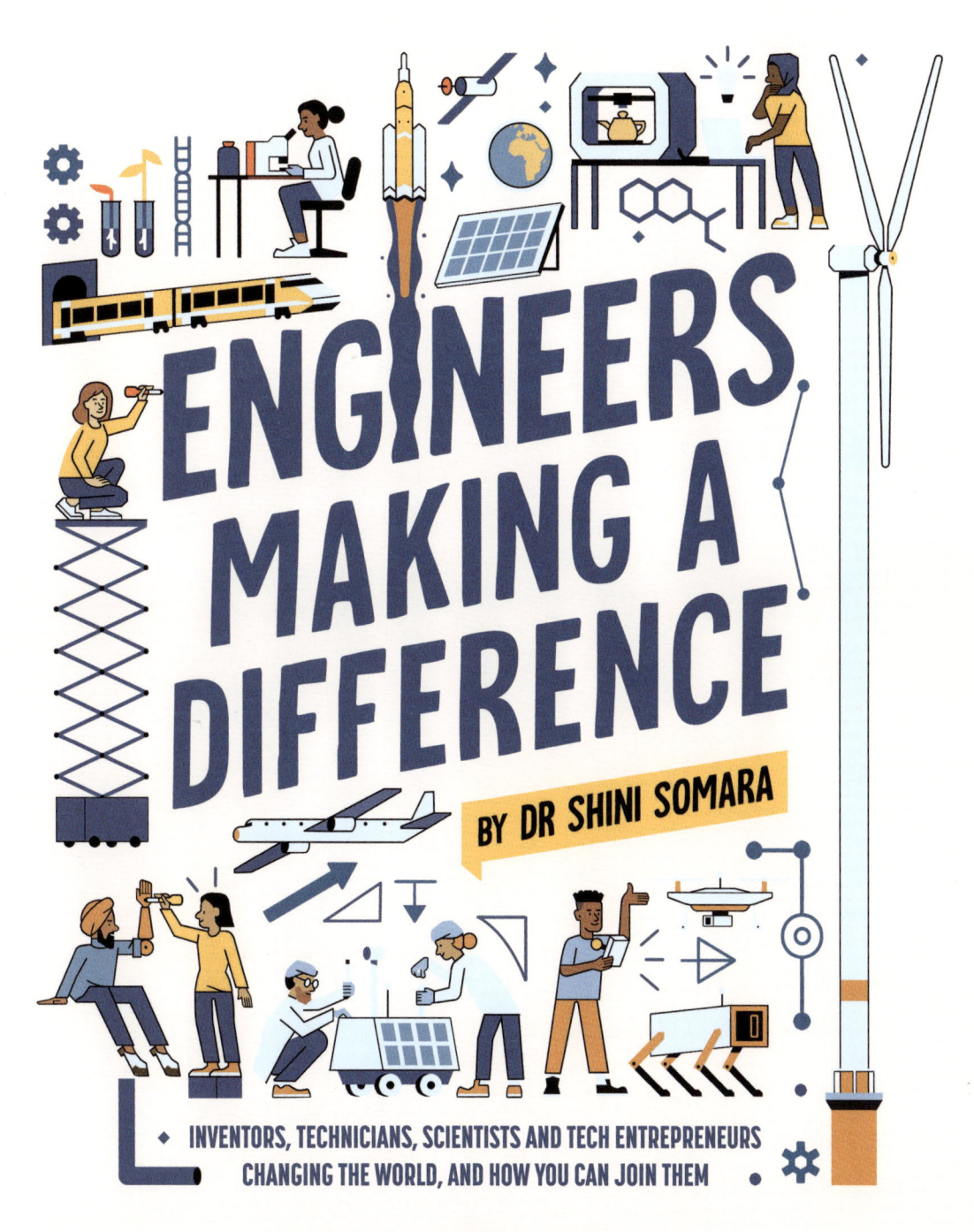

ENGINEERS MAKING A DIFFERENCE

BY DR SHINI SOMARA

INVENTORS, TECHNICIANS, SCIENTISTS AND TECH ENTREPRENEURS CHANGING THE WORLD, AND HOW YOU CAN JOIN THEM

What on Earth Books

Contents

INTRODUCTION 7
    Types of Engineer 10
    Becoming an Engineer 12

1 HUMAN NEEDS 14
    Navjot Sawhney 16
    Dr Natalia Falagán Sama 20
    Ayo Sokale 22
    FARM-FREE 26

2 CLIMATE AND ENVIRONMENT 28
    Dr Benoît Illy 30
    Anna Gates 32
    Pierre Paslier 36
    Dr Lynsey Melville 38
    Anthony Baker 40
    DRONES 44

3 POWERING OUR FUTURE 46
    Katriya Sabin 48
    Samantha Magowan 52
    Manjot Chana 56
    NUCLEAR POWER 60

4 INFRASTRUCTURE AND CONSTRUCTION 62
    Malithi (Milly) Hennayake 64
    Will Arnold 66
    Professor Anastasios Sextos 68
    Georgia Lilley 72
    Heba Bevan 74
    BUILDING WITH MMC 76

5 HEALTHCARE 78
    Alan James Proud 80
    Dr Samantha Micklewright 82
    Dr Arash Angadji 86
    Professor Molly Stevens 88
    Dr Uğur Tanrıverdi 92
    ENGINEERING GENES 94

6 ADVANCED MATERIALS 96
    Mimi Nwosu 98
    Dr Clara Michelle Barker 102
    Professor Tom Ellis 106
    Dr Elena Dieckmann 108
    SUPER CARBON 112

7 COMMUNICATION **114**
   Mike Lawton 116
   Jahangir Shah 120
   Dr Nikita Hari 124
   Professor Mischa Dohler 126
   STAYING CONNECTED 130

8 SMART MANUFACTURING **132**
   Bethany Cousins 134
   Dr Matjaz Vidmar 138
   Kate Todd-Davis 142
   Neil Glover 146
   FACTORIES OF THE FUTURE 148

9 TRANSPORTATION **150**
   Sonny Kombo 152
   Krystina Pearson-Rampeearee 156
   Todd Downs 158
   BATTERY-POWERED TRANSPORT .. 162

10 ENTERTAINMENT **164**
   Pavlina Akritas 166
   Dr David Trevelyan 170
   Michelle Hicks 174
   EXTENDING OUR REALITY 178

11 ROBOTICS AND ARTIFICIAL INTELLIGENCE **180**
   Silas Adekunle 182
   Professor Aldo Faisal 184
   Jennifer Olsen 188
   Joshua Schofield 190
   MACHINES WITH BRAINS 192

12 EXPLORING BEYOND OUR PLANET **194**
   Professor Michele Dougherty 196
   Jamie Pinnell 200
   Dr Veronica Bray Durfey 204
   WATCH THIS SPACE 206

TIMELINE OF ENGINEERING **208**

A FINAL NOTE **213**
   Glossary 214
   Index 218
   Selected Sources 220
   Picture Credits 222

Look out for QR codes throughout the book – these will take you to videos where you can meet the engineers and learn more about their work. For more information, visit:

www.engineers-making-a-difference.com

To Dad, my favourite engineer!

I'm forever grateful for your curiosity, inquisitiveness and everlasting inspiration to bring out the best in myself and others.

INTRODUCTION

I'm really excited to introduce you to a diverse group of incredible engineers who are making a real difference to all our lives. I chose to interview the people in this book because many of them are working on engineering solutions that affect all of us. I wanted to find out more about them, what they do every day at work and what motivates them — and I'm delighted to be sharing their inspiring journeys with you, in the hope that it might excite and enlighten you about the world of engineering.

Like many of the engineers in this book, I was always the kid who took things apart to see what was inside. I loved LEGO® and building things out of anything that I could find. In fact, I regularly turned our lounge upside down building dens out of sofa cushions, blankets and skipping rope, and constructed highways for my toy cars out of whatever building materials I could find nearby.

I have always been curious to understand how things work, and my dad, being a mechanical and electrical engineer himself, encouraged me to investigate. But this wasn't always a good idea… One time, I opened up the back of an old film camera and, because the film was exposed to daylight, we lost all our summer holiday photos from that year! Back then, I didn't know that was how cameras worked, but it's something I have never forgotten since! In fact, my mistakes have taught me more valuable lessons than my successes.

Growing up, my dad inspired me and my two sisters to ask questions and be curious. He was probably the main reason why I chose to follow a STEM career myself. I spent quite a bit of time in his office after school and was fascinated by his giant oak and iron drawing board and stationery collection (which included fine pens, stencils, protractors and rulers). He had to draw all his engineering plans by hand, which was such an intricate and interesting process. Today, engineers draw everything on computers using computer-aided design (CAD). To me, engineering seemed to be creative, hands-on, logical and, most of all, fun!

This drone was made by an engineering team at University College London. I was expecting it to be really heavy, but because it was made from carbon fibre it was surprisingly light!

Not everyone has an engineer in the family and that's okay, because there are plenty of other brilliant engineers out there who can inspire us. I've brought 46 of them together in this book and hope that you can find someone that you relate to and are inspired by – just as I have been. It was fun to find out about the variety of different routes that they all took into this amazing profession.

Engineers love a challenge. They enjoy understanding how things work, fixing things and coming up with ingenious ideas. That's exactly why I studied Mechanical Engineering and I loved every minute of the process – even when lessons were really tough! During my Bachelor of Engineering degree at Brunel University London, I became fascinated with fluid dynamics, an area of engineering that uses mathematics to describe and predict how gases and liquids flow. An understanding of fluid dynamics is useful to engineers when designing aeroplanes and Formula 1 cars, for example.

My fascination led to studying fluid dynamics in depth, and completing a Doctorate in Computational Fluid Dynamics (CFD) following my undergraduate degree. My doctoral research involved improving CFD algorithms, which are the calculations used to predict and simulate how air flows in buildings. This tool was useful during the COVID-19 pandemic because, by understanding how air flows in buildings, we were able to further understand how the virus travels from person to person indoors.

"I believe that engineers are undercover superheroes, who save lives in many different ways, by building safe bridges, planes, medical equipment and much more. Engineers are crucial for a better future, too, as they continue to play a major part in slowing climate change."

Dr Shini Somara

Anyone can be an engineer. You just need to find the thing that interests you most and I guarantee there will be a part of engineering that applies to it. Perhaps there is a particular problem in the world that you would like to solve? If so, then engineering might be for you. In the past, engineers have helped to overcome many big challenges and in the future, there will be many more to face. Perhaps you will become an engineer and help to make our world a better place.

Dr Shini Somara is a Mechanical Engineer, Fluid Dynamicist and Media Broadcaster of science, technology and innovation content.

Types of Engineer

An engineer is someone who designs, builds or maintains engines, machines or structures. You might already know an engineer, or you might have met one who has come to your house to fix your Wi-Fi or an appliance. Engineers work across every bit of human life, from the buildings we live in and the clothes we wear to the food we eat. There are four main pillars of engineering: chemical, civil, electrical and mechanical. From these pillars, more have been built, which cross over and connect with other disciplines. Here you'll find a list of the most common types of engineer today, but there are many more.

Aeronautical engineers work on all things flight-related, from supersonic jet engines to helicopters, drones and new flight-operating systems. These engineers design, test, research, build, produce and maintain new technology for aircraft. Some aerospace engineers also focus on objects in space, such as satellites, rockets and materials used above the atmosphere.

Biomedical engineers focus on the human body. It's the profession where engineering and medicine come together to help people live healthy and happy lives. The human body is complex, so biomedical engineers work in a huge variety of ways. They design surgical devices and artificial organs, develop medicines and maintain important computer software for hospital equipment.

Chemical engineers work, quite simply, with chemicals. Their work can be found in all sorts of day-to-day materials such as hairspray, toothpaste, food and clothes. Chemical engineers work with raw chemicals and dream up ways to transform them into different and useful substances. For example, oil has been used to create plastic, which is used in a multitude of products.

Civil engineers are experts in building. They help to design and build hospitals, bridges, tunnels, roads, water systems, railways, schools and more! A civil engineer can tackle any build with technical know-how and mathematical precision. There are a huge number of specialisations in the world of civil engineering depending on the type of construction and environment.

Environmental engineers use their knowledge of civil engineering to specifically address the environmental issues facing our world today. These engineers are trained to tackle problems such as pollution, the supply of clean water and waste disposal. Environmental engineers think up solutions for large-scale problems in order to create a more sustainable future.

Computer engineers are a tech-savvy bunch. They design and build systems to create cutting-edge computer technology. As a computer engineer, you might work in robotics, with artificial intelligence (AI), in communications or on creating new software and hardware for computer programs. Their works sits between electrical engineering and computer science.

Geotechnical engineers specialise in rock and soil. They come from a branch of civil engineers that test natural surroundings and how they might react to building work. Their jobs include analysing risks in places where there are earthquakes, building railways or installing wind turbines out at sea.

Electrical engineers cover a wide range of areas – think of all the electrical items in a single room, let alone the world! They design, create, fix and maintain electrical systems big and small, such as the power grid that keeps the lights on or microchips in small electronic devices. Electrical engineers can also specialise in areas such as equipment in hospitals or renewable energy.

Materials engineers don't just work with fabric – they get stuck into all matter, from metals and plastic to glass and clay. They could work on anything from new alloys in jet engines to turning recycled materials into new fabric. Materials engineers will often study materials science and engineering before specialising as a materials engineer.

Mechanical engineers create machinery and are responsible for machines such as trains, cars, escalators and aeroplanes. Mechanical engineers understand how things move by studying the interplay of many scientific principles – including the law of gravity and thermodynamics (the study of how heat is linked to energy) – and use that knowledge to build new machines.

Do any of these engineering jobs appeal to you? Maybe you like the sound of more than one of them? An engineer might work in just one of these fields or across many of them. As the world develops and humans face new challenges, the role of engineers will evolve with it. The sky is the limit as to what engineers of the future can do!

Becoming an Engineer

There are many different routes into engineering and many different qualifications that engineers can get along the way. Everyone has their own journey and can choose the path that is right for them. Some engineers choose an academic route that might lead them straight to a university degree after A-levels, but others might choose an apprenticeship so that they can get out into the world of work as soon as possible. Here are some of the most common qualifications in England, Wales and Northern Ireland (the educational system in Scotland has some of these qualifications, but also some different options) that will help you on your journey to becoming an engineer.

GCSEs are the last big milestone for examinations at secondary school in England, Wales and Northern Ireland. From the ages of 14 to 16, students take lessons in 10 different areas of study. Mathematics and science are compulsory and are important subjects for becoming an engineer.

NVQs (National Vocational Qualifications) are work-based qualifications that you can complete at any age. They train you on the job and grade you based on your performance at work. This can lead to apprenticeships in the engineering sector as an alternative to a standard university degree.

A-levels follow GCSEs for students aged 16+. Over two years, you will study three or more subjects of your choice. Those who are interested in studying engineering at university level should take A-level maths, plus a relevant science subject.

T-Levels are an alternative to A-levels that you can take after your GCSEs. During a T-level, you spend 80 per cent of your time in a classroom learning core subjects and 20 per cent of your time in an industry placement, learning the skills needed for your chosen career.

Apprenticeships are offered in all sectors of engineering, from aerospace to energy. An apprenticeship means working and learning on the job while getting paid. You can also study part-time for qualifications, such as a university degree, at the same time.

BSc (Bachelor of Science) is an undergraduate degree (meaning that it's your first degree), which typically lasts a minimum of three years. It covers all science and technology-related subjects. Your chosen subjects are studied in depth and will involve lectures, seminars, essay writing and lab work.

BEng or BSE (Bachelor of Engineering) is an undergraduate level of study at university in one of the engineering sciences. You might begin by studying core engineering topics and then specialise in subjects such as biomedical, chemical or electrical engineering. It is academically equal to a BSc.

BSc Honours is similar to an undergraduate BSc but is more specialised in the subject matters and more advanced. Due to a higher workload than a BSc, they are also considered to be slightly more valuable as a qualification.

MSc (Master of Science) is a postgraduate degree, which means it is taken after an undergraduate course is completed. An MSc usually lasts one year and gives you the opportunity to strengthen your technical skills and become a specialist in your area of interest.

MEng (Master of Engineering) is a specialised Master's degree in engineering and typically lasts four years. This is a great option for those who intend to work in engineering and who aim to become a chartered engineer.

PhD (Doctor of Philosophy) is the highest level of academic study available (along with the EngD – see below). It usually takes three to four years to complete if you study full-time and involves carrying out unique research to produce a thesis (a long essay). Your thesis could contribute to the growing pool of scientific knowledge and help shape the future of thought and practice in your subject.

EngD (Doctor of Engineering) is similar to a PhD, but the difference is that an EngD puts more emphasis on engineering research that suits the needs of the industry. They are intended for people who wish to advance their practical skills. At the end of both a PhD and an EngD, the person will be given the title Dr.

Chartership is a special qualification that is awarded to someone who has practical experience in industry and has proven to have the scientific and technical knowledge required for their job. An Engineering Chartership is awarded by the Engineering Council.

QUALIFICATION LEVELS

	LEVEL	TYPE OF QUALIFICATION
UNIVERSITY	8	DOCTORATE PhD, EngD
UNIVERSITY	7	MASTER'S DEGREE MEng, MSc, MA (Master of Arts)
UNIVERSITY	6	UNDERGRADUATE DEGREE BEng/BSE, BSc, BA (Bachelor of Arts)
UNIVERSITY	5	UNDERGRADUATE DEGREE BEng/BSE, BSc, BA (Bachelor of Arts)
UNIVERSITY	4	UNDERGRADUATE DEGREE BEng/BSE, BSc, BA (Bachelor of Arts)
COLLEGE	3	A-LEVEL
SCHOOL	2	GCSE Grades A–C
SCHOOL	1	GCSE Grades D–G

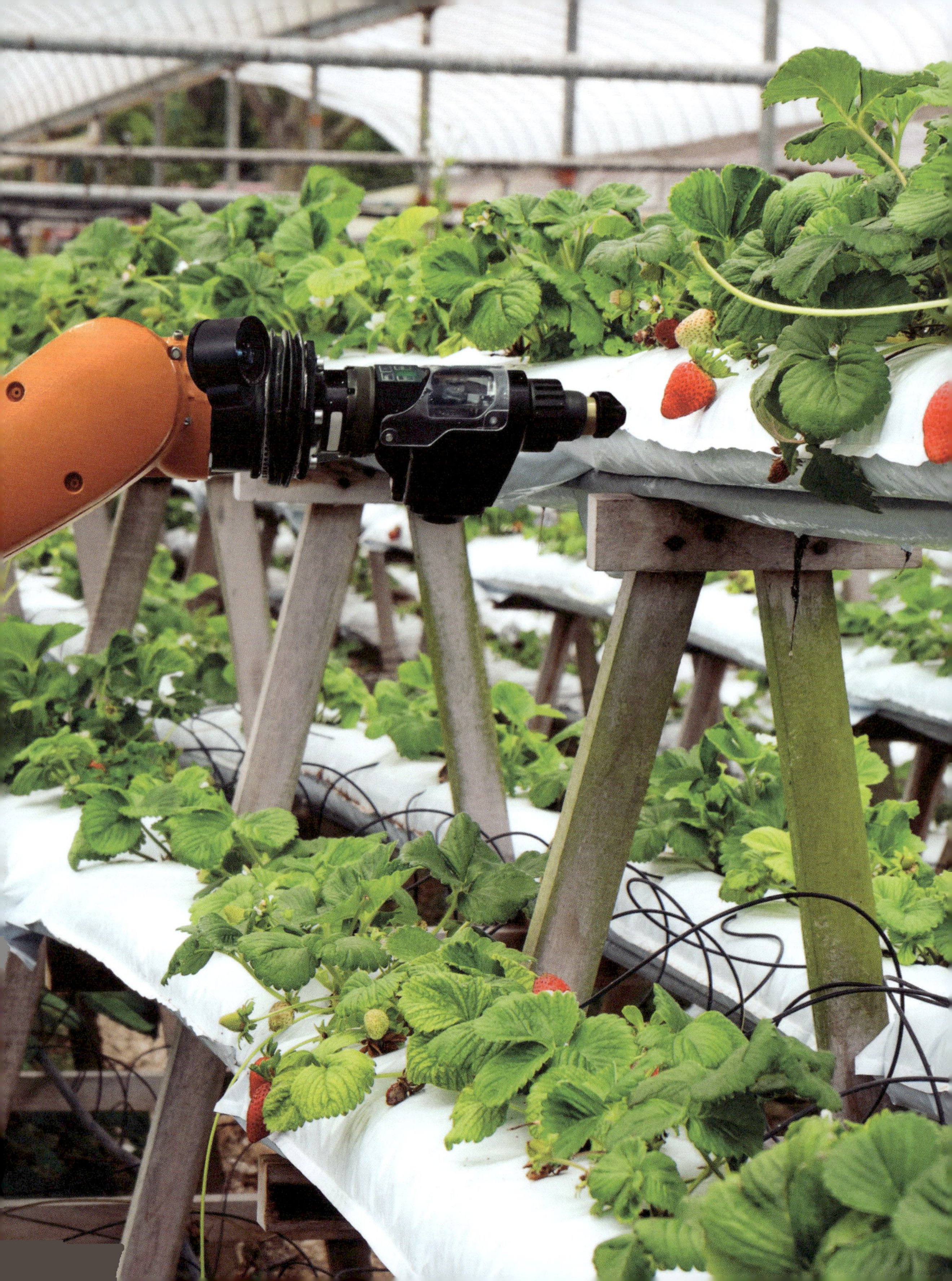

CHAPTER 1

HUMAN NEEDS

We all need certain things to survive and live comfortably: access to clean drinking water, food, a safe and secure place to live and clothes to keep us warm. Throughout history, engineers have created ingenious tools and systems to meet these needs. Spears are an example of primitive engineering and helped humans to hunt and feed themselves. Since then, many other useful mechanisms have been engineered – tractors, cranes, ovens and refrigerators to name just a few.

Providing for these basic needs will always keep engineers busy. They are often faced with challenges caused by our changing climate and rapidly increasing global population. As ice caps melt, sea levels rise and the demand for more food continues to grow, engineers must find ways to make our lifestyles more sustainable.

By the year 2050, it's predicted that there will be around 9.7 billion human beings on Earth. They will all need to be fed, sheltered and have access to healthcare and sanitation. Engineers have plenty to do to help the lives of others – now and in the future – across all sectors of engineering. In this chapter, we meet three engineers who are using their skills in mechanical, agricultural and civil engineering to make a difference to the lives of people all over the world.

LEFT: In order to save space, many crops can now be grown in vertical farms. Farmers are helped by robot assistants that can detect what the crops need to grow and stay healthy. The robots are then able to provide for these needs.

the
washing
machine
project

Navjot Sawhney

AEROSPACE, AERONAUTICAL AND ASTRONAUTICAL ENGINEER AND CEO
PROVIDING ENGINEERING SOLUTIONS TO THOSE WHO NEED THEM MOST

Navjot Sawhney is the founder of The Washing Machine Project, which designs, manufactures and distributes low-cost manual washing machines. These human-powered machines save time, water and effort for the millions of people, usually women, who have no choice but to handwash clothes for themselves and their families.

WHY DID YOU BECOME AN ENGINEER?

My parents fled India in the 1940s to escape the war that was happening there. They moved to the UK in the 1980s, and I was born in London. From an early age, I learnt of the harrowing experiences that my parents had suffered and became familiar with the concepts of loss, displacement and hard work.

> *"I wanted to use my engineering skills to help the disadvantaged rather than just create things for people who already had so much."*
>
> **Navjot Sawhney**

My father was an aerospace engineer and would often take me to air shows. I was fascinated with how massive machines could stay in the sky. Full of curiosity, I would raid my father's toolbox to take apart every home appliance, not really knowing how to put them back together again.

My father passed away when I was eight years old, so I grew up amongst the women of my family: my mum, her five sisters and my two older sisters. I truly appreciated their role in our household as I saw how much work they did and the trouble they went through just to allow us all to get by in life.

I went to university to study Aerospace Engineering where I learnt to design and build spacecraft. After graduating, I got a fantastic job at Dyson, one of the world's leading technology companies. I was in the Research and Innovation Team, and it was an awesome experience, but something was missing.

I needed a change of direction, so I applied to Engineers Without Borders for an 18-month placement in rural southern India. Engineers Without Borders started in the early 1980s to allow engineers to share their time and skills with local people. The organisation has helped to improve infrastructure in many communities around the world and as a result has had a positive impact on the health, safety and general day-to-day lives of more than 1,600,000 people.

The Engineers Without Borders project that I signed up for was to design and build stoves that ran on solid fuel, in collaboration with Prakti, an engineering organisation based in India. To me, this was the chance of a lifetime, but a difficult choice to make because it involved having to quit my highly paid job for an unpaid role. My family were worried that I was making a big mistake.

AND WAS IT A BIG MISTAKE?

No! This experience made me a better engineer. Through creating low-cost and low-emission stoves, I found purpose and meaning in engineering and reassurance that it was the right career for me.

The fuel used in Prakti stoves doesn't create as much smoke as fires that burn wood or charcoal. This is better for the health of the people using them.

Every week was productive: on Monday we would brainstorm ideas, Tuesday build prototypes, Wednesday test the prototypes, Thursday assess our results and by Friday, we might have solved one of the challenges that we were facing. We existed in a living lab, where local women used our prototypes and gave us immediate feedback.

This was only the beginning of what engineering could do for this community. During the time that I was there, I experienced first-hand the problems that these people faced – the unstable electricity, frequent power cuts, no access to fuel, open sewers and dirty drinking water. They needed a multitude of engineering solutions and this was what inspired The Washing Machine Project.

My next door neighbour in the village was a young mother called Divya. She spent hours each day doing unpaid jobs, for example waiting in line for fresh water and food and handwashing clothes. This work was backbreaking and many women suffered from joint pain and skin irritation as a result. I promised to create Divya a low-cost washing machine and returned to the UK on this mission.

HOW DID YOU DEVELOP YOUR HAND-POWERED WASHING MACHINE?

An engineer needs to fully understand a problem in order to solve it, so, a couple of engineering friends and I interviewed more than 3,000 people in 17 countries about how they wash their clothes. We learnt that techniques varied all over the world, but what people had in common was a sense of pride in providing clean clothes for their families, an enjoyment of social interaction and a need to reduce water consumption and physical labour.

We also researched existing handwashing devices on the market and found machines designed for 'glamping' trips (i.e. glamorous camping) and SpinCycle, a washing machine powered by cycling. Nothing low-cost and stand-alone existed that could help the disadvantaged. My mum's salad spinner was a source of inspiration for the gear technology in the machine, and it took one year to design and build our first prototype.

HOW HAS THE PROJECT DEVELOPED SINCE THAT FIRST TEST?

Since then our prototype has gone from strength to strength, and we have now distributed it in 15 countries. Our team has grown to six people strong and we are already working on our next projects, which include refrigeration, lighting and air conditioning. The next nine to 12 months will be a really crucial time for us as we move and scale up our production. In the next few years, The Washing Machine Project is on track to distribute 12,500 washing machines across 27 countries.

FACT FILE

Most fun thing about your job: The best thing about my job is that I get to have a positive impact on people every day. Giving people back the dignity of clean clothes is one of the most fulfilling things you can imagine.

CAREER HIGHLIGHTS

1. Quitting a high-paying corporate job to make stoves in South India.

2. Being inspired by my next door neighbour to improve her life and founding The Washing Machine Project as a result.

3. Leading an inspirational bunch of people to make a positive impact in the world.

HAND-POWERED WASHING MACHINE

The washing machine is portable and can be easily constructed.

Dirty clothes, water and washing detergent are put in the top.

The handle is turned by hand to rotate the drum and wash the clothes.

Dr Natalia Falagán Sama

AGRICULTURAL ENGINEER
WORKING TO REDUCE FOOD WASTE

One of the things that humans can't live without is food. And thanks to many people throughout history, we have lots of ingenious ways to grow, make and store it. However, with more people living on the planet than ever before, it is becoming increasingly difficult to ensure that everyone has the food that they need.

Dr Falagán Sama is an Agricultural Engineer and a Lecturer in Food Science and Technology at Cranfield University, near Milton Keynes. She is an expert in food systems and focuses her work on post-harvest solutions for fruits and vegetables, which means the ways in which we keep food fresh after it has been harvested. There are many things that Natalia needs to consider in her work, such as the temperature that the food is stored in, the gases that it becomes exposed to (which can cause it to ripen faster) and also the packaging that it is kept in.

WHAT MADE YOU WANT TO BECOME AN AGRICULTURAL ENGINEER?

I was always a very curious child, and I really enjoyed nature and building things with my hands. I discovered that agricultural engineering combined these two areas: learning about how our natural environment works and designing technology that helps us protect and use natural resources in a more efficient way. Agricultural engineering is really important because it has a direct impact on people and the food they eat.

WHAT IS MOST REWARDING ABOUT YOUR WORK?

The best thing is when I see something that I have developed actually being used! For example, going into a supermarket and seeing how my work is used to create packaging that keeps fruits and vegetables fresh for longer. In my research, I study biological processes, such as how some fruits become ripe, then help to design technology that can maintain the quality and safety of these fruits for as long as possible. In the right conditions, food can last a really long time: for example, potatoes can be stored for up to a year! But a lot of research goes into finding just the right environment for them to be kept in. By doing my job, I hope to reduce food loss and waste.

WHAT CHALLENGES DO YOU FACE IN YOUR JOB?

One challenge is that I have to work with lots of different people and organisations and often, when we solve one problem, it can create a new problem elsewhere! The supply of food is a global challenge that requires the help of everyone from engineers to energy and refrigeration experts, soil experts and even psychologists who can help us to understand the way people shop. Fixing these problems also involves the government, people in academia and food companies. It's easy to take food for granted if we live in a place where it's readily available in shops, but so much work and research is required to keep every grape and grain fresh.

FACT FILE

Most fun thing about your job: I have the chance to learn new things every day!

CAREER HIGHLIGHTS

1. Seeing the impact of my work in the real world.

2. My choice of an Agricultural Engineering degree has opened up so many possibilities for me to follow my dreams.

3. Having the opportunity to teach a new generation of food experts to tackle global challenges.

"Don't take for granted that you have food in the supermarket – think about where that food came from. If that sparks an interest, then perhaps agricultural engineering is for you!"

Dr Natalia Falagán Sama

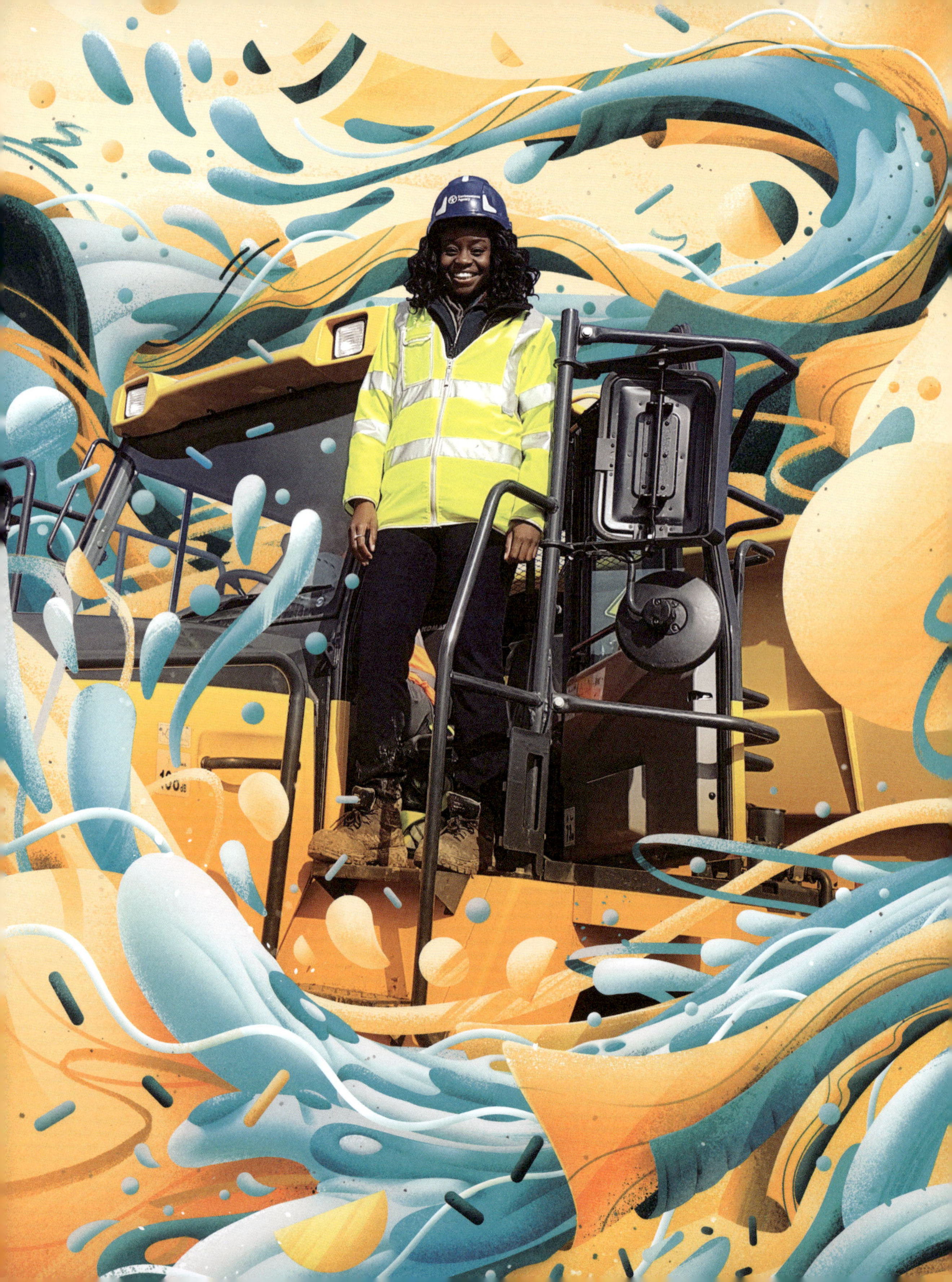

Ayo Sokale

CIVIL ENGINEER

IMPROVING PEOPLE'S LIVES THROUGH FLOOD DEFENCES

Ayo Sokale is a Chartered Civil Engineer who specialises in flood risk management and water resourcing (ensuring that water is well-managed) at the Environment Agency. Ayo works to protect environments and make them better for people and wildlife to live in. Sometimes, Ayo must find ways to contain water and stop it from damaging people's homes, other times she needs to make sure it's available in areas that it's required. It's all in a day's work for a civil engineer!

WHAT DOES YOUR JOB INVOLVE?

Many homes are at risk of flooding, which can be catastrophic for the people who live in them. Currently, 5.2 million homes in the UK are at risk of flooding, and by the year 2065 the number of properties built on flood plains is set to double. This is due to increasing populations and the effects of rising sea levels caused by global warming. So, the need for flood risk management is ever increasing and the time to act is now.

> "Engineering is about solving problems, and anyone can solve problems if they are passionate, hard-working and care about people. That's what engineering needs!"
>
> **Ayo Sokale**

My first task on a flood engineering project is to identify how an area floods. This might include visiting the site and talking to local residents to gain an understanding of how their lives are being affected. From there, I can explore ways to deal with the problem. I then work with others to find the right solution and ensure that it can be funded. Amongst many factors, we need to make sure that the solutions we create are good value for money.

I always try to find low-carbon solutions that maintain the biodiversity (the variety of wildlife and plants) in the area. There are many things that can be done to achieve this, for example using low-carbon concrete, energy from renewable sources and fuel alternatives, such as vegetable oil, to power machinery. Engineers also try to work harmoniously with the natural environment and plan our projects well in order to reduce the amount of materials we waste.

WHAT HAS BEEN THE MOST REWARDING AND IMPACTFUL PROJECT YOU HAVE WORKED ON?

The Tull Way Flood Alleviation Scheme was really rewarding. Tull Way is a busy road in the town of Thatcham in Berkshire and the project was built to help a local community that had been badly flooded. The flooding occurred when water rushed down a nearby hill after heavy rainfall and overwhelmed the sewers in the area. It took ten years from the initial flooding to develop a surface water management plan and then to progress the scheme and start construction.

Our final solution involved building a bund, or embankment, which is a structure made of earth that traps and stores excess flood water. The bund was built at the bottom of the hill to stop water from flowing across the road and into the town. It acts like a reservoir, collecting and storing the water. A structure called a penstock valve controls the rate at which the water flows into the sewer. This significantly reduced the flood risk to over 250 properties in the area.

I supervised the construction of the bund, ensuring that the work matched the design and the quality was up to scratch. A few years after construction was completed, it rained really heavily in this area and our solution was put to the test. I'm happy to say that it worked!

HOW THE BUND WORKS

Most of the bund is below ground. It was built to blend in with the scenery and become part of the landscape.

— homes

— Tull Way Road

reservoir

Pipe for water to flow into sewer.

rain

Water being held in the reservoir.

penstock valve

The penstock valve works like a tap – it can open and close to control how fast the water flows into the sewer.

WHY DID YOU CHOOSE TO WORK IN FLOOD MANAGEMENT?

I was born in Kent, but grew up in Nigeria, Africa, which is a less-developed country than the UK. During my childhood, I watched the development of infrastructure and saw how much of a positive impact it had on life there. Witnessing this first-hand showed me how important and powerful engineering is in transforming people's lives. I wanted to be able to help people in the same way.

HOW WOULD YOU DESCRIBE YOUR ENGINEERING JOURNEY?

I was determined to become an engineer from a really young age, and my parents and other people around me helped me towards my goal. I had really supportive teachers and brilliant mentors. My maths teacher gave me additional school work, which really helped me. At secondary school, I had a wonderful design technology teacher who encouraged me to join an after-school engineering club. Organisations such as WISE (Women In Science and Engineering) and the Engineering Development Trust provided courses where I was introduced to all different types of engineering. Work experience also gave me a lot of great opportunities to apply my engineering studies to real life. I have always been keen and hard-working and have followed my interests by staying curious and asking lots of questions.

WHAT IS THE SECRET TO BEING A GOOD ENGINEER?

Always be authentic to yourself – discover what your natural skills are and develop them. It helps to work out what you enjoy and what problem in the world you want to solve. Growing up, I often felt like I didn't fit in and thought that being different was a bad thing. But now I know that everyone is different, and that's great! As an engineer, working with a diverse group of people is ideal because everyone brings new ideas to the table. I was diagnosed with autism around seven years ago and I often see things from a different angle to others, which is a real asset.

My secret is that I am continuously learning, which helps me to grow and improve, and with that comes a good attitude towards failure. I live big and do big things by being comfortable with making mistakes and learning from them. Even if you feel scared, don't let it stop you! Failing is not a reflection of you, it's an indication that you tried.

FACT FILE

Most fun thing about your job: When my projects work and people are protected – it makes me feel like a superhero!

CAREER HIGHLIGHTS

1. Completing a Master's degree in Civil Engineering at the University of Plymouth.

2. Being chosen as an Institution of Civil Engineers (ICE) future leader and working on the ICE review of the Grenfell Tower accident.

3. Achieving Chartered Engineer status in just three years.

Farm-Free

The world's expanding population means there is a bigger demand for food and space than ever before. Currently, 38 per cent of land on Earth is used for the farming of animals and crops, and the numbers of fish in our seas are dwindling. A solution could lie in these lab-grown foods.

A MEATY ISSUE In 2013, the first lab-grown burger was served up on a plate. It took three months to develop under carefully monitored conditions, from a few cells taken from a sample of animal muscle. This process is called cellular agriculture, but also known by a few other names including in-vitro meat and synthetic meat. It could be the solution to challenges posed by consuming and rearing livestock, which has a negative impact on the environment. Compared to crops, farming animals requires large areas of land and water and can produce huge quantities of greenhouse gases. Growing meat in a lab could also end meat shortages, reduce the illnesses carried by animals and eliminate the need to farm animals in a cruel and inhumane way.

LAB-GROWN The complex process engineers use to create in-vitro meat is called tissue engineering. It all starts with satellite cells – a kind of stem cell that usually takes part in muscle repair. The second requirement is 3D scaffolding, which encourages the cells to grow in certain ways and shapes.

Attaching themselves to the sponge-like scaffolds, the cells multiply and form into stripes, much like the way muscle cells form fibres in living animals. A machine floods the fibres with a nutrient-rich liquid that contains animal blood. It also stretches the fibres, in the same way we stretch and exercise our muscles in the gym to encourage them to increase their size and protein content. When the tissue has grown to a reasonable size, it can then be seasoned, cooked and eaten.

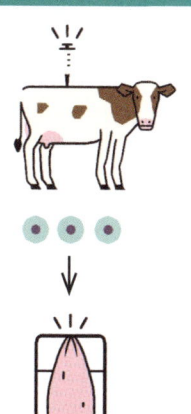

Muscle cells are taken from the animal using local anaesthetic, so the animal isn't hurt.

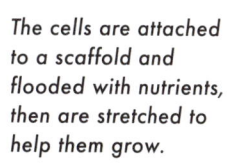

The cells are attached to a scaffold and flooded with nutrients, then are stretched to help them grow.

Once the cells have grown enough, the 'meat' can be cooked and eaten.

Synthetic meat is created by taking animal cells and encouraging them to multiply and grow in a certain shape.

SCALING UP Engineers have been working to figure out how to take synthetic meat that has been made by hand in a lab and make a lot of it quickly and cheaply. To grow cells industrially requires a large bioreactor – a high-tech vat that can provide the perfect conditions for culturing cells, but also the movement and stimulation to exercise them. A bioreactor with a capacity of 300,000 litres (about one-tenth the size of an Olympic swimming pool) could make enough meat for around 75,000 people (assuming they each eat ten kilograms of cultured meat per year).

BEYOND MEAT In-vitro fish can be grown in a similar way to in-vitro meat. This might stop the population of fish in the oceans from dropping and also make sure that the 'fish' we eat is free of plastic and metal. Real fish often eat rubbish from the water, which humans can eat without realising. But it's not just animal flesh that is being engineered – it's artificial milk and hen-free egg whites too. The possibilities could be endless!

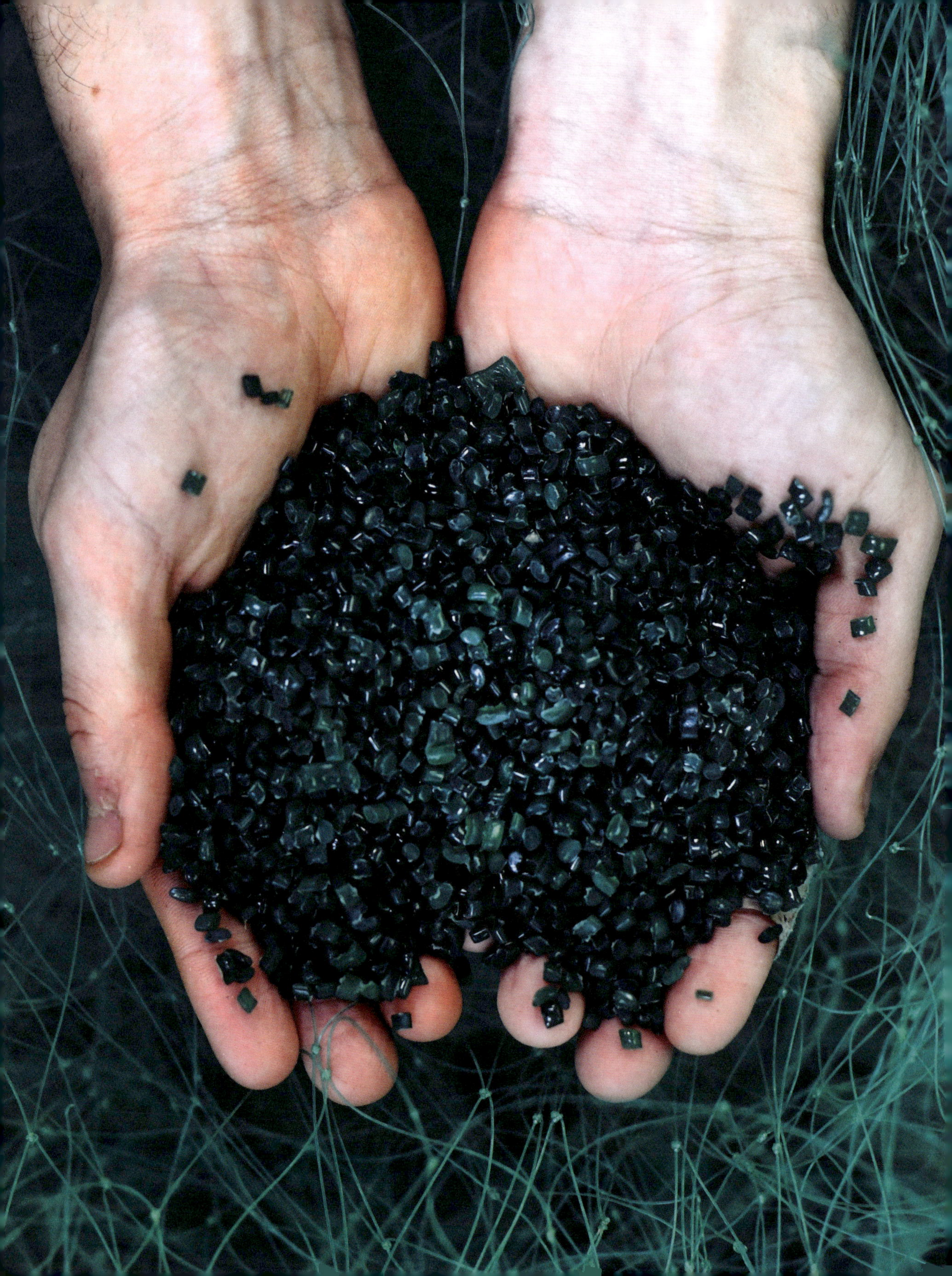

CHAPTER 2

CLIMATE AND ENVIRONMENT

Human existence puts a strain on our planet. We use Earth's resources for food, energy and materials, but in turn we create waste and pollution. Engineers have played a big part in providing us with what we need to live comfortable lives. However, as our needs increase, their focus has had to shift to finding solutions that protect the planet for future generations.

Sustainable solutions are those that are not harmful to the environment and don't unnecessarily reduce natural resources – instead they aim to be more harmonious with the planet. In the past, we have lived in an unsustainable way, only generating electricity from fossil fuels, such as coal and oil, and pumping massive quantities of greenhouse gases, particularly carbon dioxide, into our atmosphere. Over time, this way of living has caused the climate to change at a faster rate. Engineers can help us find solutions that slow down or even reverse the harmful consequences of our past choices.

Sustainability will come in the form of renewable energy, renewable materials and smart and efficient systems and processes. In this chapter, we meet five engineers who are determined to protect our environment with the innovative and exciting work that they do.

LEFT: Plastic pellets made from old fishing nets that are ready to be made into new items.

Dr Benoît Illy

MATERIALS ENGINEER
TRANSFORMING CO_2 INTO WEARABLE FASHION

Many of the things that we use every single day have been carefully engineered. Clothing, for example, can be engineered to be lightweight, warm, waterproof or durable – or all of those things and more! And increasingly, the fabric itself is engineered to be kind to the environment.

The fashion industry uses huge quantities of materials, contributing to ten per cent of humanity's carbon emissions. The production of materials and the way that they are disposed of are both causes of these excessive carbon emissions and many engineers are working to find better and more efficient solutions.

Dr Benoît Illy has used his experience of nanotechnology (the study and manipulation of extremely small things) to develop an incredible new solution. Not only does it stop carbon dioxide (CO_2) from being released into the atmosphere, but it makes something useful with it too!

WHY DID YOU CHOOSE TO STUDY MATERIALS?

I have always loved maths and physics, and this naturally led to me doing a PhD (Doctor of Philosophy) in Materials Science. I learnt that I felt completely at home in a lab, experimenting and discovering what materials could do. For my PhD, I developed cells to make solar panels more powerful and efficient. I then created a material that improves the thermal efficiency of buildings – helping them to stay warm in winter and cool in summer. This material stops heat from being wasted and encouraged me to do more to help the planet.

WHAT JOB DO YOU DO TODAY?

Today, I run a company called Fairbrics that develops an innovative textile fabric from the excess carbon dioxide in our atmosphere. My career has been driven by sustainability more than money. I am passionate about developing materials that have a positive impact on the planet.

I was determined to do something about the problem of excess carbon in the atmosphere and was inspired by the growth cycle of trees. Trees breathe in carbon dioxide and use sunlight to convert it into natural fibres. At Fairbrics, we wanted to do the same. Instead of using sunlight, we combine electricity with carbon dioxide and water to make our own polyester fibres that are wearable. As a result, our technology is a carbon-negative material, meaning that it consumes more carbon dioxide than it emits during its manufacturing. We are still at the lab stage in the development of this fabric, but our goal is to have our first product on the market in 2023, to contribute to the increasing trend of sustainability in fashion.

FACT FILE

Most fun thing about your job: When I wake up every morning, I look forward to overcoming new challenges on projects that I truly believe in. It's an adventure!

CAREER HIGHLIGHTS

1. Obtaining a PhD and working extremely hard on a topic to become a world expert.

2. Moving to the USA – leaving my comfortable position and taking a risk to build something new.

3. Creating my company and taking ownership of the problems I care about.

THE FAIRBRICS PROCESS

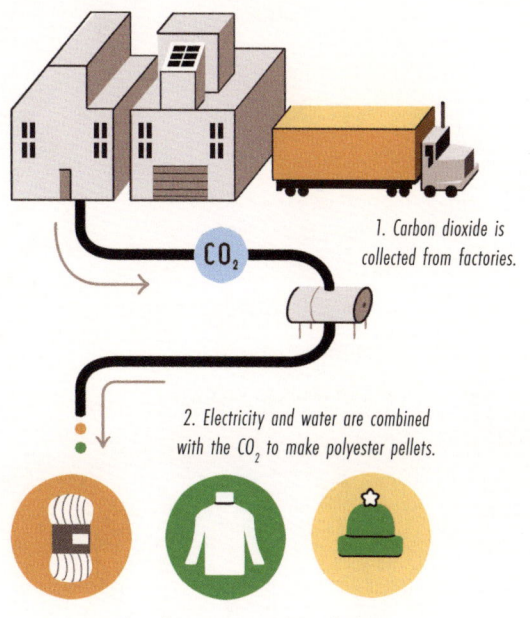

1. Carbon dioxide is collected from factories.

2. Electricity and water are combined with the CO_2 to make polyester pellets.

3. The pellets are then used to make fabric.

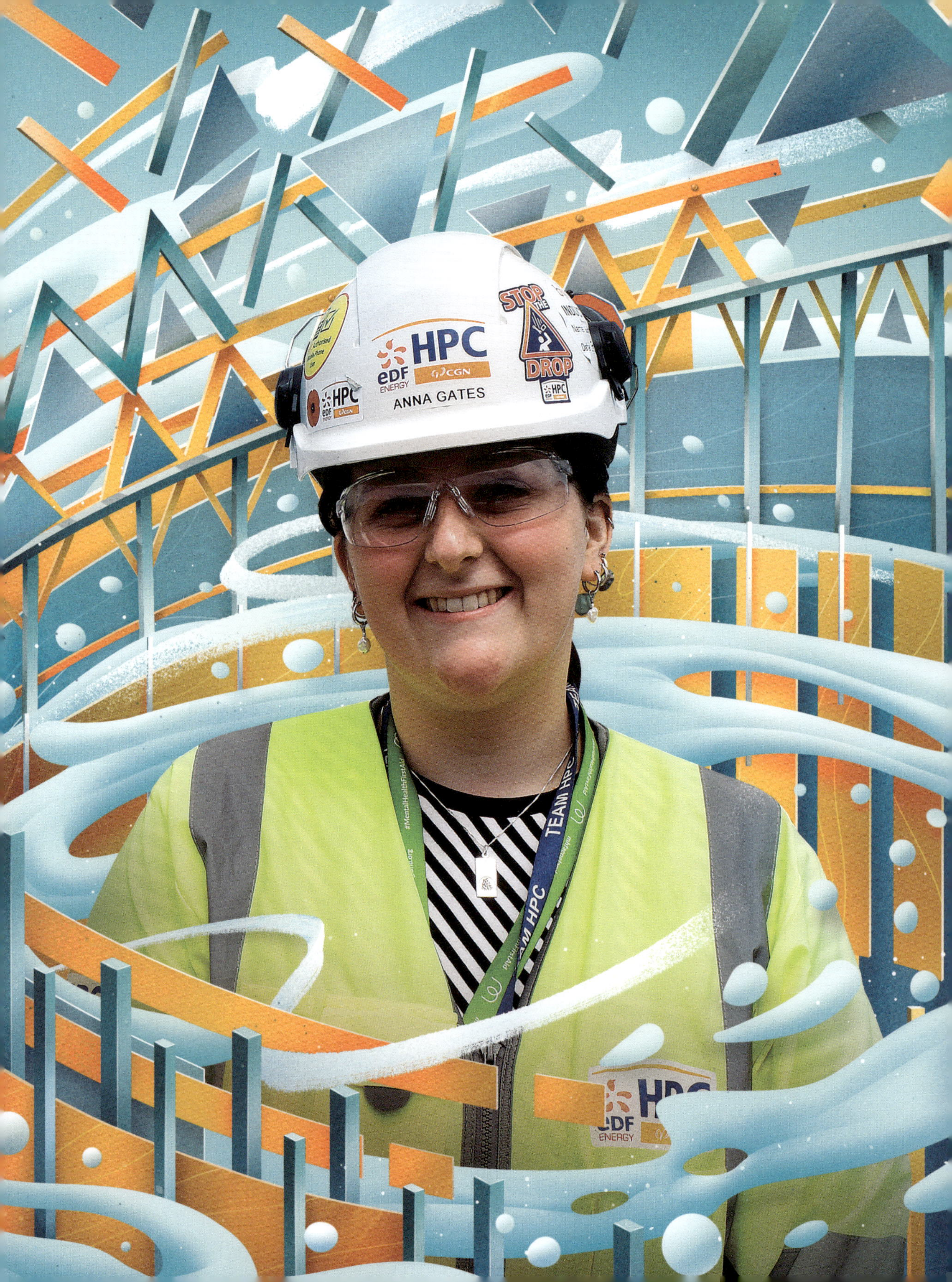

HPC
EDF ENERGY
CGN
ANNA GATES
STOP THE DROP
TEAM HPC

Anna Gates

CIVIL ENGINEERING APPRENTICE
CONSTRUCTING SAFE ENERGY SOLUTIONS

It has been a quarter of a century since the UK last built a new nuclear power station. This is all set to change in 2027 with the opening of Hinkley Point C in Somerset. It's an exciting project that will provide energy to approximately six million homes and will contribute seven per cent of the UK's electricity needs. Over the plant's 60–80 year lifetime, Hinkley Point C promises to reduce further carbon emissions. During this timeframe, it will generate less carbon dioxide than wind or solar power plants, and by avoiding the need to burn fossil fuels, the plant will save nine million tonnes of carbon dioxide a year. Even its construction has been kind to the environment – the steel reinforcement used to build the plant is made from 98 per cent recycled steel sourced in the UK. Ships are also being used to deliver materials – just one delivery by sea keeps 110 lorries off the road. Anna Gates, a Civil Engineering Apprentice, has been hard at work on this project.

WHY DID YOU CHOOSE A CAREER IN ENGINEERING?

I've always had a passion for the environment, probably because I'm part of a generation that grew up with disturbing headlines about melting ice caps and starving polar bears. It left me feeling worried and wanting to do my bit to help.

A lightbulb switched on for me, aged 15, when an employee from Network Rail gave a talk at our all-girls school about his career in civil engineering. I learnt about infrastructure and the impact it has on the environment.

"Engineering was a career where I could apply my love of maths and physics to positively impact the environment."

Anna Gates

HOW ARE YOU ACHIEVING YOUR GOAL OF BECOMING A CIVIL ENGINEER?

My school suggested I should go to university, but instead I chose a degree apprenticeship in Civil Engineering. I go to university part-time but also work for EDF Energy at Hinkley Point C. Alongside all this, I have also chosen to apply for Chartership accreditation with the Institute of Civil Engineers.

To juggle all these different commitments, I have had to make a number of adjustments, including moving away from London where I grew up and learning to manage my money. During the first two years of my apprenticeship, I struggled to stay organised, but now I'm in my third year and I'm getting into the swing of things!

CAN YOU DESCRIBE WHAT YOU DO IN YOUR DAY-TO-DAY JOB?

I am part of the Health, Safety and Environment team, so I am often on the construction site ensuring that we are meeting the strict safety and environmental standards required in the UK. I help to make sure that the 8,000 people working onsite are staying safe. I also have to communicate any construction changes to the wider team to make sure everyone's informed. Another part of my role is working with the Environment Agency and actively monitoring the air quality at Hinkley Point C.

One of the two reactors being built at Hinkley Point C.

At the moment, we are building a structure that will house a massive turbine at the power station. When the turbine is turned on, it'll convert steam into electricity. One of the highlights of my career so far has been witnessing the giant steel columns being installed.

My work is very hands-on, but at university I hit the books and study everything from structural materials to construction and site management, which are all relevant to my work. For example, this knowledge helps me to understand which engineer is best placed to answer certain questions that I might have.

WHAT IS IT LIKE WORKING WITH OTHER EXPERTS?

I started my apprenticeship as a shy 18-year-old, having only worked with others in small lab groups at school. Initially, I was quite overwhelmed. Everything seemed so new and unfamiliar, but I quietly pushed through and realised that I didn't need to know everything all the time – other people are there to help. Our teams at work are really diverse – some people are more academic and others are more practical – but everyone's skills and ideas are equally as important. Over the past couple of years, my confidence has skyrocketed. Everything I have learnt is fitting together, and I am establishing my own area of expertise. I now love learning from others and having others learn from me!

WERE THERE ANY STEREOTYPES THAT YOU HAD ABOUT APPRENTICESHIPS?

There were three: 1. Apprentices only make tea; 2. Apprentices only obtain low-level qualifications and stay at low levels for their entire careers; 3. Apprentices are not as educated and don't get degrees. So far, I have smashed all three outdated stereotypes. In fact, I wish I had time to make tea!

WOULD YOU ADVISE PEOPLE TO FOLLOW IN YOUR FOOTSTEPS?

I would 100 per cent recommend apprenticeships! I've learnt so much and gained so many friends, colleagues and experiences. I'm getting a degree while being paid a great salary – what's not to love? My advice is to be confident enough to say yes to every opportunity that interests you because you will always learn something new about yourself.

FACT FILE

Most fun thing about your job: The variety and diversity of the people I work with means we're always having a laugh while getting our work done.

CAREER HIGHLIGHTS

1. Passing my physics A-level (which at one point I didn't think was going to happen!)

2. Meeting friends for life at university.

3. The day I had enough confidence to step onsite for the first time without a manager.

Pierre Paslier

MATERIALS DESIGN ENGINEER

REDUCING PLASTIC POLLUTION WITH SMART SEAWEED PACKAGING

Millions of tonnes of plastic are discarded every year, and a lot of it is single-use food and drinks packaging. Less than a tenth of all plastic is recycled – the rest pollutes the environment. A company called Notpla (which stands for 'not plastic') was started in London in 2014 by Pierre Paslier and Rodrigo García González to address this problem. Notpla have developed biodegradable packaging, that easily decomposes, out of seaweed. The product is called Ooho and is a transparent packaging for bite-sized servings of water, juices, sauces and other liquids. Ooho is completely edible or it can be composted in four to six weeks.

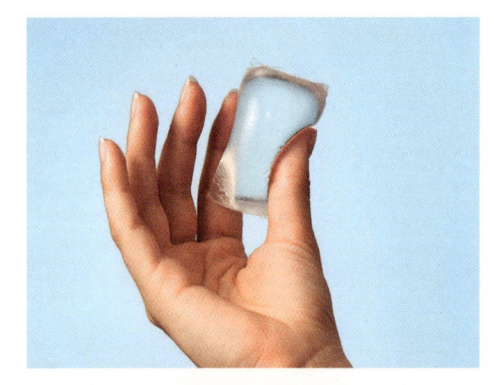

Ooho products are made using an innovative manufacturing process that transforms seaweed extracts into transparent, edible sachets and packets.

WHY DID YOU DECIDE TO BECOME AN ENGINEER?

From a young age I wanted to be an inventor. I spent hours playing with LEGO bricks and taking household products apart. I was good at science and maths, so engineering was suggested as a career path. But I also had an interest in design, which felt in conflict with engineering. At that time, France did not have any studies that embraced the crossover of these two worlds. After my baccalaureate (the French equivalent of A-levels), it was a tough choice to decide between art or engineering school. Under the good advice of a teacher, I chose engineering, as it would be easier to build a career with a more technical background.

I didn't find engineering school very fulfilling, but it did give me a solid knowledge base that I value more today than back then. After two years working as a packaging engineer for L'Oreal, I applied for a joint Master's in Innovation Design Engineering at Imperial College London and the Royal College of Art. Through this qualification, I was finally able to combine my two competing sides, and I have become a much better engineer as a result.

HOW DO YOU USE YOUR ENGINEERING SKILLS TO RUN NOTPLA?

Engineering is good preparation for entrepreneurship (starting a business) because it is all about understanding and solving problems. These days I don't spend as much time working directly on materials as I did when we first started Notpla in our kitchen. Today, I tend to work across teams and have learnt to wear either my design hat or my engineering hat.

WOULD YOU RECOMMEND ENGINEERING? IF SO, WHY?

Engineering gives you the ability to understand global challenges and make a positive impact. Our planet is full of human-made problems, and any curious engineer is going to enjoy creating solutions. Perhaps the engineering projects of the future don't exist yet but having an engineering mindset is timeless.

FACT FILE

Most fun thing about your job: Tasting all the new flavours of Oohos on Friday evenings with the team.

CAREER HIGHLIGHTS

1. Doing a one-year exchange at the Australian National University, learning English and discovering the other side of the world.

2. Quitting my job at L'Oreal and being accepted on an Innovation Design Engineering Master's course.

3. Raising £850,000 in a crowdfunding campaign from Rodrigo's kitchen.

"Our planet is full of human-made problems, and any curious engineer is going to enjoy creating solutions that can transform these challenges into opportunities."

Pierre Paslier

Dr Lynsey Melville

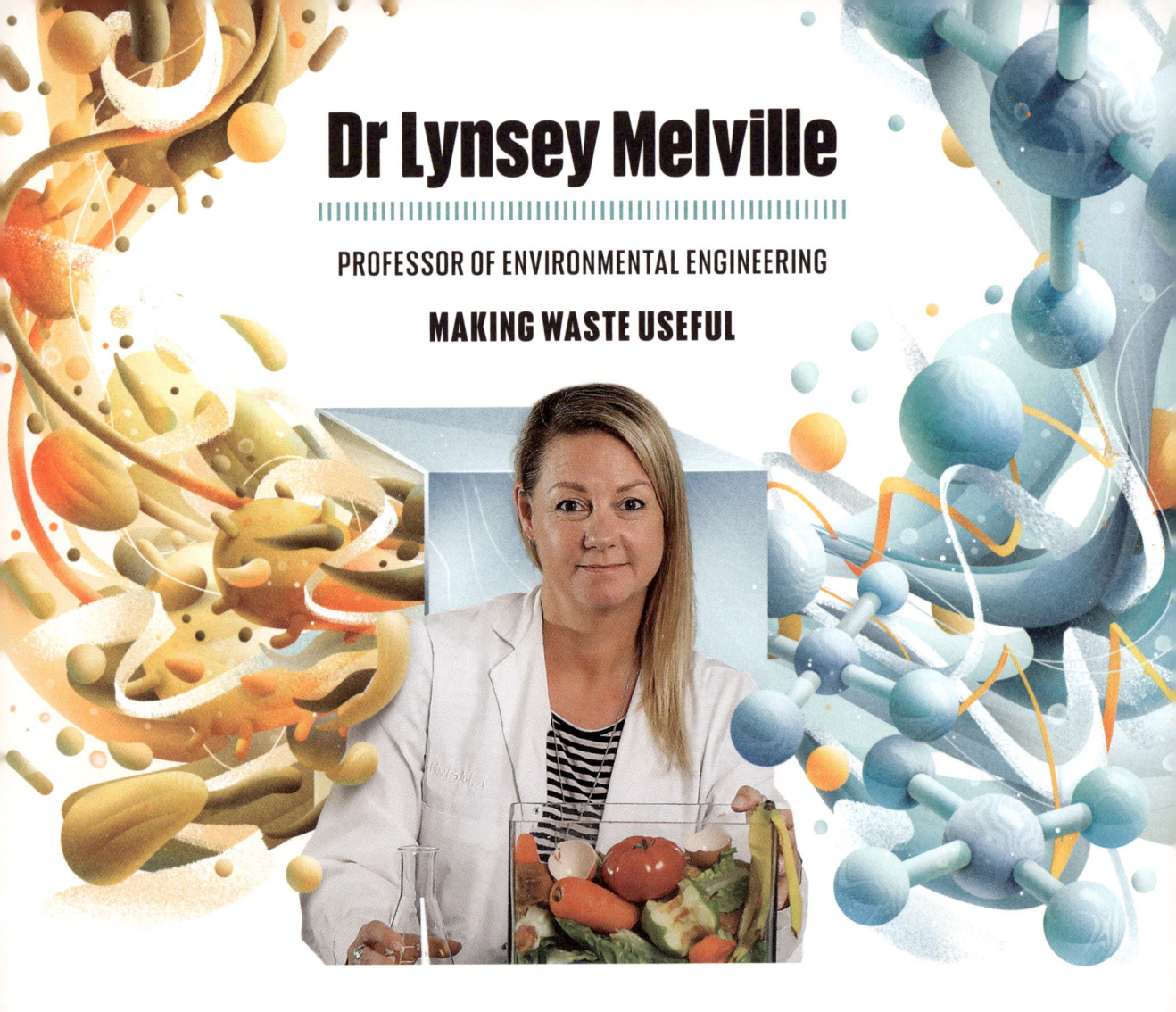

PROFESSOR OF ENVIRONMENTAL ENGINEERING

MAKING WASTE USEFUL

One of the main causes of climate change is our use of fossil fuels, so many engineers are developing ways to produce energy that won't put carbon into the atmosphere. Dr Lynsey Melville is working on a solution that produces energy from biomass, the remains and waste of living things. Biomass – including food waste, sewage and animal manures – is a great option for bioenergy because the process can capture the carbon that would otherwise be released into the atmosphere.

HOW DID YOU LEARN ABOUT BIOMASS?

I learnt young that Mother Nature is the greatest of all engineers because she never wastes a thing! Every product and by-product of a biological process has a use. After my Environmental Science degree, I worked at a water treatment company, where bacteria are used to clean wastewater.

My job was to work out how to keep the bacteria happy so that they could function effectively. I discovered that these natural processes and waste materials could actually be used in lots of different ways: to make fertiliser for growing plants; to make products, such as textiles or other biodegradable materials; or to make energy, potentially replacing fossil fuels.

HOW IS BIOMASS PROCESSED AND MADE USEFUL TO US?

It is processed in an anaerobic digester. This machine works like a cow's stomach – organic material is put in one end and bacteria digest it, creating rich sludge and gas. The sludge and gas come out the other end. Farmers use the sludge as fertiliser and the gas is contained and stored as energy. I am currently working with farmers in Europe, fishermen in Indonesia (turning their seaweed waste into energy) and tiny communities in South Africa.

WHAT IS CHALLENGING ABOUT DEVELOPING ENERGY FROM BIOMASS?

My biggest challenge today is to scale up what we have learnt in the laboratory so that other communities and industries can benefit from our research. Climate change is a huge problem requiring a variety of engineers and scientists to work collaboratively. Working with lots of different partners has been the key to finding the right solutions. I have learnt to understand how to encourage governments, communities and industries to use our technology. After all, we can engineer the most effective solutions, but if they are too complicated or expensive, people won't want to use them. Also, if people don't trust them, they won't adopt them. Then, we will have failed to make a positive impact on the world.

FACT FILE

Most fun thing about your job: The people I meet – I have friends all over the world who are trying to improve the environment. We support and inspire each other.

CAREER HIGHLIGHTS

1. Getting my PhD, which was really hard work. Being called 'Doctor' is cool!

2. Travelling the world and learning about other cultures.

3. Having my own laboratory and helping students to become environmental researchers too.

ANAEROBIC DIGESTION PROCESS

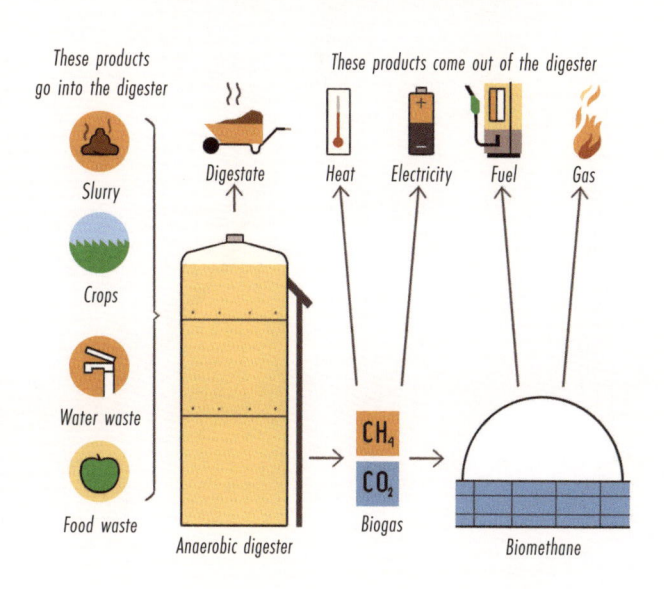

These products go into the digester
- Slurry
- Crops
- Water waste
- Food waste

These products come out of the digester
- Digestate
- Heat
- Electricity
- Fuel
- Gas

Anaerobic digester → CH_4 / CO_2 Biogas → Biomethane

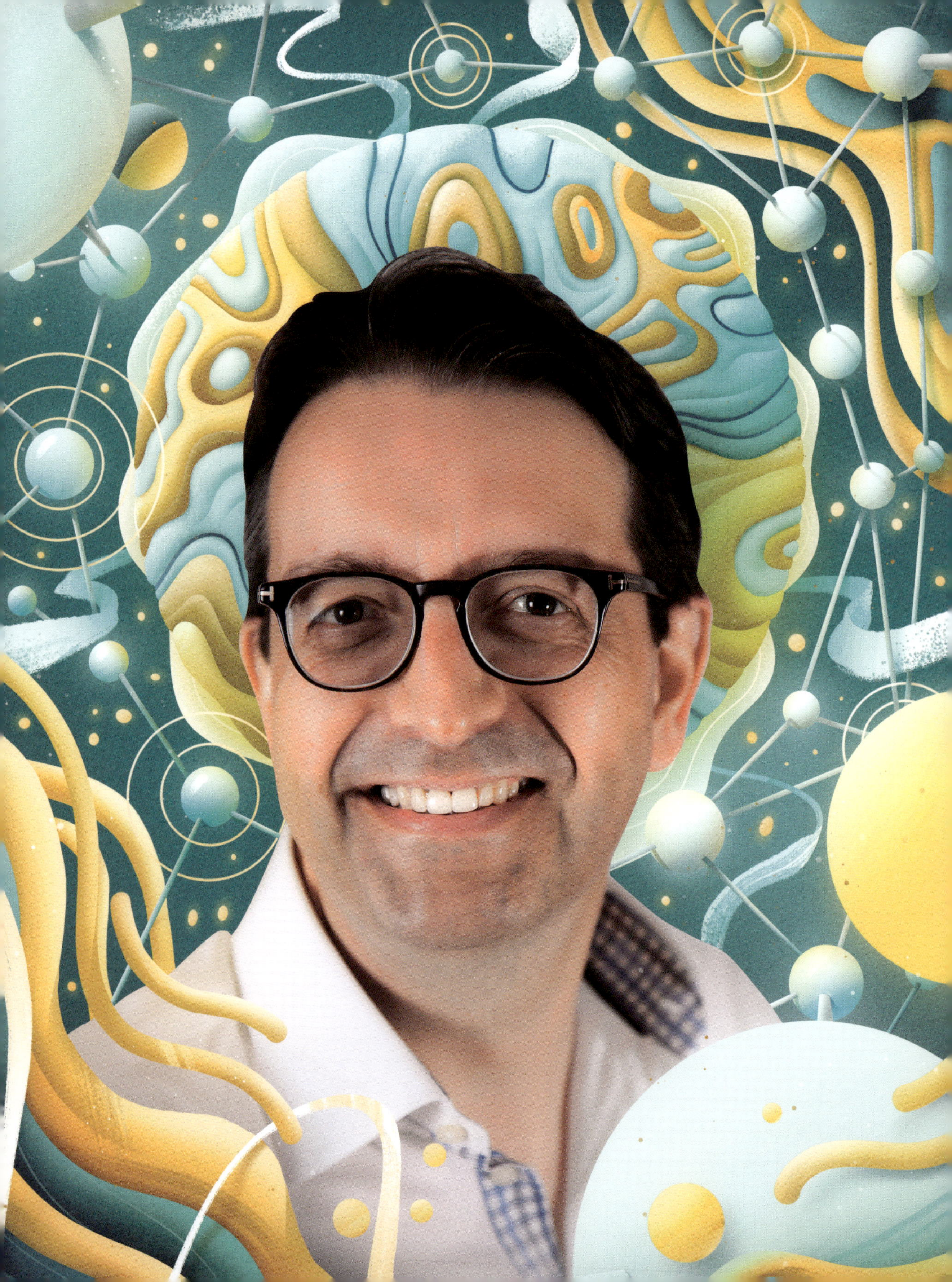

Anthony Baker

ELECTRICAL, COMMUNICATIONS AND SATELLITES ENGINEER
KEEPING AN 'EYE' ON THE PLANET

Having a bird's-eye view from space can tell us so much about the way we are living on Earth. Satellites can collect data on how and where animals migrate, how quickly the ice caps are melting or where wildfires are occurring. Satellites with thermal cameras can also create a temperature map of Earth, showing which areas are particularly hot and which are cold. Having this information can help many people, including engineers, to make better decisions for the environment and, in the case of wildfires, can help to save lives. Anthony Baker is CEO of Satellite Vu, a company that uses satellites to determine where exactly heat is being wasted, or not properly managed, from buildings or the natural environment.

HOW DO YOUR SATELLITES HAVE A POSITIVE IMPACT ON THE ENVIRONMENT?

At Satellite Vu we focus on Earth observation. We recently bought a satellite from Surrey Satellite Technology Ltd, a spin-off company from the University of Surrey, that has a camera with an infrared sensor on board. The camera takes such high-resolution images that we can look at any building on the planet and find out how much energy it is wasting. We have learnt that many factories, offices and houses could be made more energy efficient by upgrading their thermal insulation.

Before launching our satellite into space, we have been testing the camera by launching it on a plane and capturing images of Liverpool and London, Houston, USA and Berlin, Germany. The observations have identified two interesting examples of energy wastage, which both have exciting solutions. A glass factory near Liverpool generates huge quantities of heat to process glass. This heat is currently wasted into thin air but could be channelled into the nearby housing estate to keep residents warm.

Another example is in an industrial area of Liverpool. One factory has a licence to use water from the River Mersey – the river water enters the factory cold and, after various internal processes, leaves extremely hot. This hot wastewater could also be channelled to nearby residents and used in their central heating. Instead, it is being put back into the river, where it is altering the surrounding natural ecosystems.

WHY DID YOU CHOOSE A CAREER IN ENGINEERING?

My father pushed me a lot when I was young. All my Christmas presents were building, electronics and chemistry sets, and these interests stuck with me. Having grown up in the countryside, I wanted to attend a university in a big city and ended up at the University of Birmingham doing a very 'old-school' Electrical Engineering course. I was frustrated with this course because we didn't touch electronics for the first three years, focusing instead on maths and physics. I had hoped for a much more practical course and ended up taking a break for a year before completing my degree.

During this break I did a work placement at British Telecom (BT) working on their floppy disks. They were removeable storage devices for computer systems (kind of like CDs or USB sticks) and were really cutting-edge at the time! The experience made me realise that it was important for my future to complete my degree. So, I returned to Birmingham, graduated and then got offered my first job at BT, which I actually turned down! Despite finding all these experiences exciting, I still hadn't found my passion, so I travelled around South America for seven months instead.

The top image shows Stanlow Oil Refinery in Liverpool from above. The bottom image shows the same area but as seen through Satellite Vu's infrared camera. The dark red areas show the hot wastewater that is being released into the River Mersey.

While deciding what to do next, I found out that the Department of Trade and Industry was sponsoring students to go back to university to study a Master's in Satellite Communications at the University of Surrey. I jumped at the chance to be paid to be a student and the experience was life-changing. I gained expertise in a pioneering field, and it was fascinating! Finally, I had found my passion.

WHAT SKILLS HAVE YOU LEARNT THROUGHOUT YOUR ENGINEERING CAREER?

It certainly is an advantage being an engineer, especially when starting up a technology company. As a leader, it is impossible to be 100 per cent sure that your idea is going to work, but having an engineering background gives you a good chance at making an educated guess! But of course, no-one gets it right all the time, and as a result, I have also learnt how to deal with failure.

I spent five years and hundreds of millions of pounds of investors' money building a communications satellite, which took a lot longer to build than we had planned because we changed some design decisions halfway through. But then the rocket carrying it blew up on launch! It was an epic failure and a devastating setback that forced the team back to the drawing board. Although the failure was the fault of the rocket, we had to find a solution to satisfy customers and investors. We learnt to never give up hope!

I have also learnt how to lead a team and to delegate. In the past, I have been that engineer who wants to understand absolutely everything. Engineers say that with enough time and money they can solve any problem. But now I hire experts who are more specialised than me so we can quickly build amazing technology at a price that people want to pay.

WHAT IS MOST REWARDING ABOUT WHAT YOU DO TODAY?

It's twofold. One is having people join, invest and collaborate in our company because this means that they have trust and faith in us. Second is the execution of our concepts. Our technology empowers others to do better for the planet by helping them to identify what should be fixed in their energy usage. That is where we really make a difference.

FACT FILE

Most fun thing about your job: Finding new things to image with our satellite – I'm really excited about imaging volcanoes!

CAREER HIGHLIGHTS

1. Watching my first rocket launch.

2. My first job abroad in Hong Kong.

3. Starting my own business.

Satellite Vu's satellite will be one of many in a constellation – a group of satellites that work together. The constellation will be able to visit the same location on Earth multiple times a day or night.

Drone

HOW CAN DRONES HELP THE ENVIRONMENT?

SOIL ANALYSIS Crops can't grow without healthy soil. Analysing the soil before planting crops allows farmers to adjust the level of nutrients, but sending soil samples to a lab for analysis is time-consuming and often inaccurate. Using drones with precision sensors means vast areas of land can be analysed almost immediately.

WATER FLOW Special thermal and electromagnetic sensors can be fitted to drones to monitor fields to see if they're in need of water. Drones can also produce elevation models that show the lay of the land and the way the water flows over it.

SUPER-SPEED SEEDS Engineers have also developed drones that speed up the planting process by firing seeds at high speed into the soil! The seed pods have a higher chance of developing properly, as they're coated in a special gel that's rich in nutrients.

Drones are able to plant seeds much faster than humans can. They can also reach remote areas that might be otherwise difficult to access.

Drones are like flying robots and they are great for many jobs, from delivering parcels to farming. Currently, half of the world's habitable land is used for farming, which is responsible for high levels of greenhouse gas emissions. Environmental engineers develop drones to make farming processes faster and more efficient, resulting in lower emissions. This is great news for the environment!

With the help of drones, farmers can quickly and easily see which of their crops are healthy.

SCAN AND SPRAY Some drones can scan the ground and adjust their height. This means they can spray crops with the ideal amount of liquid, such as pesticides. This not only reduces waste but also means fewer chemicals soak into the ground and get into water systems.

LIGHT SHOW Drones can even be fitted with sensors that scan plants for disease. This equipment can identify the amount of light a plant reflects. A healthy plant reflects a high amount of green and near-infrared light (which is just past what the human eye can see). Using drones to capture this information means any bacterial or fungal infections can be spotted early so they don't spread.

THE BIG PICTURE Monitoring vast areas of land is a big task. Traditionally, farmers would have spent hours driving around a farm to check all was okay. Now, they often rely on satellite images to spot potential problems, such as soil erosion. Drones can also provide even more detailed and accurate images, which means any problems can be dealt with sooner.

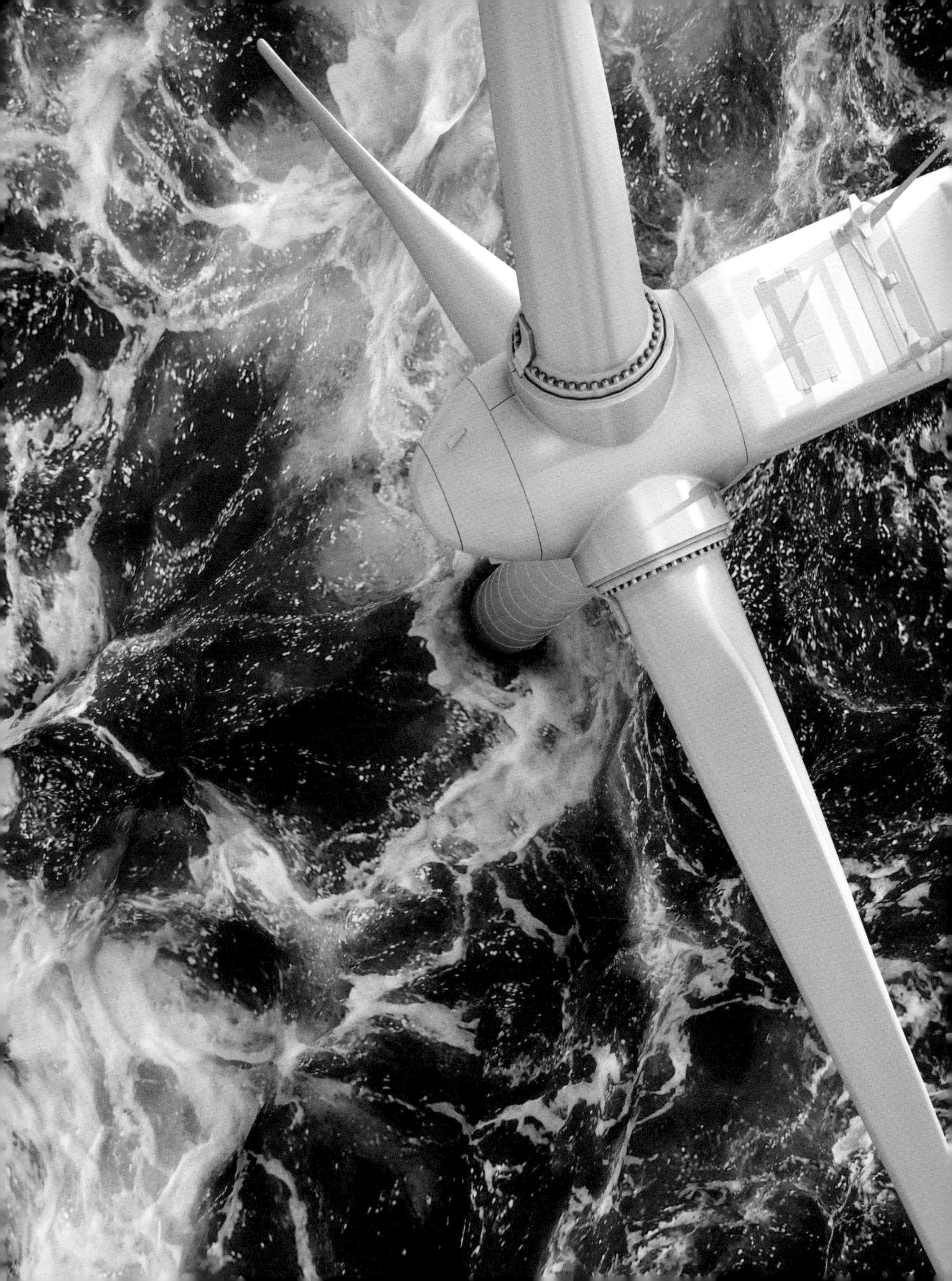

CHAPTER 3

POWERING OUR FUTURE

We need energy to do everything, which is why finding or making fuel is so important. Fossil fuels such as coal, oil and gas have taken millions of years to form underground, yet burning them can release huge amounts of carbon dioxide and other toxic greenhouse gases into our atmosphere in a matter of minutes.

Many engineers are determined to reduce these harmful consequences of our energy use by finding more sustainable and effective energy solutions. A variety of ideas have been designed and tested by engineers – even some that have been inspired by jellyfish and farting cows! But no matter how wacky solutions get, the main challenge for engineers will always be twofold: firstly, the challenge of meeting an ever-increasing demand for energy, and secondly, working out how to reduce the pollution caused by generating large amounts of energy.

In this chapter, we meet some engineers who are at the forefront of developing exciting energy solutions. They are working to slow down climate change by providing massive sources of energy, while keeping carbon generation low. Their energy solutions are both renewable and sustainable, ready to power the needs of generations to come.

LEFT: Wind turbines, such as the one shown here, are often placed at sea. The wind there is stronger and more consistent than on land, offering a more reliable source of power.

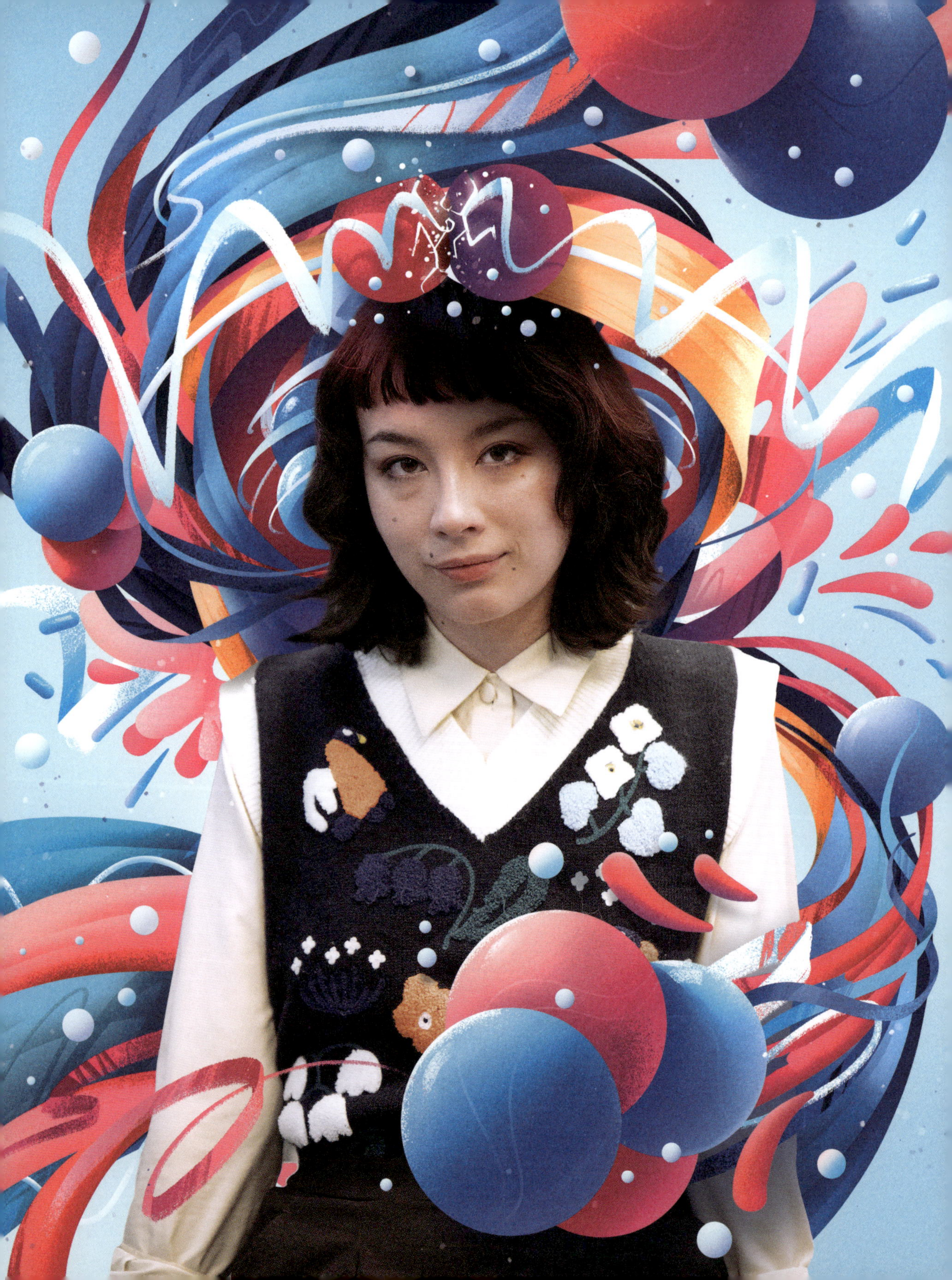

Katriya Sabin

DEVELOPMENT ENGINEER
WORKING TO MAKE FUSION ENERGY A REALITY

There are two different ways to create nuclear energy: fission and fusion. In fission, atoms are split apart. In fusion, they are smashed together so that they merge. Both processes release enormous amounts of energy. Although fission is a great source of carbon-free energy, it creates lots of radioactive waste. Fusion, on the other hand, has the potential to create even more sustainable energy, but with very little waste. Sounds great, right? But there's just one problem: we are still working out how to create fusion energy here on Earth!

Fusion is very common out in space – it is the process by which the Sun, and all other stars, get their energy. Engineers have been working on ways to capture and use the energy from fusion on Earth for decades. It's a huge challenge to replicate the conditions of the Sun on Earth. Katriya Sabin is working on a new way to harness fusion energy that avoids the difficulties others have faced.

HOW DID YOU END UP WORKING IN FUSION ENERGY?

As a child I spent a lot of time thinking and creating. I was fascinated by the Large Hadron Collider (LHC) at CERN (see page 201 for more information) on the Swiss-French border. I remember when it was about to be switched on and it felt like the world was waiting to see what would happen. In primary school I joined an after-school science club, run by a very kind and enthusiastic retired engineer. I learnt to solder, which is where you join two things together using molten metal. This seemingly simple engineering process blew my mind, especially after learning that the LHC had temporarily stopped because of a soldering issue.

> "Arts and STEM truly were the only subjects I felt passionate about at school. I wanted to find a career where these subjects overlapped, and engineering seemed to be the answer."
>
> **Katriya Sabin**

I had a tough time at secondary school. There was too much pressure and expectation to decide on a lifetime profession and attend a great university. As a result, my A-levels suffered. So, I quit A-levels after one year and followed an apprenticeship route into fusion engineering at the UK Atomic Energy Authority (UKAEA). I resumed my education with a Higher National qualification in Electrical Engineering instead.

WHAT WAS YOUR APPRENTICESHIP LIKE?

It was a rare opportunity to experience cutting-edge science at apprenticeship level. It perfectly satisfied my interest in physics, environmental activism, creativity and innovation and was very hands-on. I got to work in many departments such as Diagnostics, where we disassembled and reassembled hardware, and the Engineering Realisation Group, where we worked on making ideas a reality. I worked on cryogenics (i.e. super cold temperatures), vacuums and fuels, such as tritium, which is a type of hydrogen. During my apprenticeship, I learnt that nuclear fusion focuses on generating plasma.

PLASMA IS VERY COOL, CAN YOU EXPLAIN HOW IT'S USEFUL?

Plasma is sort of like a superheated gas. It's one of the four states of matter – the other three are solid, liquid and gas. In order to create fusion energy, we heat two types of hydrogen gas (tritium and deuterium) to such a high temperature that they squish together and become plasma. The reactions that happen within this plasma, potentially millions of them per second, are what create

UKAEA's JET fusion energy machine, the world's largest fusion energy experiment.

the energy. We use this energy to vapourise water into steam, and the steam turns turbines to make electricity. The tricky thing is that atoms don't want to fuse together, so we have had to create a container, called a reactor, that holds the plasma within a doughnut-shaped magnetic field. We set a new world record by keeping the plasma at a sustained level for five seconds. It doesn't sound long, but it is a major achievement!

WHAT HAVE BEEN YOUR FAVOURITE EXPERIENCES AT UKAEA?

There are two. One is working directly on the Joint European Torus (JET) – a fusion energy machine that generates plasma. I operated two of the eight Neutral Beam Injectors that fire a beam of high-energy particles straight into the plasma. The aim of this is to increase the temperature of the plasma.

My second favourite experience involves being in the control room, where we can see plasma being generated inside our fusion devices. So much energy and work goes into creating this moment, which lasts for just seconds, but in these moments the physicists, engineers and technicians all wait to see the outcome of hours of research and calculations. It's very thrilling to be part of this, especially knowing that it involves hundreds of technical components all working in perfect harmony.

DO YOU THINK FUSION CAN MEET OUR ENERGY NEEDS IN THE FUTURE?

With extreme weather events and environmental disasters happening all over the world, we are now experiencing the consequences of climate change. There is a push towards cleaner energy, which fusion can certainly provide, but this is not going to happen overnight. Organising the processes to create fusion energy is a huge and complex job. However, once it is up and running, I hope to see fusion energy meeting global energy demands and being distributed across borders and nations, alongside solar, geothermal and other renewables.

FACT FILE

Most fun thing about your job: Operating the Neutral Beam Injectors for JET and seeing the plasma roar as fuel is beamed into it!

CAREER HIGHLIGHTS

1. Having a great teacher at secondary school who made me realise how much I loved physics.

2. Standing on top of JET (which is high!) and installing a new plasma control system. That was unreal.

3. Co-authoring and publishing a scientific paper.

"I will always want to work on projects that focus on helping society become a fairer place."

Katriya Sabin

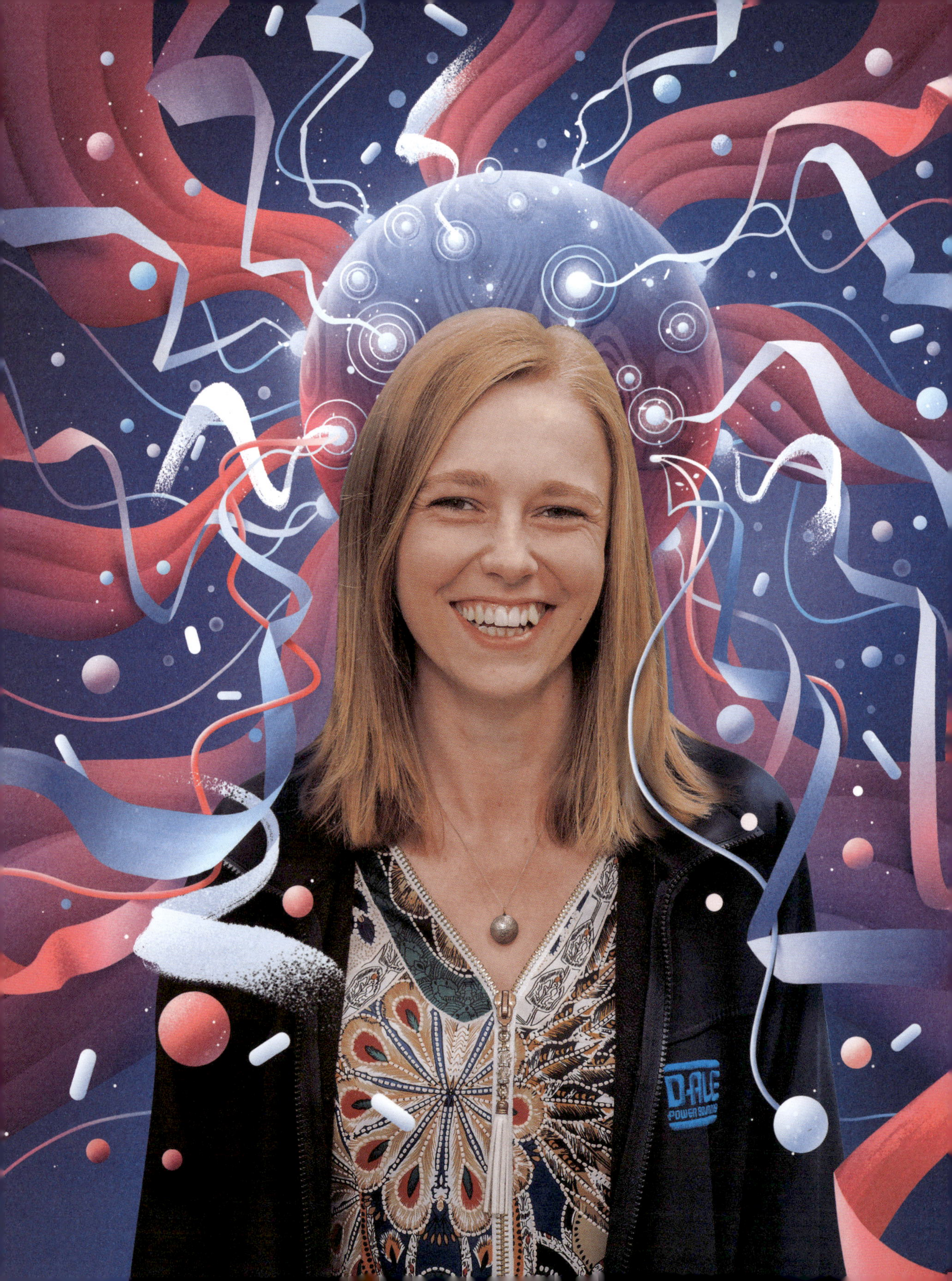

Samantha Magowan

ELECTRICAL AND ELECTRONICS ENGINEER
PROVIDING A STABLE POWER SUPPLY

Many people around the world enjoy a stable power supply most of the time, but power outages do happen. Luckily, engineers have found a way to provide emergency backup during these power cuts. This can be crucial for hospitals, businesses and infrastructure, such as train lines, but also useful to energy suppliers who may need to shut down their operations to carry out maintenance work.

Emergency power is tricky to execute effectively because back-up generators need time to power up. Valuable seconds are required to switch from a main power supply to an alternative source, which could be the difference between life and death in hospitals. These seconds can leave the system open to threats, for example from hackers who can use them to create computer glitches, causing chaos.

Samantha Magowan recently completed her degree apprenticeship in Electrical and Electronic Engineering and now works with Dale Power Solutions. She helps make uninterruptible power supplies, or UPS systems, which provide back-up power seamlessly.

Having an uninterruptible power supply means that if there is ever a power cut, a building can keep its lights on and machines working. This is especially helpful for buildings such as hospitals.

ANTI-FLASH CLOTHING *These clothes are usually made from rubber or other materials that electricity cannot flow through. A helmet with a visor can protect the worker's eyes from any sparks.*

WHAT IS A TYPICAL WEEK LIKE AT WORK?

It's a mixture of site visits and being at my desk. Once or twice a week I put on my anti-flash clothing, which prevents electricity from conducting through my own clothing, and I can be found in dusty city basements, measuring the size of the space available for our UPS kit. The information I record helps me to design the best UPS system for the client's needs.

Designing a solution for a client is like figuring out a maths puzzle. Often these basements and other spaces were purpose-built to house the original generators. Replacing or modifying them becomes a logistical challenge not just for me as the design engineer, but also for the installation engineers. Occasionally, they have had to remove walls and make other drastic alterations to discard or install kit.

HOW DID YOU GET INTO ENGINEERING?

I started a higher apprenticeship at 18 years old after receiving good grades at A-levels. I chose a route that would help me train for a specific job rather than going to university because full-time study did not appeal to me at all. I have never liked exams or revising – I was ready to be in industry.

When I applied for the apprenticeship, my CV was very short! I had never had a job, not even a paper round, so in the work experience section, I listed: 'Helping my parents with DIY', alongside my GCSE and A-level results. Luckily this was enough for me to be offered a place on an apprenticeship scheme at Dale Power Solutions.

My five-year apprenticeship was an incredible experience from start to finish. I spent between six months to one year rotating around different areas of the business, including their Factory, Design and Applications departments. I also completed a degree, attending university one day a week during termtime. Now I have a deep and well-rounded understanding of what our company offers.

Helping to build the UPS systems in the factory taught me so much about our product. After 18 months, I then learnt how to create mechanical and electrical 3D drawings of the products to reveal even more technical detail. In the Applications department, I learnt how to sell our product to customers, and this is where I have settled. I love solving a customer's problem and working together with different colleagues to find solutions.

HOW HAS AN APPRENTICESHIP BENEFITTED YOU?

I was really shy at the beginning of my apprenticeship, but everyone at work is so nice, helpful, encouraging and supportive, and that has really helped to draw me out of my shell. It has also been really inspiring seeing so many other female engineering apprentices at my work. It certainly made me feel more secure with my own choices.

The learning curve in an apprenticeship has been much better suited to me. If you make a mistake, you can get to the root of why the mistake happened by talking it through with colleagues. Being paid to work and study has allowed me to buy my own home – and I'm only 23 years old! I remember the moment I received my first paycheck: all I wanted to do was to spend the money on a holiday, but I saved it for the deposit on my home instead. Overall, I feel that the apprenticeship has really helped me to know what I want in life and that is invaluable.

FACT FILE

Most fun thing about your job: I love that my job is different every day.

CAREER HIGHLIGHTS

1. Getting a degree in Electromechanical Engineering while working.

2. Carrying out a feasibility study and research into a product range.

3. Winning the Young Woman Engineer of the Year award for apprentices.

"Engineering is such a great career and you can approach it from many different angles. You can go to university but it is also possible to go as far as you like with an apprenticeship route. This really means everyone can access it."

Samantha Magowan

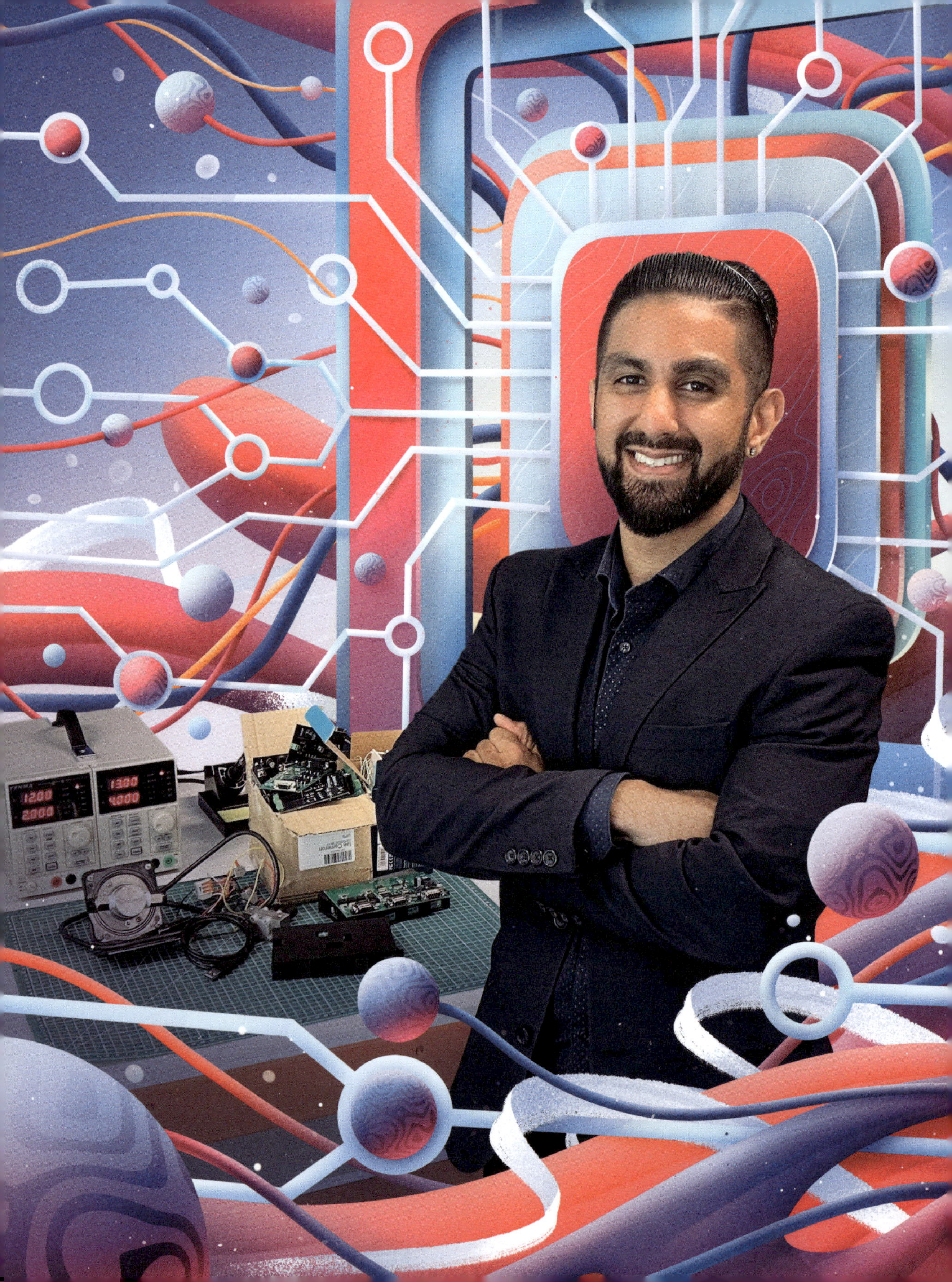

Manjot Chana

HEAD OF SYSTEMS AND INTEGRATION
DESIGNING SYSTEMS THAT TALK TO ONE ANOTHER

Hydrogen has many different uses and there are numerous ways in which it can provide low-carbon alternatives to fossil fuels. Companies such as H2GO Power have been developing hydrogen batteries, designed to store energy from renewable sources. This is incredibly useful because the Sun doesn't always shine brightly and it isn't always windy, which means that renewable energy is not always available on-demand. Manjot Chana started his career as an engineering apprentice at Jaguar Land Rover and now works at H2GO Power as the Head of Systems and Integration.

WHAT WERE YOU LIKE AS A KID? WAS IT OBVIOUS THAT ENGINEERING WAS FOR YOU?

I used to love watching Power Rangers as a kid. Every year they would release a new season involving five new robots who would join together to make one big robot. That was the best bit of the show — seeing how all of the different robots combined to make a new one. Even then I loved systems integration. At 13 years old, I was building my own computers, and a few years later I taught myself to code!

WHAT DID YOU LEARN ABOUT YOURSELF FROM DOING AN APPRENTICESHIP?

At the start of my apprenticeship, I was convinced that I was good with my head but not with my hands. I had no confidence in my practical skills and hated workshop lessons. I now realise that I developed many important skills for life at my workshops. Completing a degree and working at

Robots made of other, smaller robots are a great example of systems integration — each small robot is a system that combines to make one big system.

the same time was not easy, but I really enjoyed the intense learning experience. I grew up and matured so rapidly into a career that I love, while also financially contributing to my family. This was very important to me because after my father passed away, it was my responsibility to look after my mother and siblings. The apprenticeship has been some of the best years of my life so far.

WHAT DOES YOUR JOB TODAY INVOLVE?

Integration engineering is a combination of electrical, electronic software and network engineering. I design, make, test and put into action independent control systems that all talk to each other. At Jaguar Land Rover (JLR) I would combine control systems, for example engine subsystems and gearbox subsystems, and ensure that they could work simultaneously to propel a vehicle.

H2GO Power technology is a combination of mechanical, electrical and chemical systems. The electrical subsystems are used for monitoring faults, tracking storage capacity and monitoring external weather. These subsystems are all linked by a central control system. My job today involves writing software for the subsystems to communicate with each other, designing circuits and control boards and co-ordinating these subsystems so that our energy intake and storage units can operate safely and efficiently.

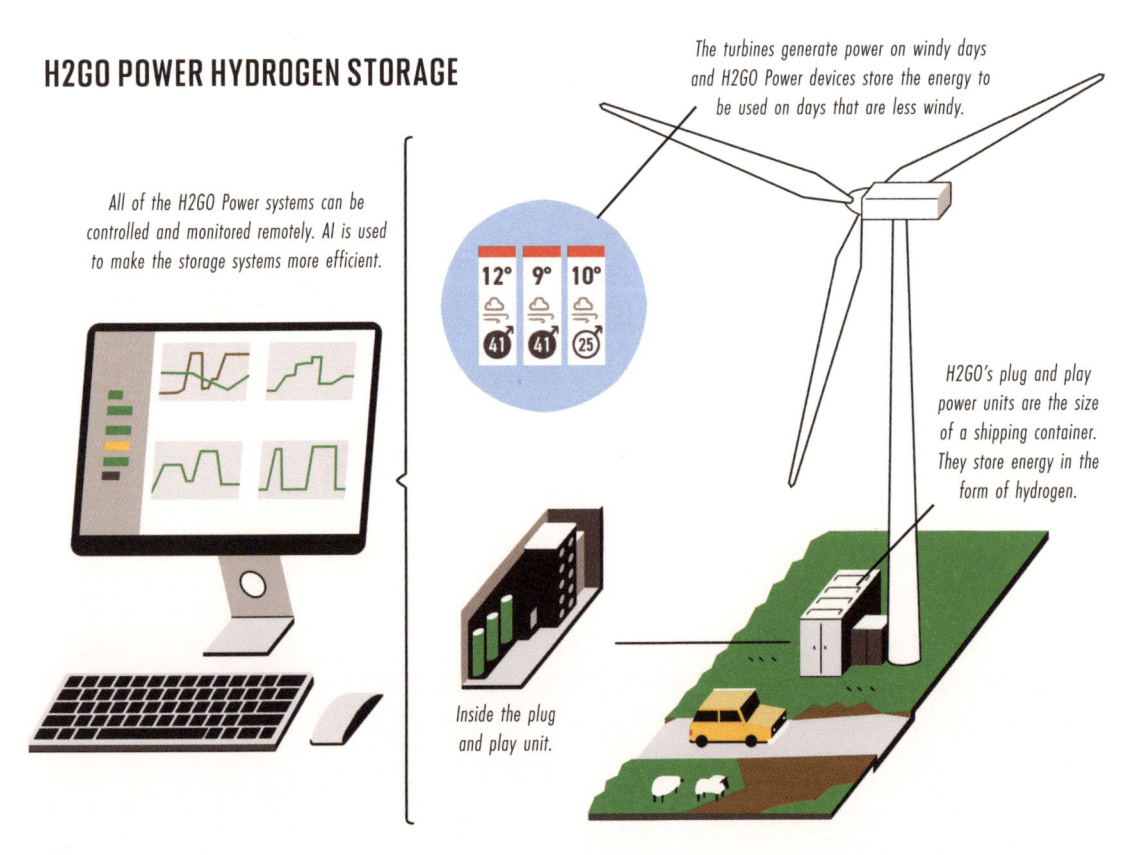

H2GO POWER HYDROGEN STORAGE

The turbines generate power on windy days and H2GO Power devices store the energy to be used on days that are less windy.

All of the H2GO Power systems can be controlled and monitored remotely. AI is used to make the storage systems more efficient.

H2GO's plug and play power units are the size of a shipping container. They store energy in the form of hydrogen.

Inside the plug and play unit.

WHAT IS THE MOST CHALLENGING PART OF YOUR JOB?

Trying not to be a perfectionist! When I was younger, I produced dubstep music. Admittedly it was a short-lived part of my life, but I made so many songs over the years and never released most of them because I was worried that they weren't perfect. When I started my apprenticeship, I uploaded everything all in one go. I wanted to face my fear that the songs weren't good enough, and I'm proud I did!

I learnt to accept my limitations because no human being is perfect. With that in mind, I am now more than happy to submit work that is unfinished, because it means I get feedback from the customers sooner. This approach opens the door to communication and collaboration and means that I am able to find the best solution earlier on in the process.

"Curiosity is everything. Double down on what interests you because curiosity is a signpost guiding you along your career."

Manjot Chana

WHAT HAS BEEN THE COOLEST EXPERIENCE OF YOUR ENGINEERING CAREER TO DATE?

The coolest thing that I've experienced in my job was while I was doing my apprenticeship. In 2017, I was part of the team that undertook the Cold Environment Testing (CET) for the new plug-in hybrid electric vehicle, Range Rover Sport. We drove these beautiful cars in a convoy from the UK into −40°C terrain through France, Belgium, Germany and Switzerland. I remember how proud and privileged I felt to be part of something so exciting, special and unique. I never dreamt I'd be involved in things like this when I was in school – at the time it really was a whole new world to me. Since then, I have worked on the Range Rover for Her Majesty, Queen Elizabeth and on vehicles made especially for James Bond movies, which was also amazing.

FACT FILE

Most fun thing about your job: Seeing a design come to life – a scribble become a circuit board or a diagram become a fully working product.

CAREER HIGHLIGHTS

1. Finishing my apprenticeship at JLR and becoming a team leader.

2. Creating CSSLaunch, an application used by every JLR engineer to work on JLR vehicles.

3. Becoming a line manager at H2GO Power and helping to deliver multi-million-pound products.

Nuclear

Nuclear power is a truly awesome field of science because it has the potential to provide more than enough energy to run the whole planet. If only it were easy and safe to produce! The word nuclear means anything relating to the nucleus of an atom – this is the centre of an atom that is positively charged and where most of the atom's mass is found. Nuclear power is energy created by manipulating the nuclei of atoms. There are two types of nuclear power: one is nuclear fission, which is where the nucleus of an atom is split apart, the other is fusion, where the nuclei of two atoms are fused together.

THE HISTORY The physicist Ernest Rutherford discovered that most of an atom's mass is contained in its tiny nucleus and observed the first nuclear reaction. This paved the way for later physicists, such as John Cockcroft and Ernest Walton, who first split an atom in a laboratory-controlled setting in 1932. Lise Meitner and Otto Robert Frisch discovered that splitting heavy atomic nuclei, such as that of uranium or plutonium, produces huge amounts of energy – a process called nuclear fission.

THE CONTROVERSY Nuclear power often has a bad reputation due to its associated dangers. Most nuclear power stations use nuclear fission and it creates dangerous waste. There have also been several terrible accidents at nuclear plants. For people to trust nuclear energy, safety systems need to be in place. Since the 1950s, more than 30 nations have built nuclear fission reactors to generate power. However, fusion is considered safer than fission because it produces less radioactive waste.

The Experimental Advanced Superconducting Tokamak (EAST) in Hefei, China. In 2021, EAST achieved a world record by maintaining a plasma temperature of 120 million degrees Celsius for 101 seconds and 160 million degrees Celsius for 20 seconds.

Power

HARNESSING THE POTENTIAL Nuclear energy could be a great solution for powering our planet because, unlike fossil fuels, it doesn't produce any carbon emissions. Also, after the initial set up, a nuclear plant is low-cost to run. It's predicted that by 2050, nuclear power could provide a quarter of the world's energy.

HOW IT'S DONE ON THE SUN The Sun has been producing nuclear fusion since the dawn of time! Its incredibly high temperatures, giant size and large amounts of hydrogen create the perfect conditions for the process. At the Sun's core, where the temperature is about 15 million degrees Celsius, hydrogen gas becomes a high-energy substance called plasma. Inside the plasma, hydrogen atoms collide and fuse together to form single atoms of helium, creating nuclear energy.

MAKING IT WORK ON EARTH Creating the Sun's nuclear fusion on Earth is so difficult because hydrogen gas is highly flammable and difficult to store. However, alternative fuels deuterium and tritium can be heated in a tokamak to create plasma. Powerful magnets inside the tokamak help the atoms to fuse. Another technique is to squeeze the plasma to encourage fusion. So far, scientists and engineers have only been able to produce energy by nuclear fusion for fleeting moments. In 2022, scientists at the Joint European Torus (JET) lab in the UK broke the world record for the amount of energy produced in a nuclear fusion experiment. They created 59 megajoules of heat energy over five seconds, which is only enough to heat about 60 kettles of water, but was a major breakthrough in the field of nuclear fusion.

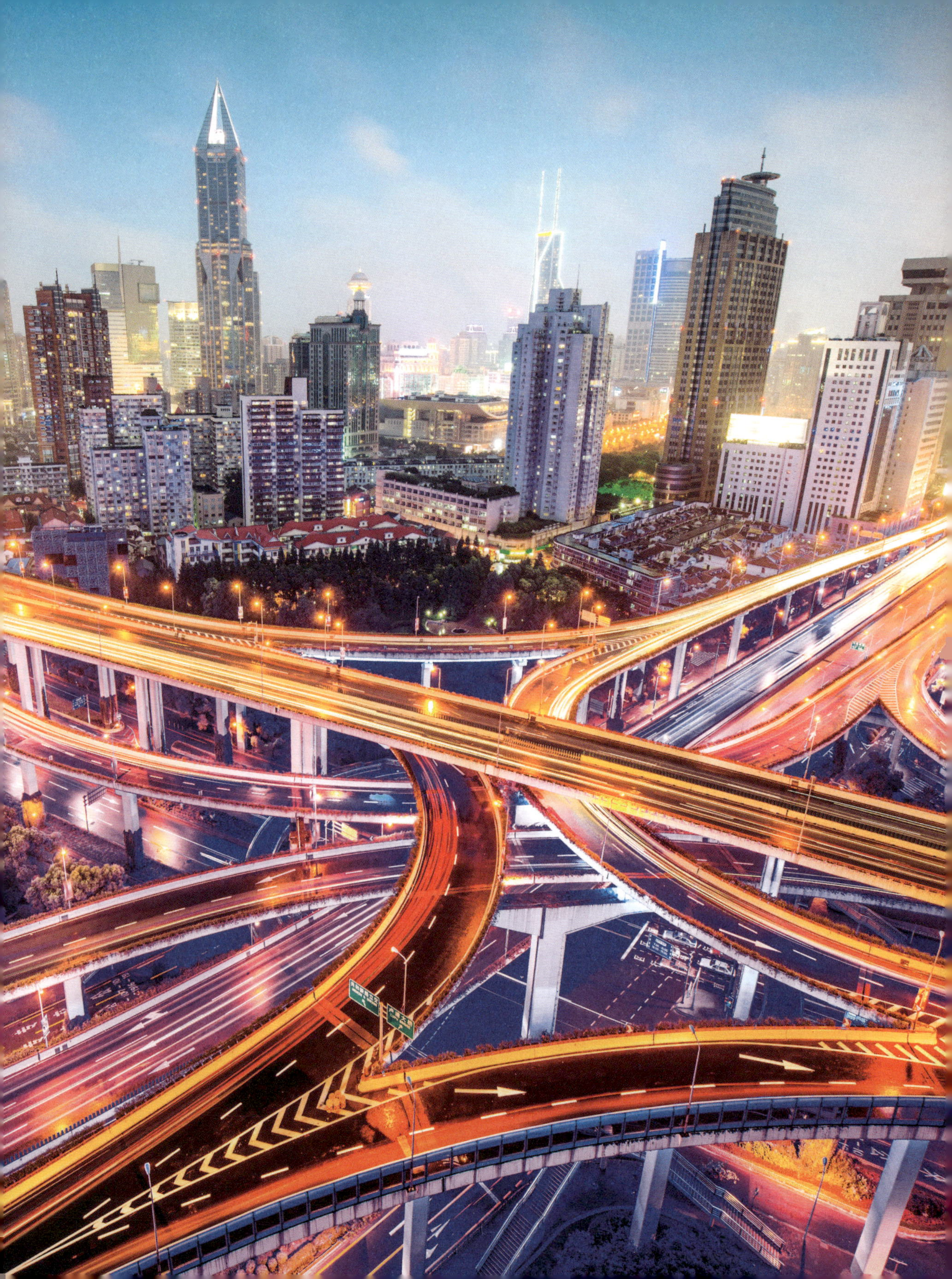

CHAPTER 4

INFRASTRUCTURE AND CONSTRUCTION

Infrastructure is a big part of engineering. It includes all the things that are needed for a society to work properly. For a city to run smoothly, it needs to have, among other things, a good transport system, communication networks, a constant supply of power and water and an effective drainage system.

Engineers are hard at work around the world creating and updating infrastructure to adapt to modern needs and a rapidly changing climate. Many engineers seek to build infrastructure that has a low carbon footprint, while keeping people safe during extreme weather and natural disasters.

Infrastructure engineers are undercover superheroes because we rely on them so much to have fully functioning lives. But we don't often see the work that they do because when infrastructure is working well, we tend not to notice it. In this chapter, we can appreciate just a few of the engineers making a big difference to infrastructure in a variety of exciting ways.

LEFT: Building upwards can help to optimise space in busy cities. The Yan'an Elevated Road in Shanghai does just that, by having roads that criss-cross over one another.

Malithi (Milly) Hennayake

CIVIL ENGINEER

HELPING TO PROVIDE PEOPLE WITH SAFE SPACES

In Ayo Sokale's profile (pages 22–25) we saw how flooding can affect people who live near bodies of water and how engineers can come up with systems to avoid serious damage. But the need for flood control is not restricted to overflowing rivers or seas. Heavy rainfall can cause flooding in built-up areas, such as cities and towns. In the countryside, rain is absorbed by the soil, but in the city, rain runs off hard surfaces such as concrete, brick, tarmac and paving stones, and can flow into the lowest floors of buildings, doing serious damage. Civil engineers make sure streets and pavements are built with drains that carry the water into sewer systems and out of the city. However, drains can get too full and overflow. This is where civil engineers, such as Milly Hennayake, step in to ensure that wastewater from flooding is managed and dealt with safely.

HOW DID YOU DISCOVER ENGINEERING?

When I was a kid, I had no idea what engineering was or that it could be an option for me. That is, until I actually saw some engineers at work. The Headstart Scheme, which is organised by the Engineering Development Trust, was my first insight into engineering and engineering degrees. Through my school I was also able to visit CERN and meet the engineers and physicists constructing the Large Hadron Collider, which was incredible! After completing my Engineering degree, I decided to work in the water sector because this felt like the best way for me to have a positive impact on communities and the environment.

WHAT PROJECT ARE YOU MOST PROUD OF?

My first job after university was at Arup, a sustainable development firm. I still work there and have been involved in designing and building flood alleviation schemes. My favourite project has been the Leeds Flood Alleviation Scheme, where we built defences to protect Leeds city centre from flooding by the river, in such a way that didn't detract from its natural beauty. I was an Assistant Site Supervisor during construction, helping to make sure that the contractor was following the design when building the moveable weirs, which are barriers put in a river to regulate its flow and reduce floodwater levels. Every day onsite, I would check the quality of construction and make sure that the contractor was working safely. I took photos and kept detailed notes to ensure that disruption to the community and environment was kept to a minimum.

WHAT KEY SKILLS DID YOU NEED TO DEVELOP AS AN ENGINEER?

Problem solving, teamwork and communication are critical because I work with many experts, organisations and the public. No engineering challenge is ever solved in isolation.

FACT FILE

Most fun thing about your job: I love the people! Often they are interesting, fun and we have similar principles.

CAREER HIGHLIGHTS

1. Working with Engineers Without Borders UK, which allowed me to see how engineering can positively impact people.

2. Volunteering with Kounkuey Design Initiative in Nairobi to design community infrastructure.

3. Moving to Lima, Peru to help with rebuilding their infrastructure after major flooding in 2017.

A WEIR IN ACTION

1.

The weir is up when the water levels are normal.

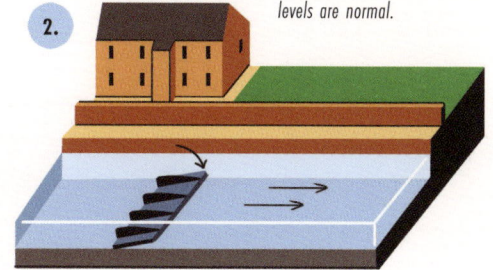

2.

When the water level rises, the weir lowers, allowing excess water to flow through.

Will Arnold

STRUCTURAL ENGINEER

STRIVING FOR A MORE SUSTAINABLE CONSTRUCTION INDUSTRY

Structural engineers design the skeletons of structures: buildings, bridges, airports, concert halls and more. They sketch, calculate and draw up the plans for the walls, columns, beams and floors using computer-aided design (CAD) software. They pay attention to the strength and durability of a structure because they are responsible for how safe it is and how long it stays standing.

The materials that an engineer chooses are essential to a structure's success – the world's most amazing buildings are made from millions of tonnes of steel, concrete, wood and bricks. But constructing, operating, repairing and demolishing them creates nearly 40 per cent of all global carbon emissions. By comparison, air travel only adds up to three per cent of global emissions. As a Structural Engineer, Will Arnold was shocked to learn of these statistics and is passionate about helping to bring about change in the industry.

HOW DID YOU BECOME SO PASSIONATE ABOUT SUSTAINABILITY IN CONSTRUCTION?

After I qualified as a structural engineer, I worked with some of the world's best architects to create amazing projects from the Macallan Distillery in Scotland to the Fubon Tower in Taiwan and the Rwanda Institute for Conservation Agriculture.

Sustainability was a key consideration for all these innovative projects. I calculated that it's often possible to save a thousand tonnes of carbon emissions by designing the structure in a more efficient way. It was shocking that many people in the industry were unaware of the impact they can have on the environment. As a sustainability specialist, my main aim is to increase awareness and offer solutions that will create a greener construction industry.

WHAT ARE THE WAYS IN WHICH YOU HOPE THE CONSTRUCTION INDUSTRY WILL CHANGE?

I would like to see the industry use less and recycle more. Demolishing old buildings and building new ones releases four times more carbon than refurbishing existing ones! It would also be great if we learnt how to effectively use lower-carbon materials, such as earth bricks, stone blocks and wooden beams. The key is finding a balance between using enough material to create strong and resilient structures and minimising the amount of material used, to keep environmental costs down.

FACT FILE

Most fun thing about your job: Speaking to people all over the world to help them make their buildings better for the planet.

CAREER HIGHLIGHTS

1. Living and working in Africa for a year and helping to design a low-carbon university.

2. Visiting the Houses of Parliament and advising politicians on how to reduce carbon emissions in construction.

3. The first time I saw a structure that I had designed in real life!

The Rwanda Institute for Conservation Agriculture is expected to be the world's first carbon-positive university. The buildings were made using natural materials, such as earth bricks and timber beams, which are good for the environment as they require minimal energy to produce.

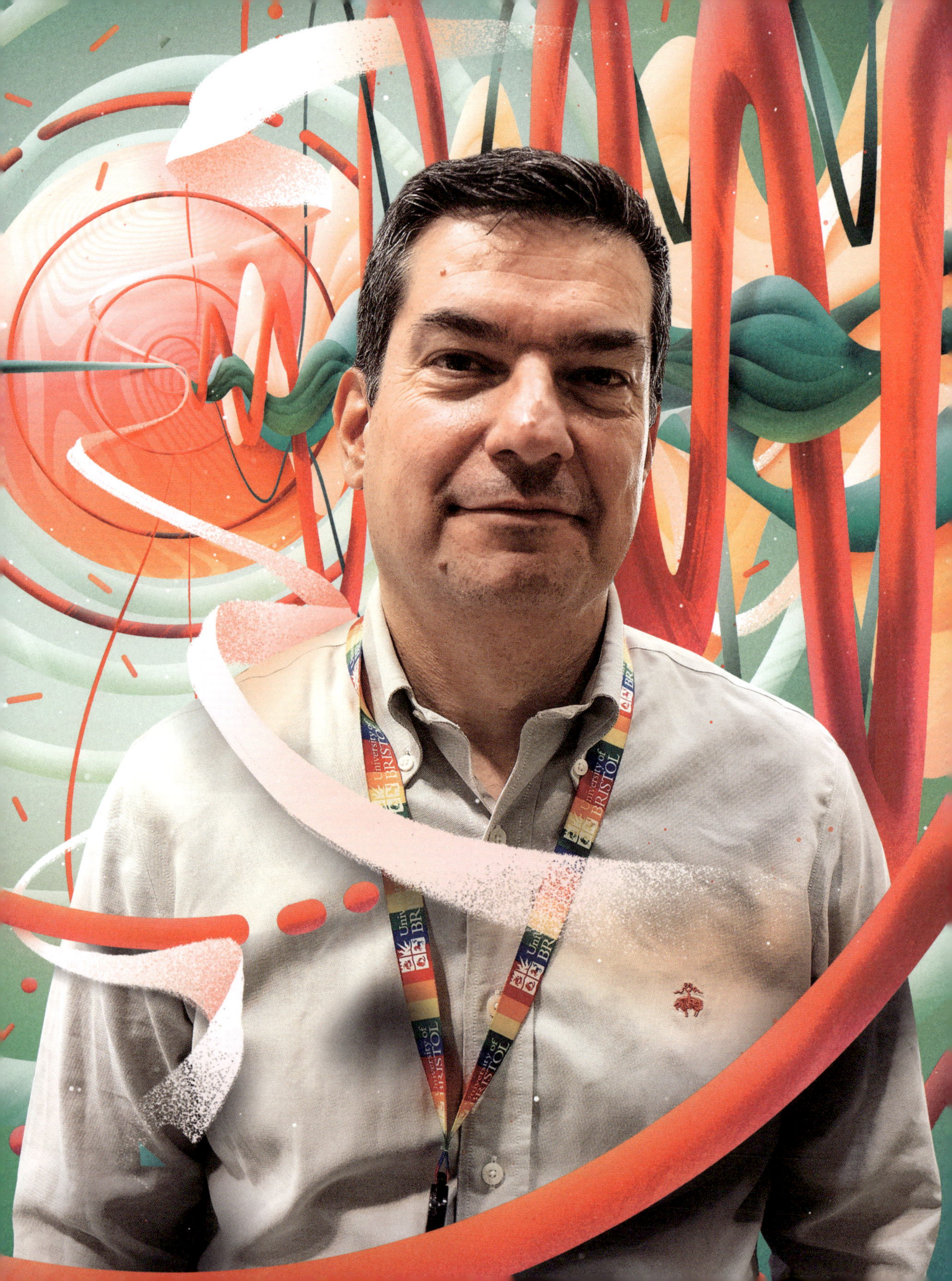
University of
BRISTOL

Professor Anastasios Sextos

CIVIL ENGINEER
MAKING INFRASTRUCTURE SAFE ON A BUDGET

Earthquakes tend to strike where the edges of tectonic plates – huge sections of Earth's surface – meet. Many places, such as Japan and the west coast of America, are prone to earthquakes because of where they are located. In many of these places, earthquake-proof technologies are incorporated into building designs.

When earthquakes strike, the amount of damage depends on three things: how strong the earthquake is, how many people live in the affected area and whether the buildings there are able to withstand an earthquake. We don't have much control over the first two factors, but in rich countries headway has been made in building earthquake-resistant structures. However, poorer countries often can't afford these expensive technologies to keep their people safe. Professor Anastasios Sextos wants to bridge that gap by developing cheap and effective earthquake solutions for all.

WHY DID YOU SPECIALISE IN EARTHQUAKE ENGINEERING?

When I was five years old, a strong earthquake struck Thessaloniki, my hometown in Greece. Fifty people were killed, and the area was devastated. My family and I had to leave home for three months until the building was inspected and confirmed as safe. It was 1978, and back then the knowledge of earthquake engineering was very limited compared to what we know now.

"Civil engineers carry a huge responsibility to protect people from the destruction of earthquakes by outsmarting them with their designs."

Professor Anastasios Sextos

The complexity of earthquakes is fascinating – they are unpredictable and have a random nature. It's a real challenge to outsmart them and I love that challenge. Because of this uncertainty, engineers not only aim to resist the forces of nature but also design ways for structures to fall in a way that creates the least damage and danger possible.

SO, HOW DO YOU OUTSMART AN EARTHQUAKE?

Current research has helped earthquake engineers to develop strategies for earthquake-resistant structures. We design the horizontal beams to be weaker so they absorb most of the earthquake's energy and we separate the building from the ground. To do this, the building can be built on rollers or bearings. This means that during an earthquake, while the ground is moving, the building can roll back and forth independently. This works like a shock absorber so that the building moves in a more gentle way than if it was attached to the ground and shaken by the earthquake. We generally build to go with the flow of the earthquake's forces instead of trying to fight them. People inside the building might experience an unpleasant wobbling sensation, but the structural damage is reduced.

These strategies can often be costly, so my team and I have been working on a cheaper alternative. We have found that building a structure on two PVC plastic sheets with a thin layer of sand grains between them can isolate the structure from the ground. The 'sand-wich' works well because there is a low amount of friction between the sand and the PVC, which allows the structure to move with an earthquake.

A SEISMICALLY ISOLATED BUILDING

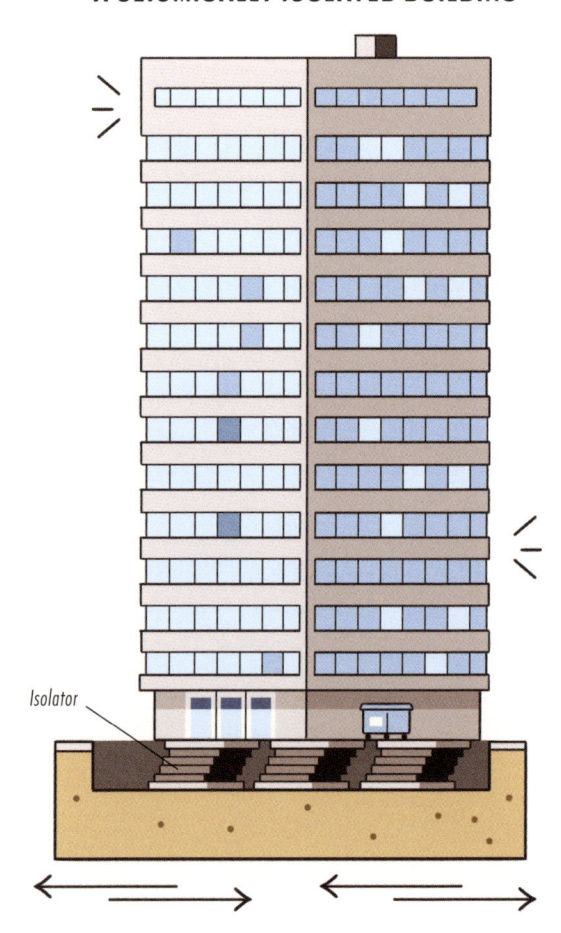

Isolator

A building that is seismically isolated is one that has been built with devices called isolators underneath it to separate it from the ground. The isolators absorb energy from an earthquake and reduce vibrations.

HOW DID YOU BECOME AN ENGINEER?

Engineering wasn't my first choice; I fell into it by accident. I was always very good at maths, so I enrolled in the Hellenic Air Force Academy, a Greek university, where I learnt to fly a small Cessna aircraft. After my first year, I decided that I wanted to contribute to society in a different way, but I didn't know how.

What was most important to me was to find a job that solved maths and physics problems and involved managing infrastructure and people. A family friend suggested that engineering would be a good choice. I had no idea what engineering was at that time since my father was a bank manager and my mother was a French language teacher.

I loved engineering from the first moments of studying it and have travelled the world thanks to my research. In 2015, I was appointed Professor at the University of Bristol after 12 years of academic service in Greece. This was a wonderful opportunity to work with brilliant academics and live in a beautiful city – I have been lucky enough to have lived in many amazing cities!

WHAT ARE THE MOST REWARDING ASPECTS OF YOUR WORK?

What is deeply rewarding is applying knowledge learnt in the lab to saving lives. This gives meaning and purpose to my life. At the University of Bristol we continue to develop a deep understanding of how to construct buildings to withstand the powerful forces of nature. We have three shaking tables in the lab, which we use to conduct scaled-down earthquakes in order to test our ideas. Often our solutions are cheap and ingenious so that all countries may benefit from our work.

It's tough to visit devastated earthquake sites, but it's nice to know that we can make a difference and help to ensure that the loss and pain people suffer will never happen again. The solutions we offer aim to make the world more equal by bridging the gap between the poor and rich because safety is a human right. Engineers can offer smartness in construction even if only small budgets are available.

WOULD YOU RECOMMEND ENGINEERING?

Definitely! And this brings an ancient Greek saying by Archimedes to my mind: 'Give me a place to stand and with a lever I will move the whole world.' This means that if we understand mechanics, we can literally move anything. If you are someone who wants to bring about change or find the best solutions to complex problems, then engineering is probably for you!

FACT FILE

Most fun thing about your job: Building structures is like playing with LEGO, just at a larger scale!

CAREER HIGHLIGHTS

1. Becoming a Fulbright Research Scholar at the University of Illinois Urbana-Champaign.

2. Being appointed Professor of Earthquake Engineering at the University of Bristol.

3. Becoming Director of the UKCRIC (UK Collaboratorium for Research on Infrastructure and Cities) National Facility for Soil-Structure Interaction.

Georgia Lilley

DESIGN ENGINEER APPRENTICE

BEGINNING A CAREER IN STRUCTURAL ENGINEERING

Engineering is all about teamwork and the best teams are those that are made up of all different types of people, from all walks of life. Georgia Lilley is at the start of her engineering journey and has a bright future ahead. Helping to design buildings in the bustling city of London, she is bringing a fresh outlook to her team at the Waterman Group.

WHY DID YOU CHOOSE A CIVIL ENGINEERING APPRENTICESHIP?

At secondary school I was good at most subjects. I went on to study biology, chemistry and physics A-levels, which is when I discovered a real passion for physics. I preferred its real-life application to the theoretical side of the subject and that made me realise that my future was in engineering. I had doubts about going to university full-time and so decided to explore alternative further education routes.

I accepted a Design Engineering apprentice role at Waterman Group. Apprenticeships are certainly not the easy route – as you have to work and study at the same time – but it has been invaluable in becoming the engineer I am today.

DESCRIBE THE DAY-TO-DAY OF YOUR APPRENTICESHIP.

My focus is on the structural engineering of large mixed-use buildings in London. I ensure that they are structurally sound and safe for occupants. I regularly visit construction sites to gather information for creating and validating 3D computer models of buildings. Additionally, I carry out calculations using the necessary building codes, regulations and standards, and sometimes use computer software to visualise the effects of more complex stresses and strains on a building.

WHAT ADVICE DO YOU HAVE FOR ANYONE THINKING OF GOING INTO ENGINEERING?

Work experience is key. Use your school holidays to try out different things because it helps to find out what you do and don't like. Don't be discouraged by any lack of representation in the construction industry, there has never been a better time to gain exposure. Be the catalyst for change that you want to see within the industry, accept new challenges and opportunities that come your way and if you want something, then go and get it!

FACT FILE

Most fun thing about your job: Finding solutions to challenges presented by climate change and the built environment in London.

CAREER HIGHLIGHTS

1. Having a significant role in the design team on the renovation of 100 New Bridge Street in London.

2. Being one of the top three teams in the Group Design Project module at university.

3. Winning the Association for Consultancy and Engineering's Apprentice of the Year award in 2021.

Computer with a 3D building model.

Heba Bevan

CEO AND ELECTRONICS AND COMPUTER ENGINEER
ADVANCING WIRELESS NETWORKS OF ELECTRONIC DEVICES

Different forms of engineering often intersect in interesting and surprising ways, and technology that was built for one industry might come in useful for something entirely different. For example, much of the electronics in smartphones have now been adapted and placed in other electronic devices to provide useful information in a variety of industries including infrastructure. Mobile phones were designed to exist in a network, needing key components such as radio transmitters and receivers to send and receive calls. Today, phones are far smarter thanks to an electronic chip, called a Central Processing Unit (CPU). Heba Bevan is one engineer who focuses on connecting all sorts of devices in order to make them smarter, more efficient and therefore more useful.

WHAT HAVE BEEN THE KEY STEPPING STONES IN YOUR ENGINEERING CAREER?

Firstly, both my father and sister are engineers. When I was a child I learnt to code and made simple video games using the programming language Basic. I have always loved solving mathematical problems and puzzles and I even seem to have transferred this interest to my daughter, who was already coding at the age of five!

During my first year at university, I did a summer internship at a company called ARM, that designs CPUs – they are basically the brains of a computer. I worked with ARM during all my holidays, and continued after graduating. During my time there I focused on improving specific technology required for smartphones, which have since become useful in other electronic devices.

Later on, during my PhD at the University of Cambridge, I researched how to make devices more power efficient. I also used artificial intelligence (AI) to record and interpret the data that these devices were collecting. The devices I worked on were sensors that were designed to be put in hard-to-reach places in infrastructure projects. When connected together, they could swap data that they had collected and use AI to smartly interpret it. Being more power efficient, they could also run for much longer on a small battery, which was great, because battery changes would have been tricky!

FACT FILE

Most fun thing about your job: Seeing our UtterBerry technology make our infrastructure 'talk back' to us.

CAREER HIGHLIGHTS

1. Completing an Electronics and Computer Engineering degree at the University of York.

2. Studying wireless sensor networks for my PhD at the University of Cambridge.

3. Being able to use my early love of computing as part of my career.

HOW WERE THESE SENSORS USED?

We used the sensors in an underground tunnel boring project in London. The tunnels being dug were surrounded by other old and significant systems of London infrastructure, some of which had been built during the First World War. We needed data from the sensors to ensure that the project was operating safely, carefully and efficiently and not damaging any of the existing infastructure. This data was being processed with AI to help the project engineers make better decisions for the project. This inspired me to start UtterBerry.

WHAT DO YOU DO AT UTTERBERRY?

We often use sensors to monitor various things to do with how structures are being used and also the conditions surrounding them. For example, a network of our sensors placed on a busy road could provide data on traffic levels. This could control traffic in real time, by varying speed limits and creating useful diversions. Our sensors help to keep our infrastructure running smoothly.

UtterBerry sensors have been placed on bridge construction projects to measure many variables, including wind speed, the number of cars travelling across the bridge and vibration – all of which is useful data for the project engineers.

Building with MMC

DIGITAL DEVELOPMENTS A key element of MMC is that a project can be digitally developed. Software called Building Integrated Modelling (BIM) is already widely used to design a building and analyse for things such as energy efficiency and sustainability. Engineers can make a 'digital twin', which is a digital model of the building that can even be used to test the effects of real-world situations. This information can be quickly shared with everyone involved in a project, even if they're not together onsite.

CHANGING ROLES Moving exclusively to MMC will inevitably involve a change in the kinds of jobs that are available in the construction industry. If more elements are mass-produced in factories, there will be fewer manual, onsite jobs and more jobs that involve digital skills.

SPEEDING TO THE FUTURE A project that is currently making use of MMC is HS2 (High Speed 2) – a super-fast railway line under construction in the UK, which will eventually go from London to Scotland. Tunnel walls, floor slabs, pillars and bridge parts are all being developed with modern methods of construction.

The construction site at the entrance to the HS2 Chiltern tunnel beside the M25 in Buckinghamshire.

Modern Methods of Construction, MMC for short, is also known as 'smart construction'. It's a way of using technology to make the building process quicker and more efficient, both in terms of the materials used and the people working on a project. There are lots of different ways this can be done, but one of the main aspects of MMC is that much of the production is done in a factory and the elements are then brought to the site to be assembled. These methods can be used for building all sorts of things, from roads and railways to big stadiums. It is hoped that using MMC can help to tackle the urgent need for more housing.

BALANCING THE PROS AND CONS Using these building methods has many benefits. It cuts down on the noise and disruption usually associated with construction sites and makes the whole process more efficient, which is undoubtedly better for the environment. Digital assessment also ensures that projects are as eco-friendly as possible from the start. However, MMC projects can be more expensive to set up and also involve the logistics of transporting some very large items.

RAISING THE ROOF MMC has opened up the possibility of more 'airspace' development, which means building upwards! Adding lightweight, pre-built modules to the top of existing buildings could create more housing in a way that doesn't need more land.

This modular unit was made in a factory and is being lifted on to the top of an apartment building. It is made of wood, which is becoming more popular in construction due to its manufacturing processes creating fewer greenhouse gases than concrete.

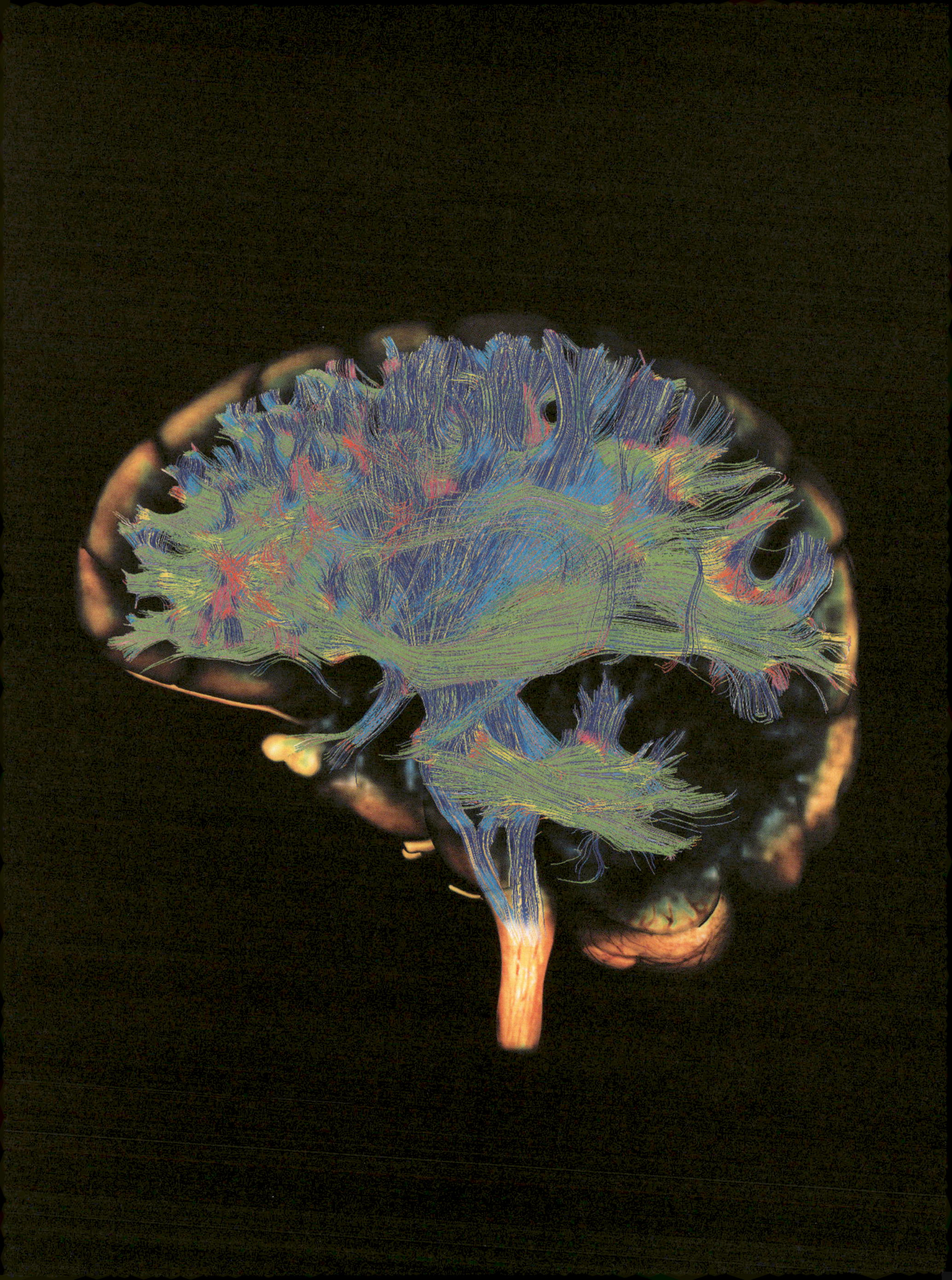

CHAPTER 5
HEALTHCARE

Engineers play a huge part in the medical industry. They have helped to create technology that allows us to see inside the body, such as X-ray and MRI (magnetic resonance imaging) machines. Robotics and AI have also helped to increase the efficiency, accuracy and effectiveness of many medical processes. Engineers are making a big difference to the way patients are diagnosed and treated and play an essential role in preventing disease from occurring in the first place.

Often, medical engineers have experience of several types of engineering along their career journeys before they land in medicine. All skills learnt in these different areas give medical engineers a broad knowledge to be able to handle a range of challenges in a rational, logical and caring way.

The engineers in this chapter all have different skills and areas of expertise, but one thing in common – their desire to help people. Let's meet five medical engineers who are advancing healthcare in their own incredible ways.

LEFT: When a person thinks, neurons in their brain use more oxygen and need more blood. An MRI scanner can detect this increased blood flow and create a map of the brain. A doctor can use a map such as this one to plan a surgical procedure, such as the removal of a tumour, and avoid damaging any of these important connections in the brain.

Alan James Proud

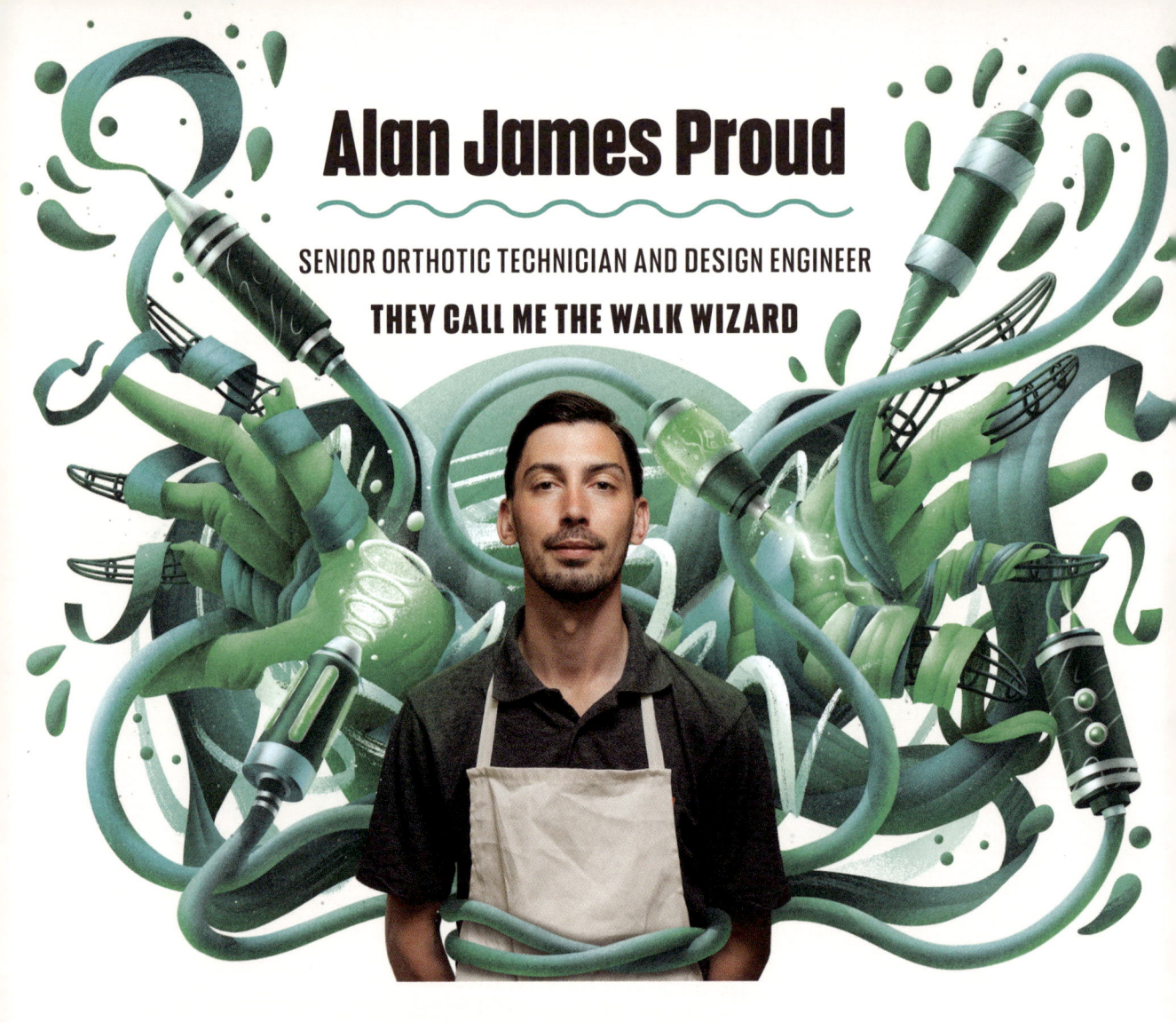

SENIOR ORTHOTIC TECHNICIAN AND DESIGN ENGINEER
THEY CALL ME THE WALK WIZARD

Accidents, injuries, birth defects and diseases can result in people losing limbs or suffering from muscle and bone deformities. These conditions might reduce a patient's ability to move or do certain things, so prosthetists and orthotists focus their careers on helping patients move freely on their own again.

Prosthetists and orthotists design and build devices such as splints, braces, footwear and artificial body parts. They use 3D imaging software to help bring their ideas to life and usually work together with medical professionals to create the best solutions for each patient. Prosthetists create and fit artificial limbs, whereas orthotists correct deformities in nerves, muscles and bones. Orthotic technicians, like Alan James Proud, design and build the devices that orthotists recommend.

WHAT DOES YOUR WORK INVOLVE?

An orthotist will prescribe a device for a patient and will usually send me a scan and cast of the patient's limb or a list of measurements. I then manufacture the device using a range of different 3D design software and machines. Knowledge of the way bones, muscles and nerves work together is essential for my job because each device is bespoke for the patient. No two days at work are the same! The best bit about my job is hearing gratitude and appreciation for the difference that our devices have made in patients' lives. This makes me love my career even more.

WHAT INSPIRED YOU TO GET INTO ORTHOTICS?

From a young age, I have always loved creating useful objects, but I struggled with reading and writing. I had no confidence when it came to most school subjects. After being diagnosed with dyslexia, I realised that I viewed the world differently to others and today I use that as a superpower. School teachers helped me develop my skills and talents, and it became evident that an apprenticeship was a much better fit for me than university. I went on to study more National Vocational Qualifications (NVQs) to become a senior technician and have since won a few awards, including the Technician of the Year award – run by the British Association of Prosthetics and Orthotists – in 2020. I am also an ambassador for the Royal Academy of Engineering.

FACT FILE

Most fun thing about your job: Working with my hands and making solutions to problems – then seeing the outcome.

CAREER HIGHLIGHTS

1. Winning the British Association of Prosthetists and Orthotists' Technician of the Year award.

2. Seeing the products I've made help people.

3. Every day being different. There are always more highlights to come!

3D PRINTING A PROSTHETIC LIMB

A blueprint of the prosthetic is created using computer software.

The design is sent to the 3D printer.

Plastic thread is heated until it melts, then 'printed' on to the plate where it cools into the shape needed.

Heating device

Spool of plastic thread

The prosthetic is built up, layer by layer.

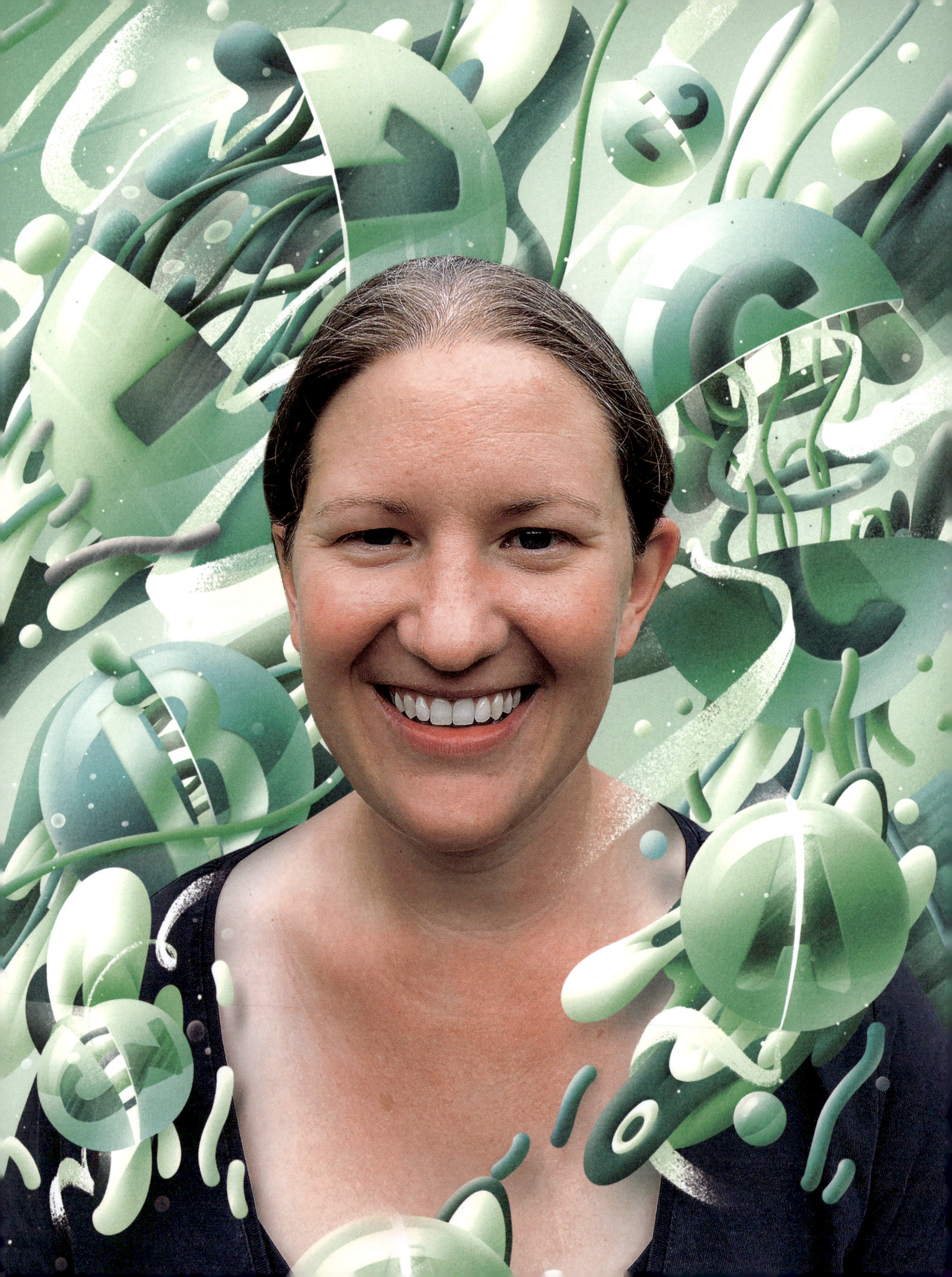

Dr Samantha Micklewright

BIOMEDICAL ENGINEER
HELPING PATIENTS TO COMMUNICATE

The only way for a medical professional to really understand if a treatment is working for a patient is to speak to them about their experiences. But some patients have difficulty with communication, which is where biomedical engineer Dr Samantha Micklewright can help. She is a Clinical Scientist working at the Sussex Community NHS Foundation Trust, where she provides tablet computers, electronic devices and associated access methods to patients who are unable to speak.

WHAT WAS YOUR JOURNEY INTO MEDICAL ENGINEERING LIKE?

Medical engineering wasn't a clear choice for me in the beginning. As a result, I spent many years studying and didn't have a very straightforward educational journey. During my first Master's degree I spent a year working at a packaging machinery company. This felt odd for me, but I gave it a go because there were no medical engineering placements available. I learnt many skills there that have made me a better medical engineer today. To enter the NHS, I needed to complete another Master's in Clinical Engineering, and while studying for this I also worked full-time at the Clinical Engineering department in Salisbury Hospital. This was a great experience as they specialise in using Functional Electrical Stimulation (when an electrical current is applied to a muscle to help it move) and Clinical Gait Analysis to analyse and improve how a patient walks.

ANALYSING HOW A PERSON WALKS

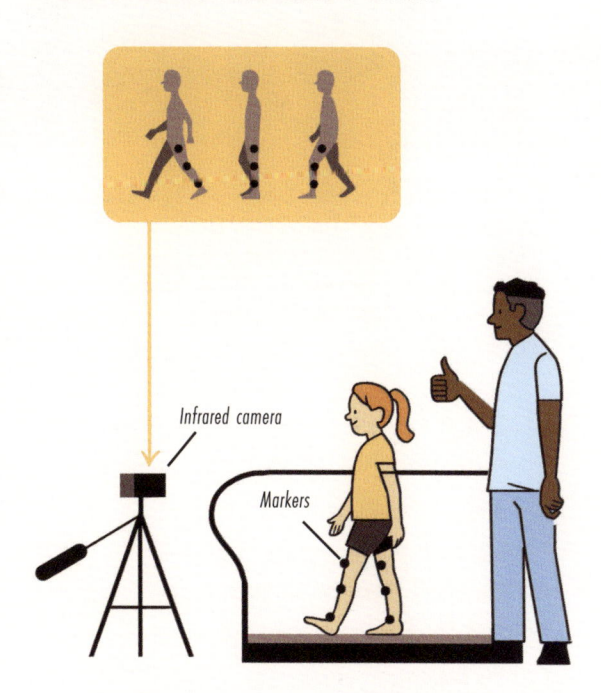

The doctor attaches reflective markers to certain points on the patient's body, then the patient walks along a walkway. An infrared camera tracks the position of the markers and sensors in the floor measure the forces that are exerted from the patient. All of this data is analysed to show how the patient walks.

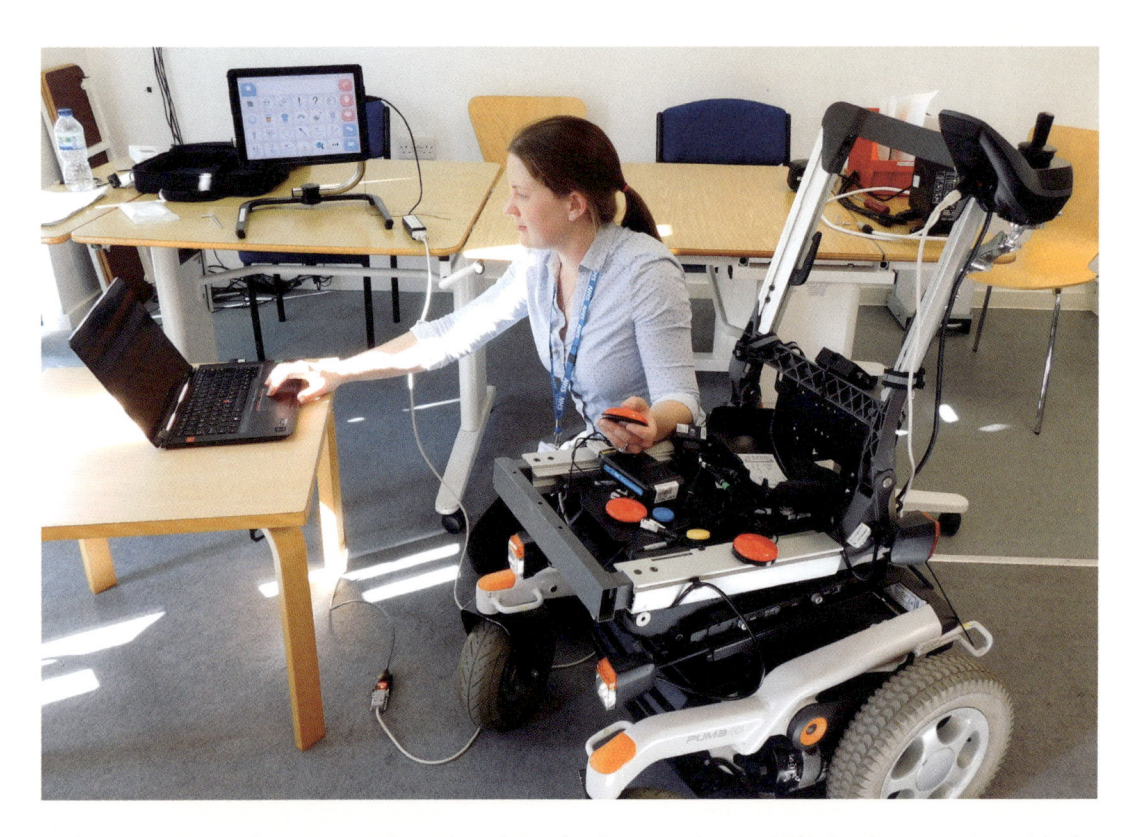

In this picture Samantha is testing a bespoke solution for 'integrated access'. This is where a patient wished to use their only access method (a switch) to be able to independently control both the driving of their power chair as well as the tablet on the table behind, which has the voice output communication software on. So, she programmed an additional function into the power chair to add the communication – the switches now drive the chair and allow the patient to select cells on the tablet accordingly.

I have always been particularly fascinated by knees and hips because, from an engineering perspective, they allow us to do so much. Parts of the knee can withstand huge forces (in normal daily activities your knee joints can experience forces that are 9.7 times your body weight) and the integration of artificial knees and hips into the human body is incredible. During my PhD at the Centre for Orthopaedic Biomechanics at the University of Bath, I learnt about the structure, function and motion of the knee and how it can heal. I can now apply this knowledge to my bioengineering work in the NHS.

WHAT WERE THE KEY ENGINEERING LESSONS YOU LEARNT DURING YOUR TIME AT THE PACKAGING COMPANY?

I learnt a lot from having to solve problems that would often occur with the high-speed packaging machinery. Production lines processing 300 packages a minute could suddenly puff into a cloud of smoke, forcing us engineers to use logic and high-speed cameras to fix these issues. This process allowed me to develop confidence in suggesting my own solutions.

WHAT DOES YOUR CURRRENT DAY-TO-DAY JOB INVOLVE?

I perform clinical assessments of patients with speech and mobility difficulties. Working together with speech and occupational therapists, I design and provide solutions that allow patients to use computer technology as their voice. For example, if someone can't speak or use their limbs, we could trial a head-switch activated iPad, which would allow the patient to type text messages or allow them to select pre-set messages in specialist software.

If head movement isn't possible in a patient, we could trial eye-gaze technology, where cells on the tablet screen can be selected by tracking where the patient looks. Their eyes can activate a voice output of what they would like to say.

All these solutions often need to integrate with other aspects of the patient's care, such as driving their wheelchairs. My work involves finding and assessing the best fit of technology for the patient's needs.

WHAT ADVICE DO YOU HAVE FOR ANYONE THINKING OF BECOMING A MEDICAL ENGINEER?

Hard work and determination are key. I chose a university route into my profession and had an incredible time, making friends for life. But there are also apprenticeship routes, which are equally valuable. Qualifications are essential, but I have learnt more through experience and have gained the most confidence through doing my job well. I put extra time into my work because it gives me confidence knowing that I am up to date with the latest research in my profession.

FACT FILE

Most fun thing about your job: Knowing that my team and I have found solutions to improve patients' quality of life – this isn't always possible, so I appreciate it every time that we can.

CAREER HIGHLIGHTS

1. Finishing my PhD at the Centre for Orthopaedic Biomechanics at the University of Bath.

2. Presenting my research at international conferences.

3. Completing the Scientist Training Programme in Clinical Engineering.

"I enjoy making a positive difference in people's lives and the direct interaction I have with my patients. It's easy for me to be passionate about my work."

Dr Samantha Micklewright

Dr Arash Angadji

MEDICAL ENGINEER

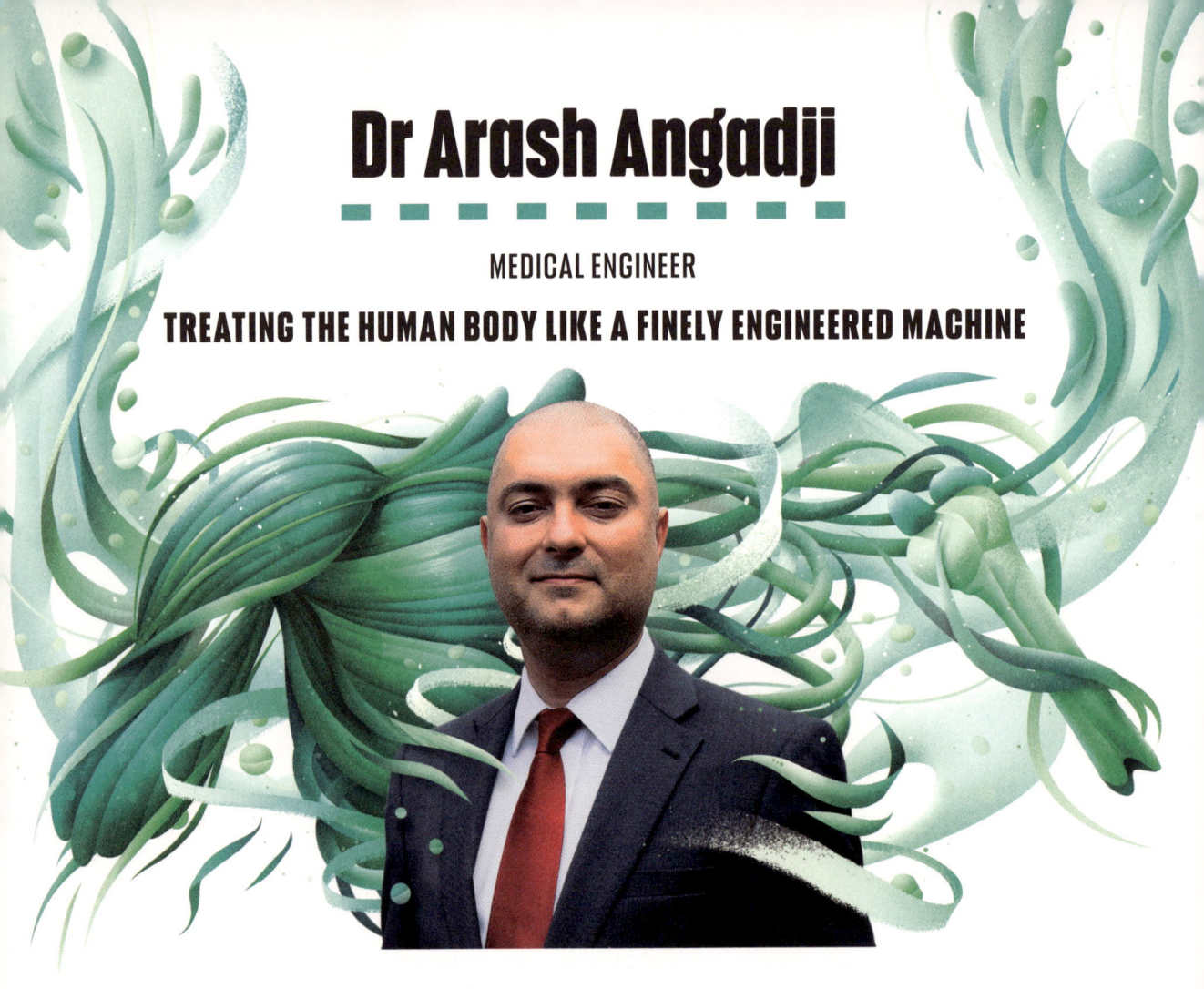

TREATING THE HUMAN BODY LIKE A FINELY ENGINEERED MACHINE

Dr Arash Angadji leads Orthopaedic Research UK, a charity dedicated to advancing musculoskeletal health, which is to do with keeping our bones, joints and muscles functioning well. He gives funding to start-ups in order to help get new healthcare technologies out to patients.

"When you can think like a true engineer, I believe the world is your oyster."

Dr Arash Angadji

WHAT DOES ORTHOPAEDIC RESEARCH UK DO?

At Orthopaedic Research UK, we support healthcare professionals in reaching academic and clinical standards, which involves training and educating the next generation of clinicians. We aim to improve patients' quality of life and help reduce pressures on the NHS. We started a scheme that helps to bring brand new new ideas and designs to patients sooner. This was started because there is often a delay between innovations being developed and then being put into use. Research that is done by academics more often than not ends up in a library gathering dust once the researcher completes their qualification, and patients lose out.

WHAT ARE SOME ENGINEERING START-UPS YOU HAVE SUPPORTED THROUGH YOUR SCHEME?

We have supported a fantastic researcher from the University of Southampton who came up with a substance called Nanoclay, which is used to fill the gaps between fractured bone parts. Nanoclay also contains medicine to aid healing. Another company uses sensors and AI algorithms to achieve a better fit of prosthetic devices. Better-fitting prosthetics reduce the number of trips to the hospital and improve the quality of life for the patient. Luckily my knowledge of engineering has been so useful in helping me see the value in all these great entrepreneurial ideas and identify which ones to support.

HOW DID YOU END UP IN MEDICAL ENGINEERING?

I was born in Aberdeen, Scotland, when my father was doing his MSc in Agricultural Engineering. We stayed in the UK until I was five years old before moving back to Iran where my parents are from. I went to school in Iran and wasn't a great student, but I enjoyed maths and physics. I was fascinated by space and new technologies, so I knew that I wanted a job in engineering.

When I was 18, I returned to the UK to go to university. I started Electronics Engineering, but needed to work a couple of part-time jobs to support myself. At the time I had a flatmate called Amir, who was doing his PhD in Medical Engineering. I would often visit Amir in his lab and thought his experiments were awesome. They involved incredible mechanical setups that replicated the human body and made biology seem really fun. So, in 2004, I transitioned from Electronics Engineering to Medical Engineering.

I then went on to do a PhD where I researched artificial hip replacements. After my PhD I struggled to find a job due to the recession. Companies were hesitant to hire people, but I came across a charitable foundation who were looking for a researcher to manage the orthopaedic research projects that they were funding. On my first day, I was handed a key to a little cabinet to sort through all their research files. I have been there ever since.

FACT FILE

Most fun thing about your job: Supporting entrepreneurs to accelerate innovation in our field.

CAREER HIGHLIGHTS

1. Being able to successfully rebrand (change the corporate image) of the charity after completing an MBA degree in 2010.

2. Becoming one of the youngest CEOs of a medical research charity in the UK in 2016.

3. Becoming the first musculoskeletal charity in the UK to actively invest in entrepreneurs and start-ups.

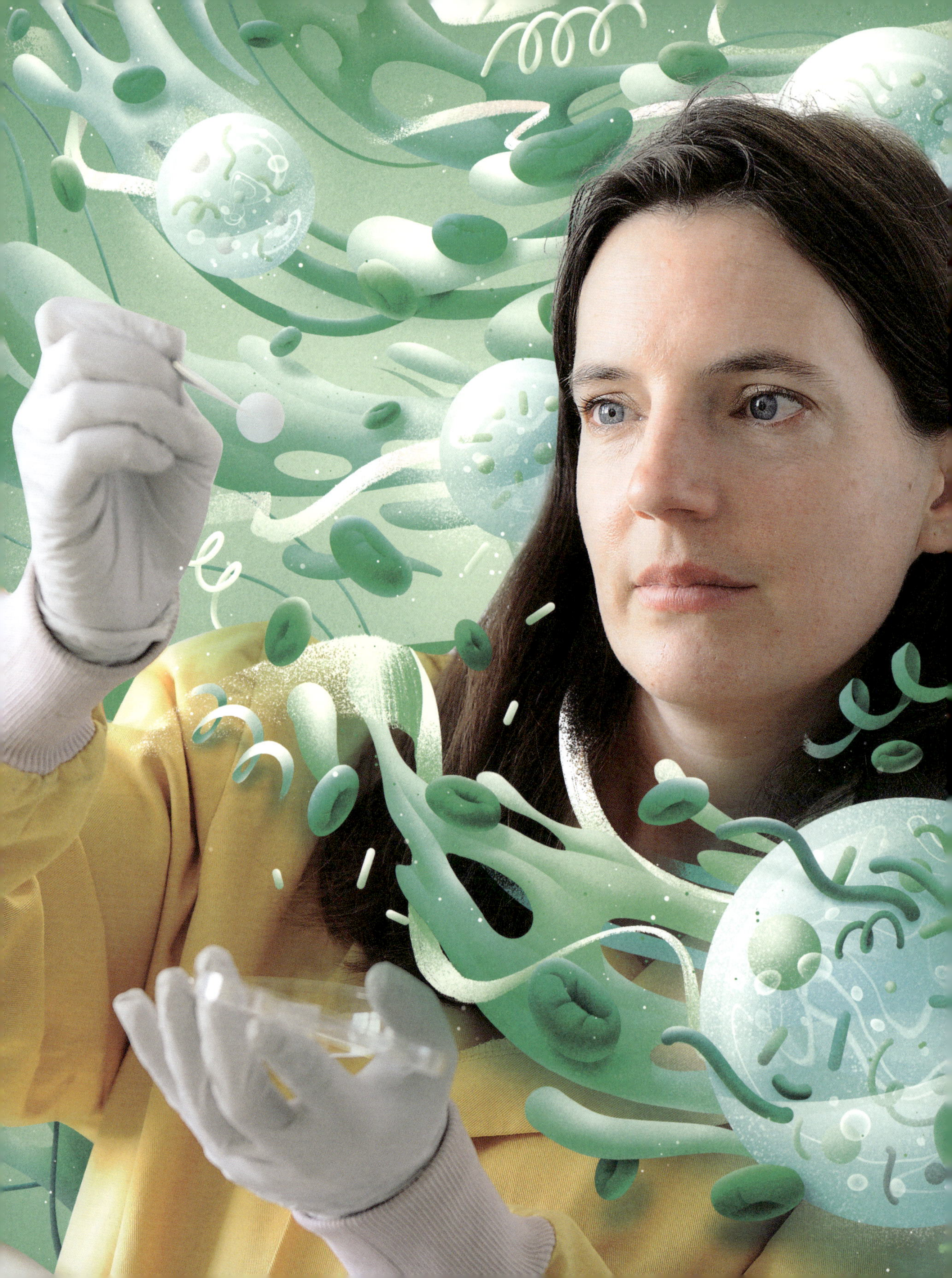

Professor Molly Stevens

PROFESSOR IN BIOMEDICAL ENGINEERING
MAKING AN IMPACT IN BIOENGINEERING

Healthcare usually involves treating the symptoms of diseases and injuries, but regenerative medicine takes a different approach. It seeks to replace damaged or malfunctioning tissues or organs with novel bioengineering, which is when engineering processes are used to create technologies for healthcare. Biosensors are a significant part of regenerative medicine. They can be placed inside the body to provide data on what is happening there by detecting key molecules, called biomarkers, and analysing what the body needs to be well.

Professor Molly Stevens is a Research Director within the Institute of Biomedical Engineering at Imperial College London. Her research group is made up of engineers, chemists, cell biologists, surgeons, physicists, mathematicians and computer scientists. Pooling together this range of expertise has led to the development of innovative and unique materials, often organised at a nanoscale. At the moment, a number of their technologies, including their advanced diagnostic tools (that help to diagnose problems), are being transferred from the lab and are being supported with samples from patients with a range of illnesses.

WAS IT OBVIOUS FROM A YOUNG AGE THAT YOU WOULD END UP IN BIOENGINEERING?

Not at all! I was always interested in a range of subjects but went down the science route taking A-levels in maths, chemistry and biology (and also French literature!). I continued my other interests alongside my A-levels through my love of travelling. I have always been open-minded and passionate about learning. I like to stay intellectually engaged and always learning new things.

WHAT WERE THE SIGNIFICANT STEPS IN YOUR EDUCATION?

I started off with an undergraduate degree in Pharmacy, where we studied drug design and pharmacology. After that, I went travelling for a year in India, Nepal and South East Asia. I then decided to do a PhD because I really wanted to challenge myself. I chose the really difficult research topic of single-molecule biophysics, despite not having A-level Physics. After my PhD, I wanted to pursue something that could have a massive impact on society, particularly in global health.

WHAT IS UNIQUE ABOUT WHAT YOU DO IN YOUR RESEARCH GROUP?

We are interested in how biology interacts with materials. Our research is where the human body and materials engineering meet. The knowledge we gain from this research is used in regenerative medicine or the creation and delivery of medication and biosensing. Biosensors tell us what is happening inside the body, which informs us on how to best control and treat conditions with our technologies.

My team recently invented a brand new instrument called SPARTA (Single Particle Automated Raman Trapping Analysis) that can study the chemistry of single nanoparticles in a way that hasn't previously been possible. This technology has been really useful in gene therapy (altering a person's genes to prevent or treat diseases), studying vaccines and other small particles called exosomes, which are released from all cells, including cancer cells.

Today, we work with materials that are structured at the nanoscale. We use 3D visualisation software to see on a computer screen what is happening at the nanoscale, which is so exciting.

WHAT HAPPENS INSIDE SPARTA

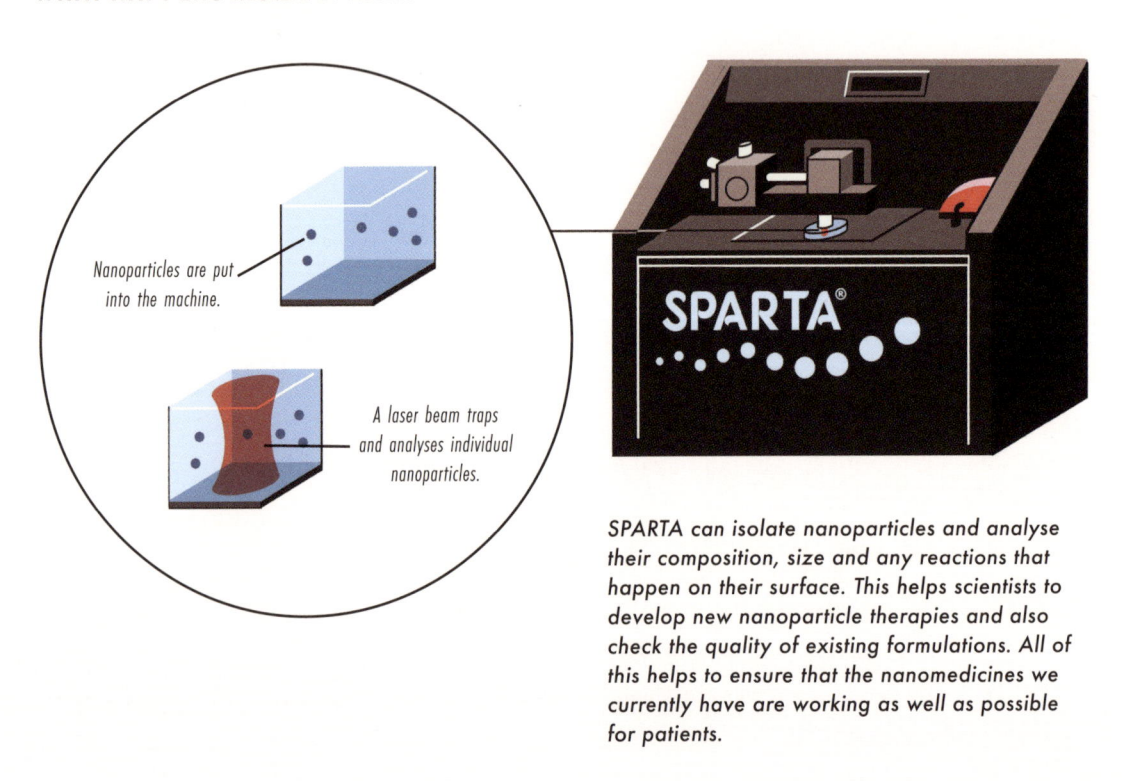

Nanoparticles are put into the machine.

A laser beam traps and analyses individual nanoparticles.

SPARTA can isolate nanoparticles and analyse their composition, size and any reactions that happen on their surface. This helps scientists to develop new nanoparticle therapies and also check the quality of existing formulations. All of this helps to ensure that the nanomedicines we currently have are working as well as possible for patients.

WHAT ARE THE HIGHLIGHTS OF YOUR CAREER?

For me, it's about the work we do in the lab and ensuring it has a greater impact in the wider world beyond. The instruments that we have developed came about from the research we were doing on nanoparticle systems. There was no technology available that could do automated chemical measurements of individual particles, so we invented SPARTA. We satisfied an engineering driven challenge, and now many companies are interested in using our technology. That has been very rewarding.

I think our work in new nanomedicines will continue to be transformative, because we are taking the time to deeply understand it. This is a highlight of our research and underpins everything we do. But there is so much more to do that there are never enough hours in the day! I find myself constantly assessing how to prioritise the different things that need doing. It keeps me on my toes for sure.

DO YOU HAVE ANY ADVICE FOR STUDENTS HOPING TO FOLLOW IN YOUR FOOTSTEPS?

I took some quite sizeable gaps in my training to travel before my PhD, and after my PhD I spent quite a while in South America. I was never trying to race to the finish line of my career. I was just somebody who wanted to stay curious.

We should always engage in the things that are interesting to us, but also think about the impact we are having on the world, and choose our careers wisely. Each one of the limited hours in our week is really precious.

Travelling and learning about other cultures, visiting places and meeting new people have been essential and really valuable to me. I don't think anyone should overlook the importance of these types of experiences. I also think it is essential to surround yourself with great humans – for me, that is a priority.

FACT FILE

Most fun thing about your job: Working with a group of wonderful researchers and brainstorming new ideas together.

CAREER HIGHLIGHTS

1. Being named in Technology Review Magazine's TR100 list and over 20 other major international awards.

2. Being elected as a member of the US National Academy of Engineering.

3. Being elected as a Fellow of the Royal Society.

"I have always been driven by learning, and the opportunity to work on things that contribute to society – to me, that is the most important thing. Working with a great team is key to my research."

Professor Molly Stevens

Dr Uğur Tanrıverdi

MEDICAL DESIGN ENGINEER

MAKING PROSTHETICS COMFORTABLE AND ADAPTABLE

Our bodies change shape throughout the day, but prosthetic limbs are not so adaptable. At the end of the day, an artificial limb that felt fine in the morning might have become uncomfortable or even unusable for the amputee. Dr Uğur Tanrıverdi and his company Unhindr aim to address this problem. They are developing automated prosthetic limbs that quickly adjust to suit the wearer's needs.

HOW DOES YOUR TECHNOLOGY WORK?

Our technology has hardware and software that work in tandem. The hardware part is the wearable robotic system, while the software part communicates with the hardware using AI. The AI learns about the amputees' preferences via a mobile phone app. With this technology we hope to reduce clinic visits, allowing amputees to be more comfortable and less reliant on medical services.

WHAT INSPIRED YOU TO FOUND UNHINDR?

I always wanted to be a mechanical engineer. My first word was 'maquina', which means 'machine' in Turkish. I went to a science high school to study mechanics and science, but I also learnt about the human body and medicine. I considered becoming a doctor because I have always wanted to help people, but then I found biomedical engineering, which is all about designing and developing devices for human medical applications. That was my eureka moment. I realised I could design machines and help people at the same time. Being Turkish, I couldn't get a student visa in the UK and so I decided to start my own company instead. I later completed two Master's and a PhD at Imperial College London to gain expertise.

HOW DO YOU CREATE A PROSTHETIC?

I start by sketching ideas on paper and then transferring them onto a computer. These designs are then 3D printed or otherwise built cheaply using different moulding techniques to make protoypes. We then run trials with amputees to test our prototypes. Unhindr has been in development for over six years now. We are working towards a final product, but we are not there yet.

> *"If you want to make a change in someone's life, then become an engineer!"*

Uğur Tanrıverdi

AN UNHINDR PROSTHETIC AND APP

Instant comfort adjustments can be made to the prosthetic (the hardware) via the app (the software). The prosthetic includes a kind of sock that the patient wears under the prosthetic. The sock is filled with a type of fluid that makes the prosthetic more comfortable and is adjusted by rollers inside it.

FACT FILE

Most fun thing about your job: Turning my ideas into things that people can use and interact with.

CAREER HIGHLIGHTS

1. Getting rejected from the Master's programme that I wanted to study – but as a result doing one that was more interesting!

2. Turning a bad experience into a good one and founding my own company after being rejected from many jobs for not having a European passport.

3. Co-founding Unhindr.

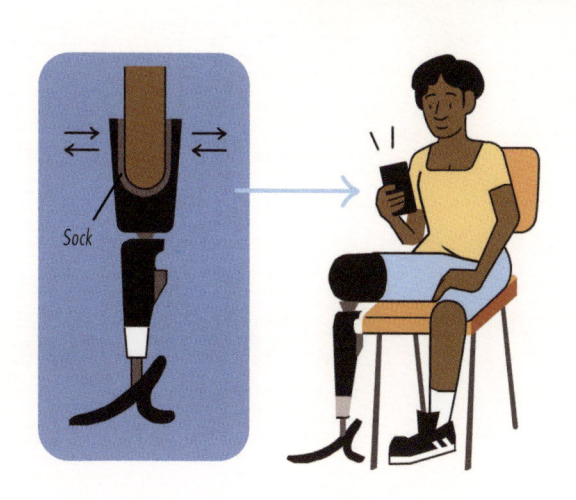

Engineering Genes

HOW IS IT DONE? Since the 1970s, when the concept of genetic engineering was first established, many different methods of genetic engineering have been developed. One of the biggest breakthroughs came in 2012, using a tool called CRISPR. The tool can target a section of DNA and cut it, like with a pair of scissors. This cut section of DNA could be repaired, altered or deactivated. It's the first technology we have that's truly capable of changing the chemistry of who we are.

Here are some of the ways genetic engineering can be used:

These tomatoes have been engineered to have more vitamin D than usual.

IN ANIMALS We can edit animals' genes to make them hardier and more resistant to disease. Genetic engineering could also eliminate problems associated with particular breeds, such as breathing issues or blindness.

IN CROPS Genetic engineering can be used to modify crops to make them stronger and more resilient. For example, scientists have modified cotton plants to make them poisonous to the insects that would damage them. In 2022, it was announced that tomatoes could be engineered to boost their vitamin D content.

All living things have DNA. It is a chemical that's present in the cells of every living thing and acts as an instruction manual for how something should grow and function. Genes are short sections of DNA, containing the genetic code that gives living things their individual characteristics. We inherit half of our genetic code from our biological mother and half from our biological father and it determines many things such as our hair and eye colour and the way we laugh. Genetic engineers can read and record segments of DNA in a process called 'DNA sequencing'. This information can then be used to change some bits of DNA by instructing cells to grow and develop in a different way. It's so precise that it's now often called 'genetic editing' and it has many uses.

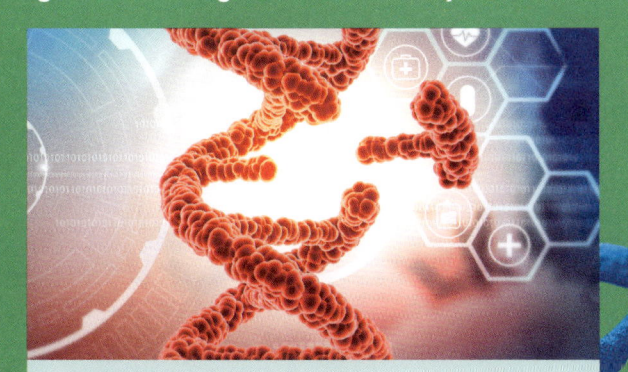

CRISPR can be used to activate or deactivate certain genes. This helps scientists work out which genes cause certain diseases.

IN MEDICINES Genetic engineering is already used to produce important medicines such as insulin, human growth hormones and the hepatitis B vaccine. CRISPR technology is now set to revolutionise the process of drug development.

IN HUMANS Scientists are developing gene technology that would enable humans to fight off certain cancers and viruses, such as COVID-19. Gene editing could be used to prevent or treat many types of serious, inherited diseases, including cystic fibrosis, sickle cell anaemia and muscular dystrophy.

ETHICAL ISSUES There is much debate around the use of genetic engineering. For example, if certain conditions are edited out of existence, some people argue it will mean less suffering, while others say it will lead to a less inclusive world.

... AND IN MUCH, MUCH MORE! This amazing technology is being used to create many things, from mosquitoes that don't spread disease to algae that produce large amounts of biofuel, and there are many more exciting developments on the horizon.

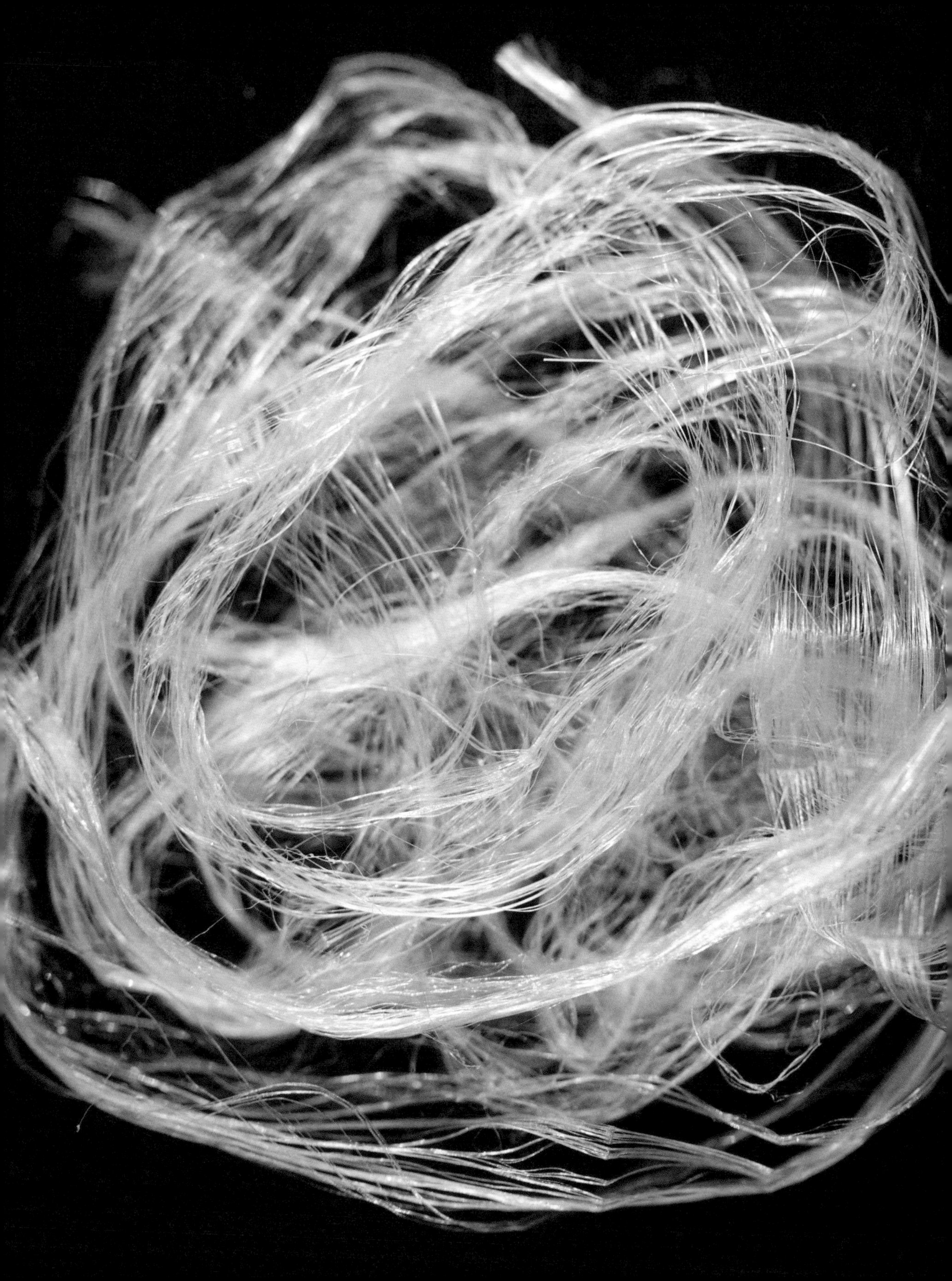

CHAPTER 6
ADVANCED MATERIALS

Construction, transport, packaging, healthcare, communication technologies and fashion all require materials that have been engineered in some way. Engineering is used either to collect raw materials from the ground or transform them into products. Sometimes, advanced engineering technologies can even be used to carefully build new materials, atom by atom.

All materials have specific properties and are chosen or made because of those properties. The mechanical properties of a material might be its hardness, how easy it is to shape, how tough it is or how it breaks. Ceramics, for example, tend to be great thermal insulators, so are an excellent choice to make containers, such as pie dishes, that can be put into the oven. Sometimes, an engineer might need a combination of properties that can't be found in one single material – that's when new materials are created.

Engineering advanced materials has allowed us to travel faster, see further and explore deeper and beyond what is humanly possible. Materials engineering vastly improves our quality of life on a daily basis – let's find out how.

LEFT: *Spider silk is thought to be one of the toughest fibres on Earth, but engineers have now found a way to create a material that has the potential to be even tougher. Artificial spider silk has been developed by genetically engineered bacteria and could be used in the future to replace many plastic-based fibres.*

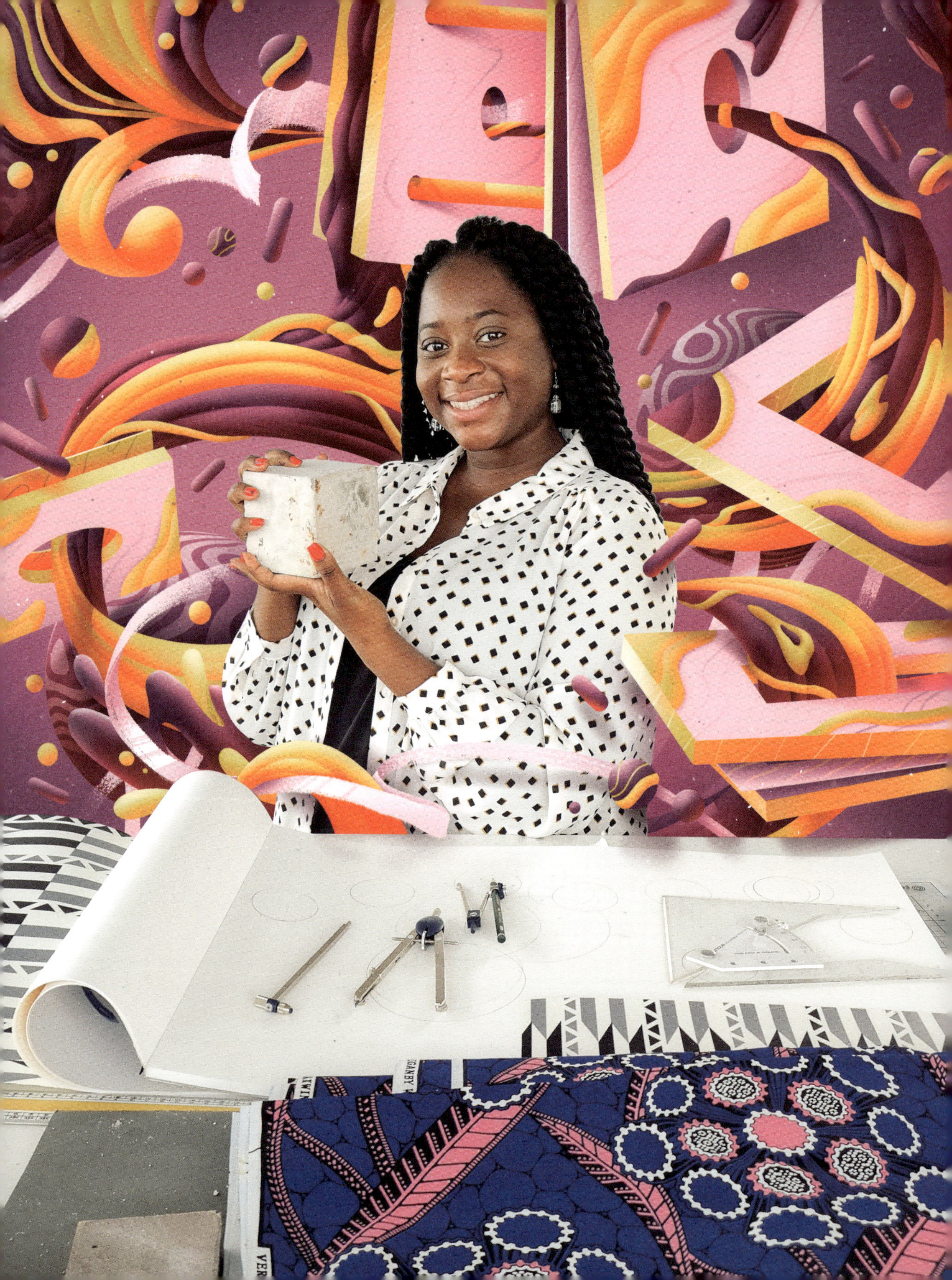

Mimi Nwosu

CIVIL ENGINEER

A MATERIAL GIRL IN A MATERIAL WORLD (CONCRETE EDITION)

In the UK, we spend approximately 90 per cent of our time inside buildings – at home, work or school. Most of the buildings we occupy were made using concrete, which is the most widely used material in the world. It was first used by people centuries ago and comes in a variety of forms depending on the mix of its key ingredients: cement, air, water, sand and gravel. The quantity of each ingredient in the mix determines the concrete's mechanical properties – how it responds to certain forces. All forms of concrete are strong, durable and versatile (meaning that it can be used in lots of different ways and for different purposes). But it has a downside: cement, one of concrete's key ingredients, is not good for the environment. It contributes to eight per cent of the world's carbon dioxide emissions.

Mimi Nwosu is a multi-award-winning Civil Engineer who specialises in concrete and has worked on many high-profile construction projects in London. She reviews concrete mixes and offers her specialist knowledge and advice on reducing the amount of cement used, or suggests cement replacements.

INGREDIENTS FOR CONCRETE

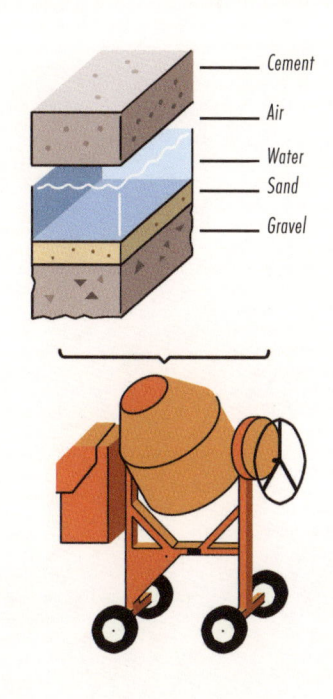

Cement
Air
Water
Sand
Gravel

WHY DID YOU DECIDE TO SPECIALISE IN CONCRETE?

It may not look like it, but concrete is such a wonderful and versatile material. I love the innovation required to work with it and also the challenge of how to make it more environmentally friendly for infrastructure projects. My interest in concrete first developed during university. One particular module that we studied was Soils and Materials and we learnt about various different construction materials. I was fascinated by concrete and its incredible mechanical and physical properties. I decided I wanted to further explore one of these properties – its natural fire resistance.

I then focused my final year university assignment on ultra-high-performance fibre-reinforced concrete (UHPFRC) at extreme temperatures. This turned out to be very helpful because one of the first projects I worked on as a civil engineer used just this type of concrete! This boosted my confidence, as I had some expertise on the strength and durability of this concrete in fire conditions. It was a perfect fit.

HOW DID YOU GET INTO CIVIL ENGINEERING?

I knew that I wanted to help save lives! I was the kid who always asked 'how' and 'why' and science usually provided me with those answers. I went down a STEM route at GCSE and A-level and had high hopes of becoming a doctor. I studied biology, chemistry, psychology and religious studies, but didn't get the grades that I needed to study medicine, so I ended up studying a general science course that didn't interest me at all. After a few months I almost dropped out of science completely, until a chance incident, which changed the course of my career.

One afternoon, I accompanied a friend to his lecture. At that time, I was feeling as though I had lost faith in what I was doing and needed a break from my course. My friend's lecture turned

Mimi worked with concrete quality and production for the construction of many HS2 projects, such as the Colne Valley Viaduct, which will be the longest railway bridge in the UK. Mimi's work involved testing the concrete in a lab and optimising it for use onsite.

out to be about bridge design and construction methods, and I was blown away with how fascinating this subject was. I took three pages of notes and asked the lecturer loads of questions afterwards – he was full of passion and enthusiasm for his subject. I remember thinking: 'Wow, civil engineers are such unsung heroes, they actually save billions of lives every day!' It took me 15 minutes to switch to studying Civil Engineering at the University of Portsmouth, and so began my engineering journey.

WHAT ARE SOME OF THE JOBS YOU HAVE UNDERTAKEN AS AN ENGINEER?

As a civil engineer with expertise in concrete, I am able to engage in a range of projects. I have been part of projects constructing bridges, tunnels, roads, towns and airports. I have worked in a range of environments too: in a laboratory testing the performance and properties of concrete; onsite (usually in a hard hat and high vis clothing) making sure projects are constructed on time and that the concrete quality is good; in an office managing health and safety and budgets, or analysing data, writing reports and giving presentations to clients, directors and other colleagues.

I have also worked as a Graduate Highways Engineer where I designed and supervised projects that help create our roads. This included designing road layouts, cycle lanes, pavement design, road markings, roundabouts and traffic signals.

WHAT ADVICE DO YOU HAVE FOR ANYONE WANTING TO BE AN ENGINEER?

I would say that it helps to have a plan. Find opportunities where you can use the skills that you enjoy most and develop the skills you lack. It is important to regularly learn new things. Looking back, I wish I ignored all of the people who told me engineering may not be for me. Today, I show up to work as my true self and I am willing and excited to learn. I hope that trait never leaves me.

FACT FILE

Most fun thing about your job: Seeing projects from start to finish and being able to say to people 'I built that!'

CAREER HIGHLIGHTS

1. Completing my Engineering degree, even though I didn't have A-levels in maths or physics.

2. Winning many awards and being named as one of the Top 50 Women in Engineering in the UK in 2021.

3. Expanding my career into television presenting!

"Let engineering be the career you want it to be and try not to fit into any mould of what an engineer 'should' look like."

Mimi Nwosu

DON'T FORGET TO LOVE EACH OTHER

Dr Clara Michelle Barker

ELECTRICAL AND MATERIALS ENGINEER
BUILDING THIN FILMS ATOM BY ATOM

Many items, from windows to camera lenses, sunglasses and touch screen phones, have thin coatings on them. And each of these coatings has a different purpose. For example, the insides of glass tomato ketchup bottles are lined with a thin film that ensures all the ketchup easily comes out. These thin films can be built atom by atom (and sometimes are only a few atoms thick), allowing engineers to control the specific properties of the film and to purpose-build them for their particular job. Dr Clara Michelle Barker is a specialist in thin film technologies whose work has already had an impact across several different industries.

WHAT KIND OF PROJECTS HAVE YOU WORKED ON?

Thin films are used in a range of industries. I have worked on coating everything from solar cells to crisp packets and even medical implants (to help integrate them into the human body). Recently, I have been working on creating thin film superconductors, which have unusual and incredible electrical and magnetic properties when kept at extremely low temperatures. When superconductors go below a certain temperature, they trap magnetic fields and have no electrical resistance – this can make them seem to float if placed above magnets. This technology is used for things such as Maglev (magnetic levitation) Trains, which use superconductors to make the trains levitate above the track! This eliminates friction and means that the train can travel super fast.

Superconductors have lots of other uses too, such as in MRI machines, which are often used in healthcare, and in nuclear fusion reactors, which will hopefully supply us with vast quantities of energy one day. They can also be used in quantum computers, which will be used to help us solve the world's most complex problems in the future.

The materials we use are often chosen because they are cheap and easy to make. This is where my work as a researcher comes in. I investigate how we can make the best materials for their application, and how to make them more reliable and perform better.

HOW DID YOU GET TO THIS POINT IN YOUR CAREER?

I grew up on a council estate in North Manchester, where few people from my primary school went to university. I needed to prove to myself that I could do it. I started A-level maths, physics, chemistry and biology but never finished them because I needed to focus on my mental health. Eventually, I did go back to education, completing a foundation access course to get into a university degree.

Electrical Engineering was a good choice of degree for me. I like fixing things and making them work – this can be anything from a bookcase to a computer. For a long while I wanted to make gadgets and wrote lots of code. During my degree I did a one-year placement at a company that made vacuum deposition equipment, which is a type of technology that coats objects with thin films. This placement led to my first job at the same company. I helped to improve the technology that coats the inside of crisp packets with a thin film of metal to keep the crisps fresh. I really enjoyed this placement, which led me to do a PhD in Materials Science. It's amazing to think that I didn't even know what a PhD was until I was asked to do one!

YOU MENTIONED QUANTUM COMPUTERS – WHAT ARE THEY AND HOW DO THEY USE THIN FILMS?

Quantum computers are very fast computers. They can carry out calculations much faster than standard computers, which makes them great for complex tasks such as measuring the movement of Earth or predicting weather patterns. However, they are very hard to make.

Qubits (or quantum bits) are essential components of quantum computers, and are so small that we cannot use standard wires to connect them – instead we use thin films. I work together with quantum physicists and other scientists to provide them with superconducting thin films. These are currently made from aluminium oxide, which is not the best superconducting material for a qubit, but it is good for now because it can be made easily and cheaply. The aim of my research is to find better solutions for the future.

A QUANTUM COMPUTER

Communications (data) between a regular computer and the quantum computer pass through the top plate. The data can be converted here, so that the computers can speak to each other.

The further down the system the plates are, the colder the temperature is. This plate is held at −270 °C.

The qubits, which do all of the quantum computer's work, sit down here. This plate is held at −273.14 °C.

Case

5 metres high

For a quantum computer to work properly, all but the top layer must be sealed in a vacuum – a space with no air in it.

WHERE ELSE CAN YOUR THIN FILMS BE APPLIED?

We also use them in nuclear fusion reactors called tokamaks. We want to make superconducting magnets for these reactors that can carry the largest amount of current possible and create high magnetic fields. There are certain materials we would like to be able to use, but we cannot make them easily right now – so we're working on that!

Also, the inside of reactors are very hostile environments. The materials inside them get damaged by radiation, so we need to understand how this damage affects the thin films. Alongside this work, we are also attempting to make superconducting magnets that can be replaced by robots instead of humans, but to do that, we have to understand more about the connections between the superconductor magnets.

WHAT IS IT LIKE BEING A WOMAN WHO IS TRANSGENDER IN ENGINEERING?

If I'm honest, it is nice to stand out. People remember who I am and that allows me to help make a difference and drive further change. That does not mean that it has been easy. For a long time I was worried that people wouldn't accept me if I came out as trans, especially as there were no trans role models around me. So, I kept myself hidden or I tried harder to fit in – neither of which was good for my mental health. Things have improved a lot over the last ten years because I have found the confidence and strength to be myself. Also, with a small number of engineers like me in the world, it means that a lot of people look up to me. I have become a role model for some people, even if this was never my intention. These are things I am proud of.

WHAT ENABLES YOU TO BE THE BEST VERSION OF YOURSELF?

The support and acceptance of other people in achieving my potential have been key and this has also involved accepting and believing in myself. Meeting other people like myself, and seeing role models I can relate to, has empowered me to stay in science, technology and engineering and know that I belong where I am.

FACT FILE

Most fun thing about your job: Every day is different – I might be fixing equipment one day, and meeting young scientists on a school tour of my lab the next.

CAREER HIGHLIGHTS

1. Being offered my first postdoctoral position in Switzerland.

2. The first time someone told me that my personal story had had a positive impact on them.

3. Being supported by my group to apply for, and get, my first research fellowship funding.

Professor Tom Ellis

PROFESSOR OF SYNTHETIC GENOME ENGINEERING

BIOENGINEERING NEW TRENDS IN FASHION

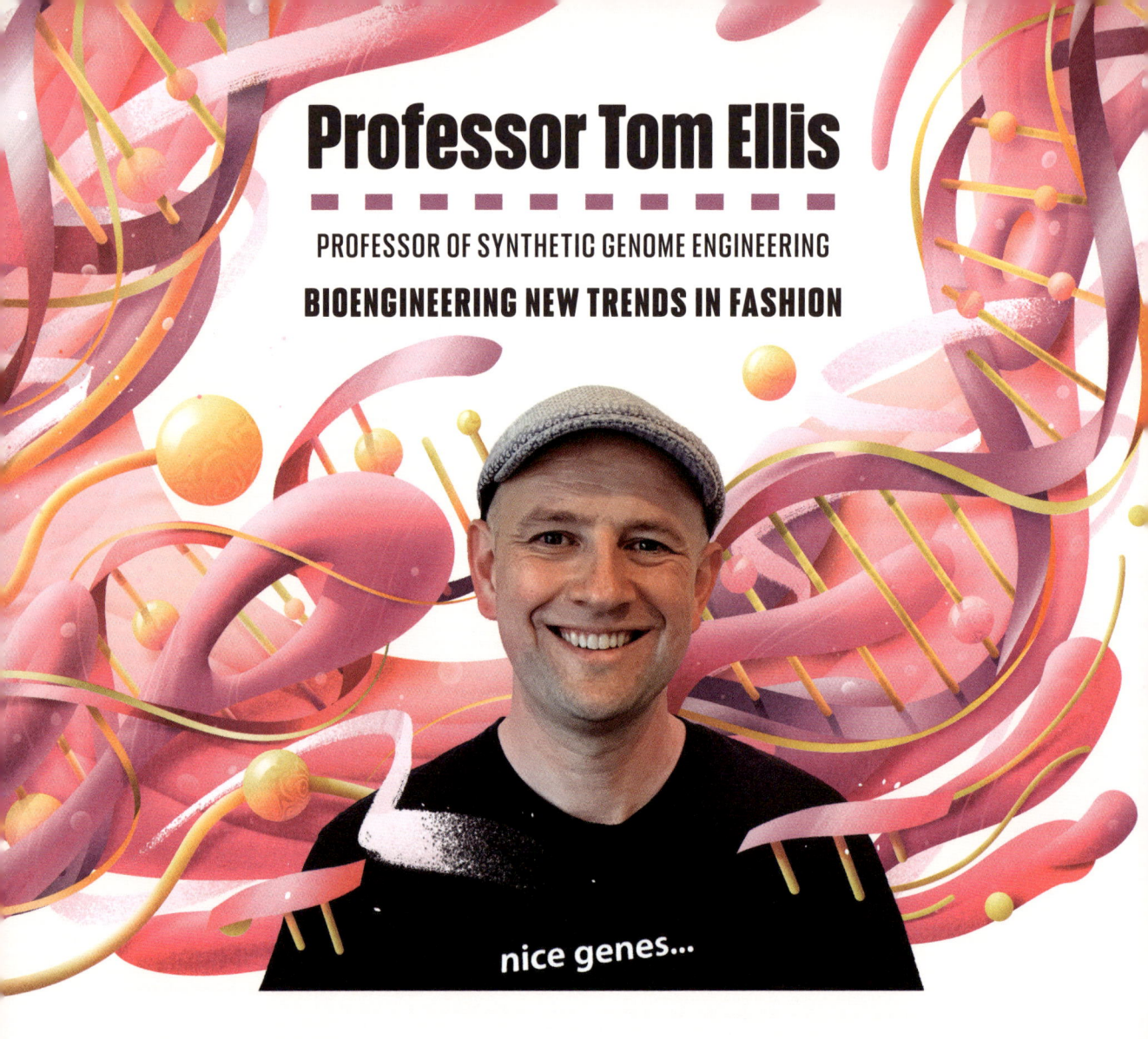

Synthetic biologists figure out ways to grow materials with certain characteristics. To do that, they have to be able to understand and manipulate DNA – the long twisty molecule found in every cell of every living thing, which encodes instructions for everything the organism does.

DNA tells an organism how to develop and tells each cell what sort of proteins to make so every different part of the body can do its job. You have DNA and so do all other living things. Synthetic biologists have learnt to edit DNA strands to make new codes that tell living cells to grow in ways they never would have grown naturally.

Professor Tom Ellis and his colleagues in the Department of Bioengineering at Imperial College London use this method to grow brand new materials that can be used to make clothing.

WHAT ARE THE AMBITIONS OF YOUR RESEARCH GROUP?

My group has two major ambitions. The first is to understand the different ways of recoding DNA inside cells, and the second is to make brand new materials for a number of different industries, including fashion.

We have been consuming and wasting natural resources for too long, so it's time to start engineering our own materials. Fashion brands, such as LVMH (who own Dior and Louis Vuitton), recognise the importance of being environmentally conscious, and are now looking for lab-grown materials to help make alternatives for leather, fur and toxic chemical dyes.

My team is equipped with knowledge on how to meet these exciting and necessary challenges. Today, we are able to grow yeast and bacteria in a lab, and recode their DNA to have particular properties or colours. Other biological engineers can even recode DNA to grow leaf cells or tree bark cells in a lab without cutting down a single tree.

WHAT ARE EXAMPLES OF SYNTHETIC BIOLOGY MAKING A DIFFERENCE?

Plants and animals don't get their colours from toxic dyes – they have instructions in their DNA. For example, black sheep produce black wool. With synthetic biology we can also add the DNA instructions for colour into the cells growing materials. We've used this method to grow vegan leather in white, brown or black. Faux fur could also be made more real using synthetic biology.

WHAT INFLUENCED YOU TO COMBINE BIOLOGY WITH ENGINEERING?

As a kid, like most engineers, I was fascinated with LEGO. I liked building and putting things together. I was influenced by both my mum who did botany at university and by moving to Cambridge as a teenager. In Cambridge there are reminders of the discovery of the structure of DNA on every street corner.

Synthetic biology is such a fascinating, fresh, new and interdisciplinary subject in engineering. At Imperial, biologists from life science and engineers from bioengineering work together. These students are striving to safeguard their futures by using synthetic biology to reduce pollution, slow down climate change and build a better future. They inspire me.

FACT FILE

Most fun thing about your job: Writing DNA code with my students and then having it made in real life is always exciting!

CAREER HIGHLIGHTS

1. Getting a weekend job when I was 16, where I helped sequence DNA for the Human Genome Project.

2. Setting up the first biology labs for a drug company in London.

3. Supervising a team of students to the grand final of an international synthetic biology competition.

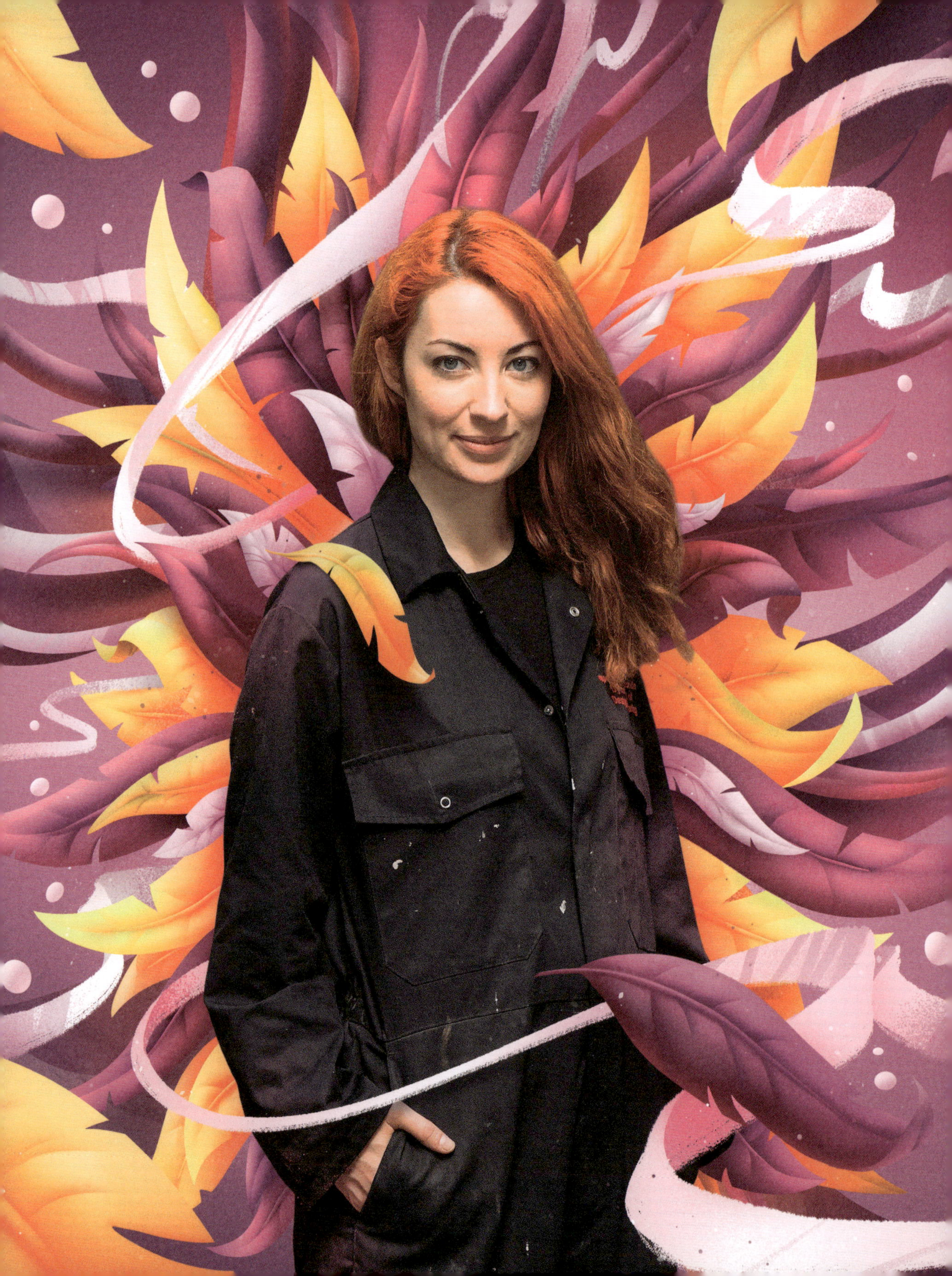

Dr Elena Dieckmann

DESIGN ENGINEER

HATCHING A PLAN TO REUSE WASTE FEATHERS

Engineers need to be very good at thinking logically, but they also need to be creative! To dream up solutions they often need to think outside of the box. Dr Elena Dieckmann is a big fan of creativity in engineering. After completing her undergraduate degree, Master's and PhD, she co-founded a materials technology start-up called Aeropowder. She and her team are developing a material for packaging that uses waste chicken feathers. She can now confidently say that she is the world's leading expert on chicken feather waste management and is keen to play her part in addressing the climate emergency through engineering.

HOW AND WHY DID YOU GET INTO ENGINEERING?

As a child I was pretty interested in problem solving and creating my own things. Nowadays, we don't just talk about STEM (science, technology, engineering and maths) – instead we talk about STEAM, to include the arts. That was certainly my pathway into engineering because I was allowed to explore my creative side throughout my education.

I was good at maths and physics; however, looking back, it was more important that I was curious. I always wanted to understand how things worked. I think these characteristics are very important for the mindset of an engineer. I don't think you necessarily need to be a maths genius, but you do need to be interested in how things work.

I had a German education and after my undergraduate studies, I ended up in the German car industry. I was originally interested in mobility around cities, so I started working at BMW. I then moved to Volkswagen to work for their emerging markets in the Middle East and Africa. Throughout these experiences, I was always looking for a task that could have a high impact and do good for society, but that need wasn't being fulfilled for me in the car industry.

Then by accident I found a Master's programme called Innovation Design Engineering (IDE), a joint Master's between Imperial College London and the Royal College of Art. I loved the idea of developing my skills in creative engineering, and it was here that I could explore my interest in materials, textiles and waste and have a real impact on environmental issues.

WHY WERE CHICKEN FEATHERS SO INTERESTING TO YOU?

The focus of my Master's projects and PhD research was on textile engineering and waste conversion. There are lots of different natural fibres on the planet, and chicken feathers are one of them. Chicken feathers have several properties that make them attractive for different uses, but the sheer quantity of them that ends up as rubbish is a big environmental issue. And unfortunately, there are very limited options for recycling them. Chicken feathers are often unusable when they come out of the slaughterhouse because they are heavily contaminated and very dirty.

While I was doing my PhD, I co-founded a company called Aeropowder with Ryan Robinson. He leads the business side of the company, while I manage the research. The aim of the company is to address the climate emergency through clever packaging.

In the last five years we have developed a cleaning and conversion process to convert waste chicken feathers into a textile that is clean, easy to handle and that can be used as a wrapper in packaging. We now have a product successfully on the market and we are still continuing to grow and develop it – it's a continuous journey.

At the moment, we are in the process of expanding our business from the UK to Europe. The need for our packaging is increasing because people are ordering goods to their homes more than ever. What we hope to achieve is a product that can be reused over and over again. Ultimately, we are hoping to replace traditional packing materials, such as polystyrene, which are made from non-renewable ingredients.

WHY ARE CHICKEN FEATHERS SO USEFUL?

Feathers are great at insulating, so they can be used in packaging to keep things fresh and cold. But that's just one use. Another great property of feathers is that they repel water but absorb oil very effectively. So, it is possible that the materials we have developed from the feathers could be used to clean up oil spills.

Pluumo chicken feather packaging acts as an insulator to keep food cool while it is being transported.

WHAT DOES A TYPICAL WEEK LOOK LIKE FOR YOU?

As a Senior Teaching Fellow at the Dyson School of Design Engineering, I teach students who often come to me with project proposals. I support them in making their ideas a reality. A student recently approached me about creating a new material, so I went with them to the lab to try out some ideas and potential material development processes. We then tested the materials and ran software simulations. My students have lots of great ideas, so every day is different and exciting.

WHAT ARE THE HIGHLIGHTS OF YOUR WORK?

I love problem-solving and being creative. And I like working at a start-up because you can see the impact of your work very quickly. When you work in big companies you're just a small cog in a big machine, and it's sometimes very difficult to see the impact of what you do. I also really enjoy teaching and it is fascinating and inspiring helping my students with their innovations.

WHAT ARE THE BIGGEST CHALLENGES YOU FACE IN YOUR WORK?

The product that we are developing is constantly changing due to customer-related requests. In these situations, I must improvise and find new ways of doing things. Feathers can be formed in hundreds of different ways for packaging, with all solutions having cost, production and time implications. At the same time, it's magical to test out a new idea and see it work.

WHY IS SUSTAINABLE PACKING SO IMPORTANT TO YOU?

The world is drowning in 'stuff' and packaging is a huge polluter that contributes to the global waste crisis. With people buying more and more items online, there has been an increase in home deliveries, which adds to our waste problem. The way we pack and ship items could make a real difference. Our packaging materials are very durable, so we can use them several times and even recycle them. We cannot continue to extract materials for single use, we need to find smarter systems to keep them in the loop. Converting feathers into a range of different materials also has the potential to replace non-renewable materials made from plastic – for example, those used in home insulation. I am lucky to have found my passion – I believe that when you do, you are destined to succeed.

FACT FILE

Most fun thing about your job: Meeting brilliant minds every day.

CAREER HIGHLIGHTS

1. Watching my product rolling off the production line for the first time.

2. Driving a large truck full of feathers to France.

3. Getting people excited about reusing waste.

SUPER CARBON

Carbon is an element, which means it's made up of a single type of atom. The atoms in carbon can join together in different arrangements, causing it to make different materials. Diamonds and the graphite in your pencils are both made from carbon atoms. These different forms of carbon each have special characteristics – diamonds are very hard, while graphite is very soft. Scientists, materials engineers and nanotechnologists (who work at a tiny scale) are transforming various carbon structures into some of the lightest and strongest materials on Earth. Here are just some of the ways this technology is being developed.

AEROGRAPHENE A mix of graphene (a thin sheet of carbon atoms) and aerogel (the lightest solid material in the world), aerographene is thought to be the world's lightest material at around 7.5 times lighter than air! It is very flexible and sponge-like, with the ability to absorb up to 900 times its own weight in water or oil. This could make it ideal for cleaning up oil spills quickly, reducing the impact on the environment.

Aerographene is so light that it can sit on the petals of a flower without crushing them.

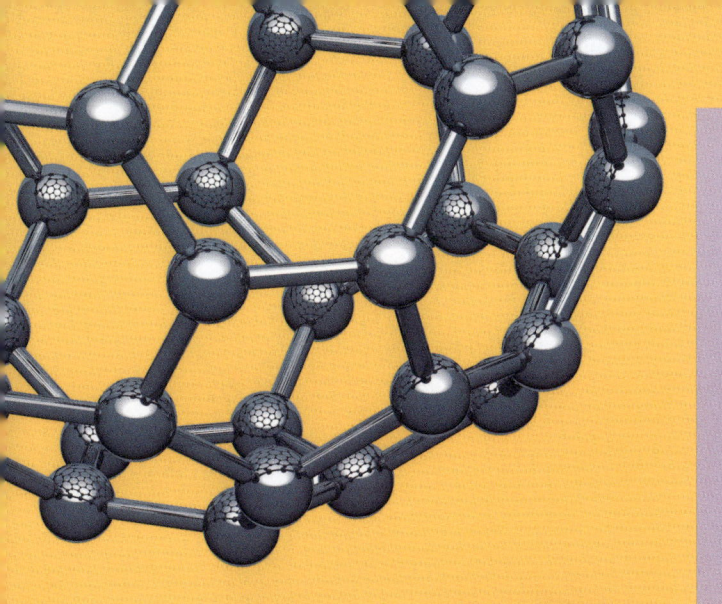

3D GRAPHENE Graphite is made up of layers of graphene, which is a substance so thin it's considered to be 2D. Researchers have now found a way to fuse graphene flakes together with heat and pressure to make a 3D material with superpowers! 3D graphene is incredibly light in relation to its volume, but also ten times stronger than steel. This could replace the carbon fibre used in cars and aircraft, and is also useful as a chemical filter to purify water or air.

AEROGRAPHITE Created from a network of hollow carbon nanotubes, aerographite is 75 times lighter than Styrofoam. Aerographite can be formed into different shapes, and it conducts electricity well, so it could be used in electric vehicles and to make much lighter batteries.

This carbon nanotube array is made of vertically aligned carbon nanotubes. It could be used in many devices, such as solar cells or computers.

CARBON NANOTUBES Sheets of graphite one atom thick can be rolled into carbon nanotubes. The bonding between the atoms is very strong, so the tubes make great conductors for electricity. Nanotubes can be used as a better alternative to silicon computer chips. They would be more efficient, would require less material and could make faster, more powerful computers. Replacing silicon chips with carbon nanotubes also promises higher resolution cameras, smaller phones and more efficient batteries.

QUANTUM DOTS Carbon quantum dots are tiny, fluorescent particles that are controlled by light rather than electricity. When used for television screens and electronic displays, they give an extremely high-quality image. These nanodots can also be used to enhance solar technology and to improve cancer screening.

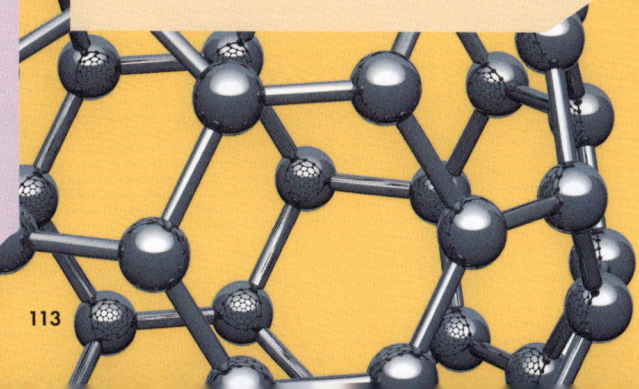

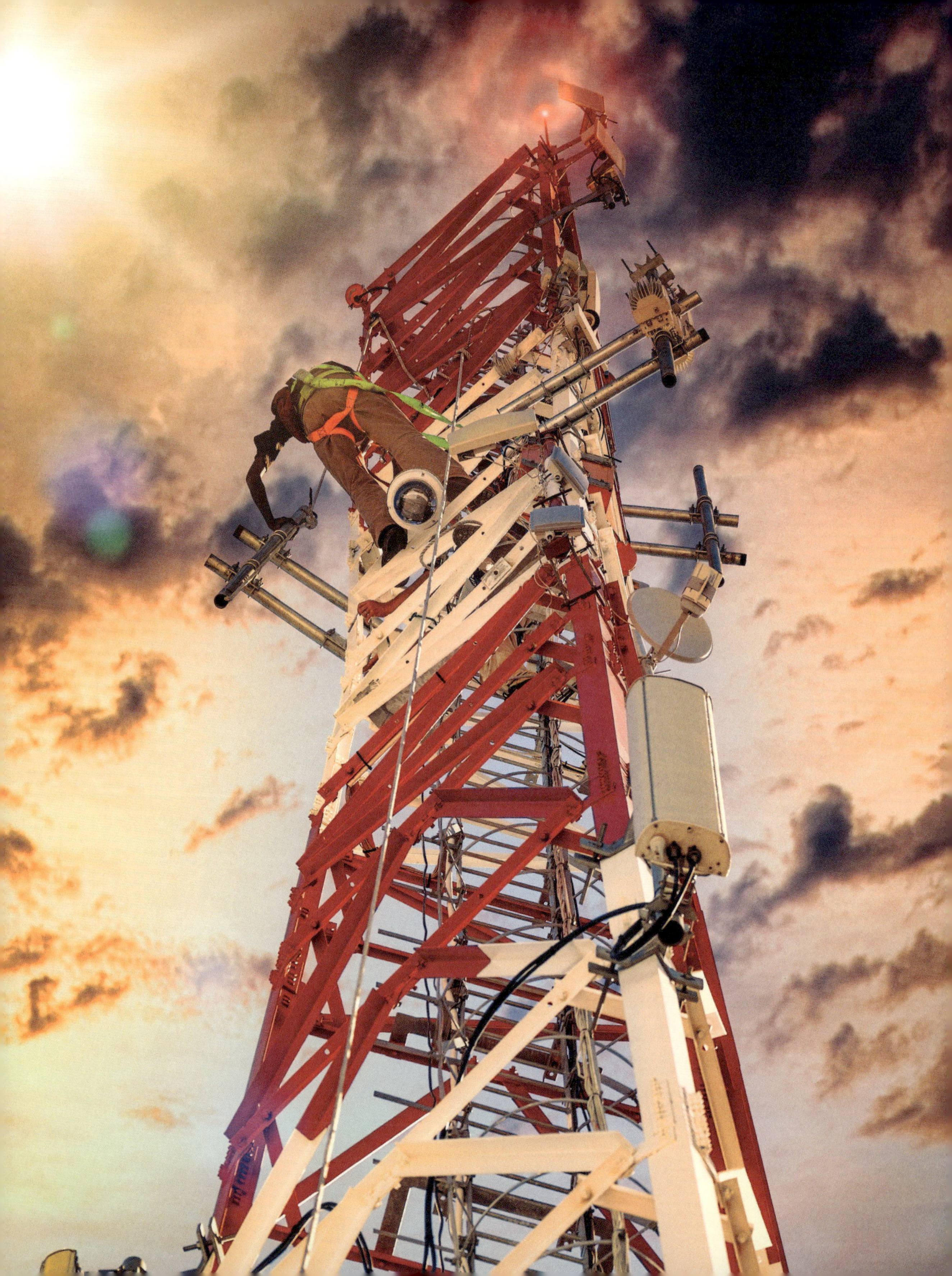

CHAPTER 7

COMMUNICATION

Communicating with one another has always been very important for humans. In the modern age, being connected means that we can talk to loved ones near and far, allowing us to share news and smoothly operate our systems and infrastructure. The way we communicate has vastly changed over time and our systems are now so good that we can even send messages to people in space!

Around the 1900s, the UK established fixed-line communication by putting up telegraph poles and connecting them with copper wires. It was a complex and expensive task, which only the richest countries could afford. However, advancements in communication technology meant that developing countries could leapfrog over technologies to adopt brand-new ones, such as wireless technology.

Leapfrogging is now happening with wireless technologies too. The telephone masts and fibre-optic cables that the internet so heavily relies on are being replaced with portable antennas and satellites. But there is still more work for engineers to do to connect everybody. The engineers in this chapter are working with a broad range of communication methods. They combine different fields of media, which allows various technologies to merge, emerge and evolve.

LEFT: Worker in Africa climbing to the top of a telephone tower to perfom maintenance work. Telephone towers are so tall that when something needs fixing, the only way for engineers to get to the problem is for them to climb hundreds of metres into the air.

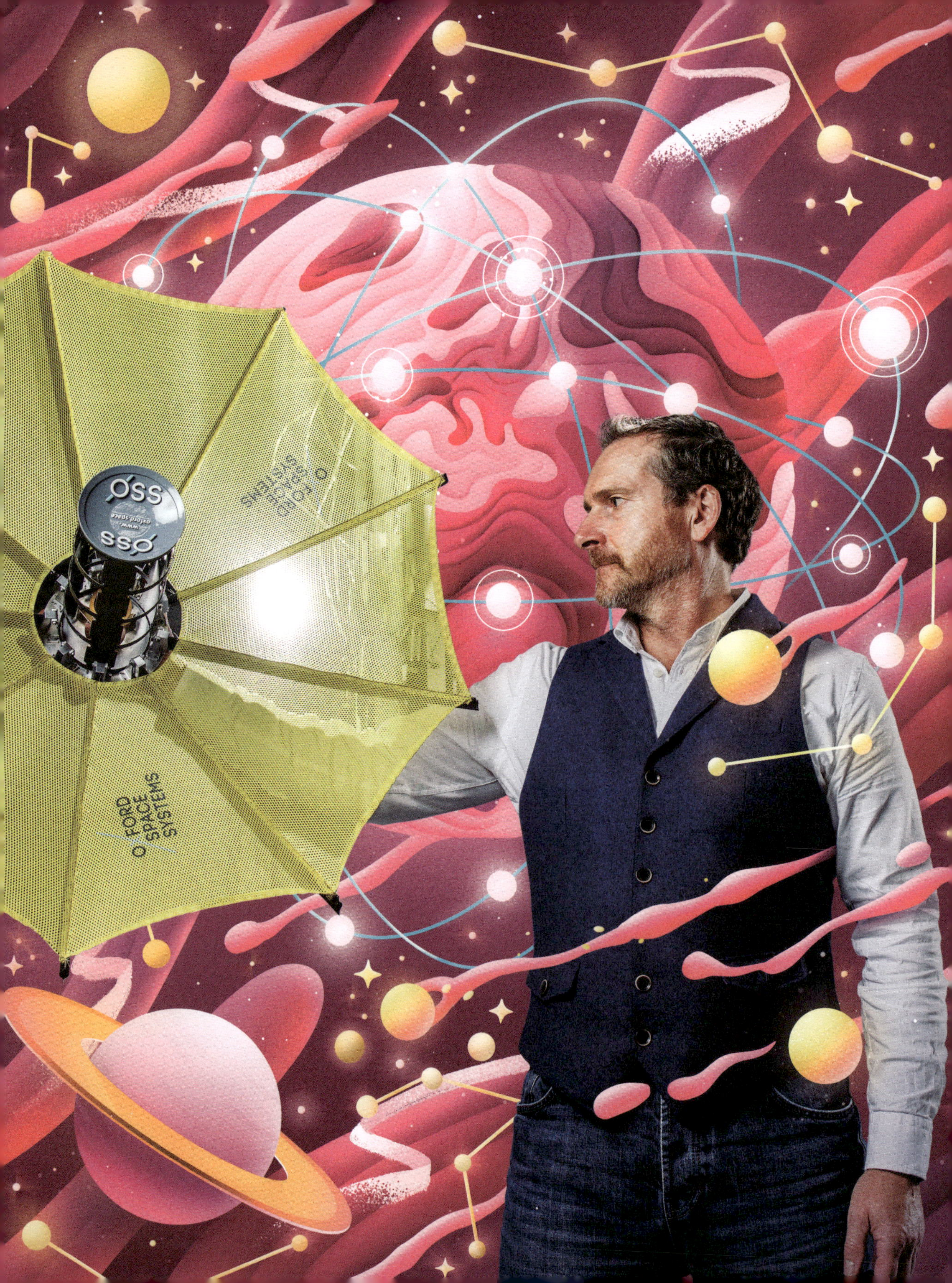
OSS
OSS
OXFORD
SPACE
SYSTEMS

Mike Lawton

ELECTRONICS ENGINEER
KEEPING SPACECRAFT CONNECTED TO EARTH

Teams around the world are working on sending crewed spacecraft to Mars and beyond, however there are many challenges to overcome first. One such challenge is how to keep astronauts connected to teams back on Earth. Mike Lawton and his team at Oxford Space Systems have come up with a clever antenna that can fold up small for the journey to space, but then pop open so it's big enough to send important data and messages back home.

WHEN DID YOUR INTEREST IN ENGINEERING BEGIN?

As a small kid, I was constantly in trouble for fiddling with things. I took the vacuum cleaner apart to try and figure out what created its powerful suction. I opened the back of the piano to see how the different noises were made. I also took my parents' television apart to understand what was creating all of the colours on screen. Back then, televisions contained different components that could be dangerous and, in all my curiosity, I managed to electrocute myself! Oddly enough, this was the beginning of my interest and excitement about electricity.

HOW DID YOU GET TO WHERE YOU ARE TODAY?

I have had a varied engineering career spanning 32 years. When I left school, I was one of 140 people starting an apprenticeship at HMNB Devonport, Plymouth, one of the largest naval bases in Europe. The apprenticeship was like being a kid in a sweet shop for me. I worked on the electrical systems of warships and submarines and it was very hands-on. I got plenty of grease under my fingernails fitting radar systems and fixing electrical issues in submarines. I also went to night school to learn electrical engineering theory, so I could pass my degree.

At the same time, I worked for the local hospital radio station, which led to a part-time job at the local BBC radio station. This is where I really developed an appreciation for communication engineering.

"You can learn a huge amount by building things; so dive in, play around and build stuff."

Mike Lawton

After completing my degree, I got my first professional engineering position with a space company called Space Innovations Ltd. My job was to help design a power system for a satellite. This involved figuring out how to get solar panels and batteries to work together to provide smooth and consistent power. This was my first taste of space engineering and as a fan of *Star Trek*, *Star Wars* and *Doctor Who*, this job was a dream come true!

After three years in the space industry, I decided to move to work in telecommunications as an R and D (Research and Development) Engineer. My job was to work out the best way to transfer data through fibre-optic cables. If there's lots of data, moving it in the most efficient way through the fibre is a huge challenge, so I worked in a team to find a solution.

HOW DID YOU END UP WORKING BACK IN SPACE ENGINEERING?

Eventually, I felt like a change again so put my 'space cap' back on to become an Entrepreneur in Residence for ABSL Space Products. My job was to figure out what technology was needed in spacecraft that currently wasn't available. My answer was deployable space antennas that could be set up and used as and when they're needed. This technology is necessary for communicating between the spacecraft and Earth. I became obsessed with deployable space antennas, and together with two other ABSL colleagues, we founded Oxford Space Systems to develop them.

WHAT CHALLENGES DID YOU HAVE TO OVERCOME TO MAKE THE ANTENNAS?

The biggest challenge was to make big satellite antennas that could fit into a small space rocket. We needed to develop something that could almost build itself once in space. My team experimented with rolled-up carbon fibre, which could unfurl like a tape measure, and metal spokes like that of an umbrella, which could pop up into the required dome shape. We also had help from Professor Zhong You from the University of Oxford – a world expert in origami!

A satellite deploying its antenna

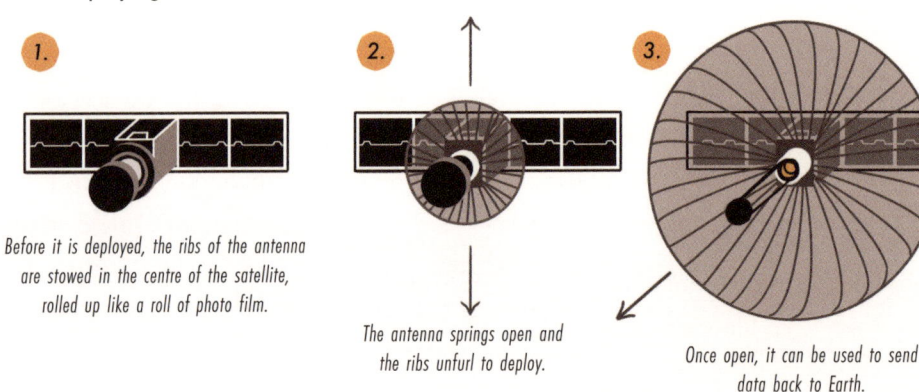

1. Before it is deployed, the ribs of the antenna are stowed in the centre of the satellite, rolled up like a roll of photo film.

2. The antenna springs open and the ribs unfurl to deploy.

3. Once open, it can be used to send data back to Earth.

HOW DID YOU MAKE SURE THE ANTENNAS WERE READY FOR CONDITIONS IN SPACE?

We use a wide range of test equipment to mimic conditions in space. Space can be very cold and hot, so we use a thermal vacuum chamber to go from −150°C to +150°C. My favourite test is the vibration table. This is used to simulate the huge vibrations encountered when a rocket fires its engines and soars into orbit. I've seen engineers shed a tear when their designs unexpectedly shatter into pieces due to the high forces caused by vibration!

Satellite being shaken on a vibration table.

FACT FILE

Most fun thing about your job: Solving a tough engineering problem with my teammates is a fantastic buzz!

CAREER HIGHLIGHTS

1. Getting an Honour's degree in Engineering.

2. Winning NASA's Ignite the Night Engineering Pitch competition in the USA.

3. Setting a world record for the fastest time from product conception to succesful in-orbit demonstration with our AstroTube Boom.

WHAT DO YOU THINK COMMUNICATION ENGINEERS WILL BE WORKING ON IN THE FUTURE?

Communication engineers will be focused on moving more data, over longer distances and using less power. We will also be trying to make communications technology smaller and stronger – especially for technologies that go to space. It is highly likely that AI will have a big role to play in this too.

WHAT ADVICE WOULD YOU GIVE TO ANY YOUNG PEOPLE WISHING TO FOLLOW A CAREER IN COMMUNICATIONS ENGINEERING?

Although studying and understanding the theory of engineering is important, it helps to get as much practical experience as you can. Even if you end up in a different sector of engineering, all experiences are good experiences. It's great to learn by building things too. That way you'll learn what's possible and what's not. This will make you more confident and ultimately a really valuable engineer. And who knows – maybe you'll be the next big tech entrepreneur!

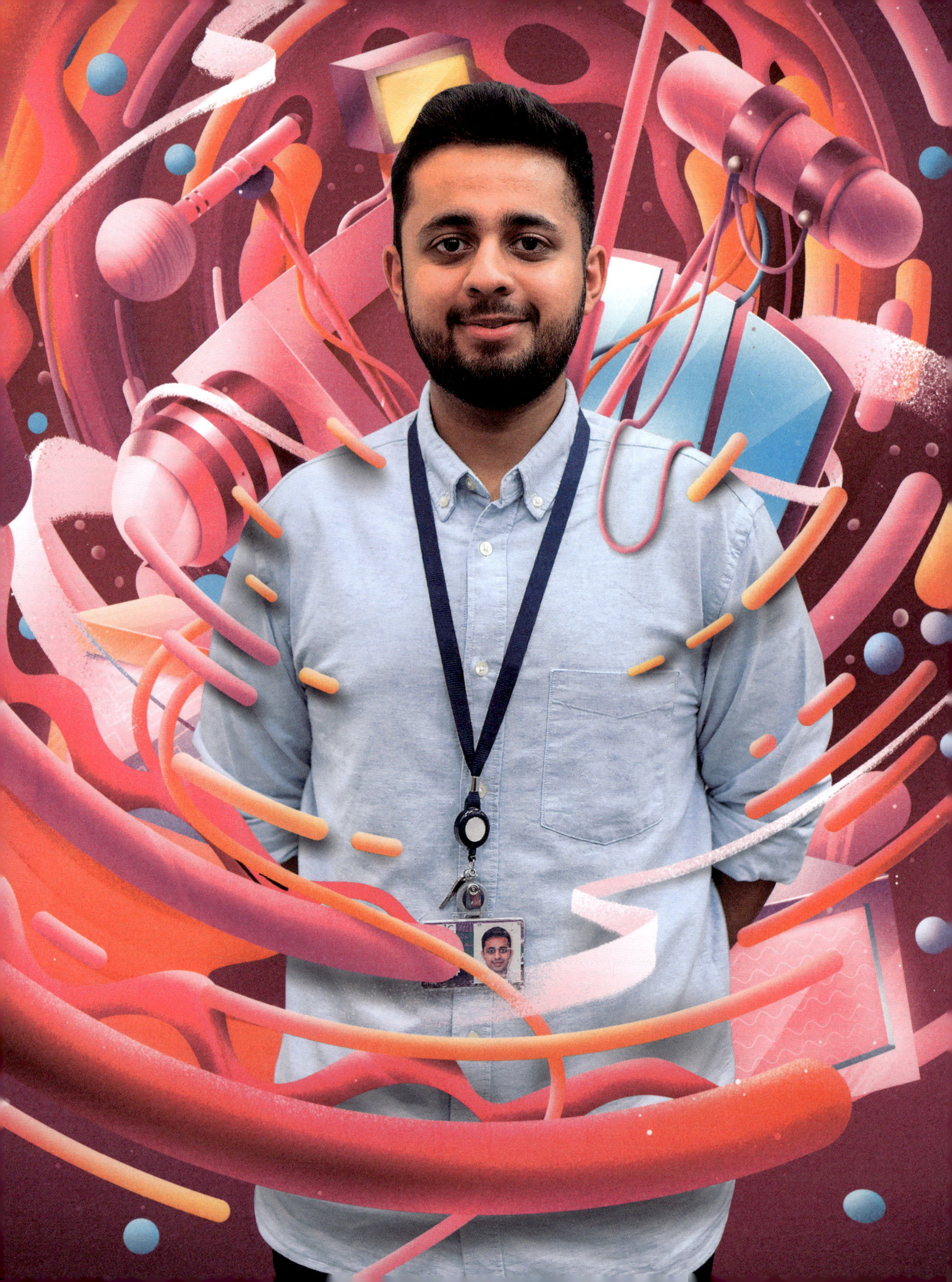

Jahangir Shah

PROJECT ENGINEER
HELPING TO GET YOUR FAVOURITE SHOWS TO YOU

Broadcast Engineering is an industry that includes electrical engineering for radio and television. Jahangir Shah started his Broadcast Engineering apprenticeship at the BBC, a great place to get hands-on experience. He now works for Sky, finding practical solutions to broadcasting shows from almost any location.

HOW DID YOU GET INTO BROADCAST ENGINEERING?

Initially, I wasn't focused on any particular career in engineering. I studied maths and physics A-levels and I had an opportunity to do some work experience at Muslim Television Ahmadiyya (MTA) International, a television channel mostly run by volunteers. At MTA, I got to see how everything in television works, such as how the studio is run, how shows are produced and how the cameras and microphones work. I also got to experience the thrill of live television broadcasts, which is something that has always fascinated me. As a kid, I wanted to know how the moving images got to my television. It baffled me that something happening far away could end up in my living room.

I discovered Broadcast Engineering and the BBC Apprenticeships scheme. I was so excited that they offered this, as I had often visited the cafe of New Broadcasting House in London to watch BBC live news broadcasts. It was a dream of mine to work there one day.

The BBC newsroom is home to the newsdesks and also the studio from which programmes are broadcast.

To my surprise, the BBC offered me an interview! The interview itself was more like an assessment day where interviewees took part in various teamwork tasks and technical tests at the BBC drama studios in Wales. It is a day I will never forget, as I got to walk around the *Casualty* set and see the *Doctor Who* TARDIS. It was surreal!

Despite being very shy and lacking in confidence, the BBC offered me an apprenticeship. I was delighted at the opportunity and spent the next three years learning everything about the industry by moving around all their departments so I had time to work in each. I also acquired a degree during this time and stayed with the BBC for a further two years after qualifying.

WHAT DID YOU DO AFTER THE BBC?

After the BBC, I decided to try working in outside broadcast as a change from being in the studio, so I joined a company called Nep. Outside broadcast means filming events and shows from remote locations, for example filming at a sporting event or a music festival. After a year, I moved to Sky, where they do both outside and in-house broadcasts.

Broadcast engineers need to have a wide knowledge of all the equipment used in the different control rooms – whether outside or in-house. Outside broadcast control rooms are usually in the form of a van with a big dish mounted on the top of it.

Broadcast engineers are there to build and assemble the equipment that makes live broadcasts happen and fix any technical problems, including audio or video mixing (choosing which sound and images the viewer sees when there are multiple cameras filming) or problems with cameras or microphones. No two days are ever the same at work due to the variety of technology and solutions available. I have loved being part of some really incredible events, such as football games and the BAFTAs.

Outside broadcast van

WHAT IS YOUR CURRENT ROLE AT SKY?

My current role at Sky is as a Project Engineer. I am responsible for providing the right equipment to cover a certain event. There are so many different ways to do the same thing and solutions change all the time because hardware and software are changing all the time. YouTube has been really useful in learning about emerging technologies and solutions in my field, and I really enjoy learning on the job, compared to being behind a desk!

The best part of my job now is seeing a project through from concept to delivery and then seeing it in use. It's rewarding when someone comes to you with a problem and you are able to come up with a solution for them.

WHAT ENGINEERING TOOLS DO YOU USE?

We use CAD to do the technical drawings and designing, but I also often sketch with a pencil and paper to create high-level diagrams. These diagrams consist of simple building blocks showing connecting lines to indicate how equipment fits together. I am often working closely with the design engineers, project managers and a wiring team, and these technical drawings are an essential communication tool.

WHERE IS YOUR JOB HEADING IN THE FUTURE?

The future of broadcast engineering is heading into the clouds! By this, I mean the cloud storage system that runs on the internet. We can get signals in and out of the cloud, and this is changing the way we broadcast content here at Sky. It makes us question whether we want to invest money into new equipment that lives here onsite when we could achieve the same results virtually with less hardware. This means that broadcasts can be controlled in-house, instead of from the remote location. Today, we can set up a whole control room within 20 minutes of switching on some servers in the cloud, and this technology is only becoming more cost-effective and efficient with time.

WHAT PIECE OF ADVICE WOULD YOU GIVE TO READERS OF THIS BOOK?

During my apprenticeship, I heard over and over again that now is the time to make mistakes and learn from them. That way, when you go into the 'real world', you will be ready for anything that your work can throw at you.

FACT FILE

Most fun thing about your job: Working with the latest technology in broadcast engineering and on large-scale projects.

CAREER HIGHLIGHTS

1. Volunteering at MTA International.

2. Completing the BBC Broadcast Engineering Apprentice and Sponsored Degree.

3. Working for the largest and most reputable broadcasters in the UK, such as BBC and Sky.

Dr Nikita Hari

ELECTRICAL AND ELECTRONICS ENGINEER

IMPROVING ELECTRONIC DEVICES FROM THE INSIDE OUT

In our modern world we are more reliant on our smartphones than ever before. We need our internet connections to be stronger and battery lives to be longer. Dr Nikita Hari has been doing essential research into improving our smart devices by looking at the electronics that are used to build or power them.

TELL ME ABOUT YOUR ENGINEERING JOURNEY.

I grew up in India with two parents who had degrees. They ran an electrical goods manufacturing unit and so I grew up surrounded by electronic goods. It felt like a natural decision to follow in their footsteps and study electronics in particular.

I dreamt of studying abroad, but that was not an option for women in our traditional Indian family.

I was top of my school with excellent grades. I was especially good at STEM subjects and had a keen interest in physics, but I was expected to go to the local engineering college because I was a girl. The mindset at the time was that girls didn't need the best education, they just needed to be able to raise a family.

Despite the fact that girls in my community were not supposed to pursue higher education, I decided to follow my dreams and eventually my family came around to the idea!

WHAT WAS YOUR PHD ABOUT?

My research was based around comparing a material called gallium nitride (GaN) to silicon, with the goal of making electronic devices more efficient. When your mobile phone feels warm it's usually a sign that valuable energy is being wasted as heat. But this can be reduced by changing the materials used inside the device.

All electrical devices have switches inside them that are usually made from silicon. I researched how we could make devices smaller, faster, denser and lighter by making the switches from GaN instead. I designed many prototypes and ran simulations and experiments to see how GaN devices would function under a variety of conditions, and I collected lots of data. I used machine learning and AI to help me quickly spot patterns and trends in this data. Once I had found the optimal conditions, I was able to share this information with other engineers so that they too could build better GaN devices.

WHAT HAVE YOU LEARNT FROM YOUR CAREER JOURNEY SO FAR?

It is okay to not want what everyone else wants, and to have different interests at different times of your life. Over time, I have learnt not to compare myself to others because I have come from very different circumstances. In letting these things go, I now have the freedom and space to do exactly what I want.

FACT FILE

Most fun thing about your job: I get to build, blow up and build back better – powering lives, powering the world!

CAREER HIGHLIGHTS

1. When I was awarded a scholarship for doctoral studies by the University of Cambridge.

2. Being awarded a Schlumberger Postdoctoral Fellowship at the University of Oxford.

3. Converting my passion into a purpose and inspiring young people to engineer a better world.

"I have engineered a world of my own where I feel comfortable and happy with who I am."

Dr Nikita Hari

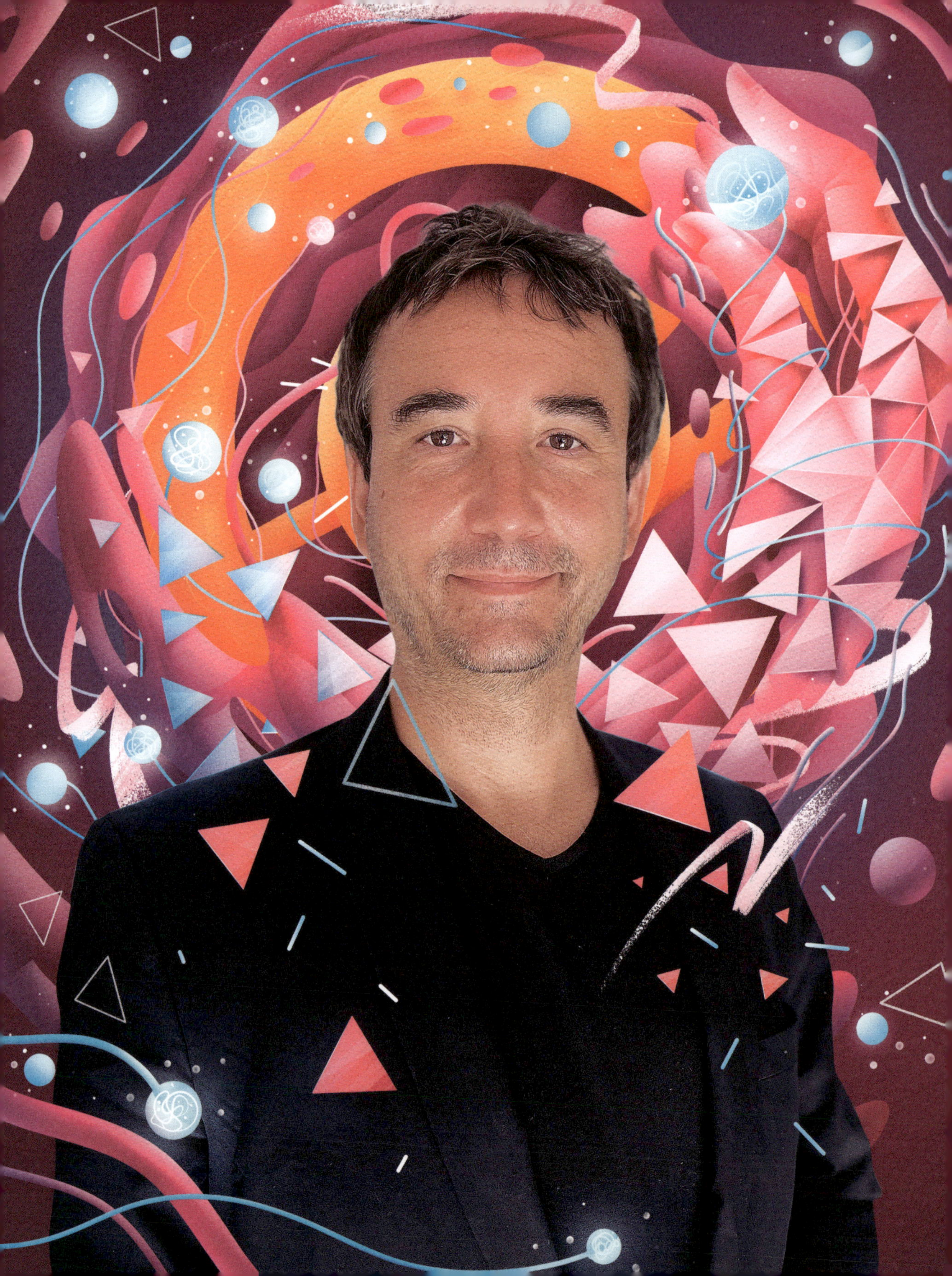

Professor Mischa Dohler

ELECTRONICS ENGINEER
BRINGING CREATIVITY TO ENGINEERING AND INNOVATION TO ART

The internet has gone from strength to strength since Sir Tim Berners-Lee invented the World Wide Web in 1989. Many people have worked hard to make it the incredible resource it is today, including Mischa Dohler, a Professor of Telecommunications who has contributed to several aspects of its exciting advancement. He pioneered technologies required in 5G systems – a faster and more advanced type of mobile network – and also the Internet of Things (IoT), a system of devices that can transfer data to one another without requiring human interaction. Mischa is now developing The Internet of Skills (IoS), a project to help us share skills and virtually connect with one another.

WHAT IS THE IOS?

The IoS is the ability for us to transfer skills through the internet. This will allow us to use the internet to control and move physical objects. For example, a doctor could conduct surgery without even being in the same room but controlling a robot's movements. The IoS requires a really good network and most of my work has been on improving technologies so that we can transmit and receive information with little to no time delay. Latency, or the time delay between a real-time action and what we see at the other end, is a big problem for 2G, 3G and 4G networks. But 5G provides very low latency, which is important for things such as robotic surgery. This system is so useful, because if a patient and specialist doctor are on different sides of the world, the doctor can still operate on them.

In the meantime, I have also helped to develop the devices needed for the IoS, such as augmented reality glasses, which enhance our view of the real world with data and images, and haptic, or touch-sensitive, gloves and suits.

Modern hearing aids can be controlled by smartphones – just one example of the IoT.

HOW DID YOU GET INTO ENGINEERING?

I have always loved physics and music and have excelled in both. I won a few national physics competitions when I was a teenager and recently released my fifth music album. Upon the advice of my parents – who are both highly accomplished in engineering and technology – I studied Physics at university and ended up converting to a degree in Electronics Engineering. I started in Germany but ended up at King's College London, where I did my Master's and PhD.

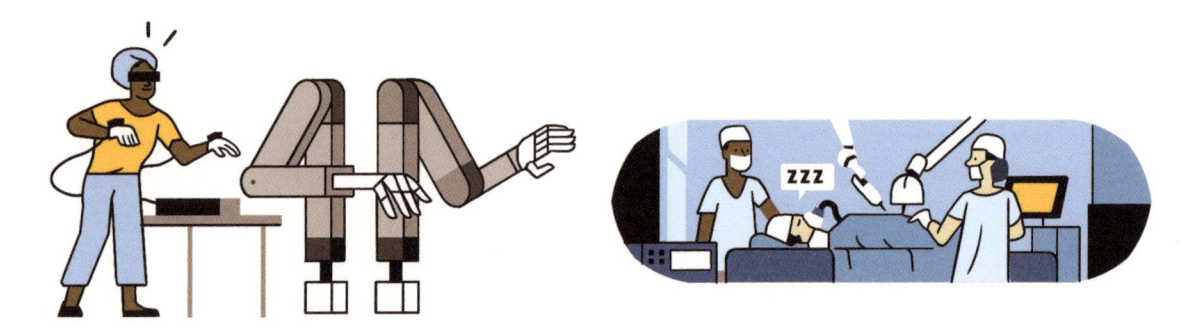

A surgeon using haptic gloves to remotely operate a robot and perform surgery.

WHAT EXPERIENCES HAVE INFLUENCED THE DEVELOPMENT OF YOUR CAREER

I took some time out from King's to take a job at France Telecom, where I developed the Industrial IoT, together with two other people. This is a system that connects industrial devices and machinery so that they can 'talk' to one another. I then moved to Barcelona to start my own company, Worldsensing, which is now one of the biggest companies in the world to offer technology that monitors infrastructure – making sure that it is always safe. Afterwards, I returned to King's to lead their Centre for Telecom Research.

WHAT ENGINEERING PROJECTS EXCITE YOU THE MOST?

I have always loved being at the forefront of new technologies. At King's, we started designing 3G when the internet hadn't yet gone live. We started designing 4G before the iPhone existed and we started designing 5G when augmented reality glasses weren't around yet. Similarly, we are now designing 6G without knowing what we can use it for.

Perhaps 6G will allow for people to have more immersive experiences over the internet. Holographic glasses, for example, could allow us to experience each other's presence in 3D even when we're far apart. Or the future could involve nanobots in your body that use 6G technology to deliver medicine more precisely than current methods.

The next big thing coming out of Silicon Valley is the metaverse, a digital environment that mimics the real world in a more detailed way than holograms can. Engineers in telecommunication need to continue to improve network speeds and capacity in order to make these things possible.

WHAT DO YOU LIKE MOST ABOUT YOUR JOB?

Engineers are a very collaborative crew, and I love that. Smartphones are a masterpiece in mechanical engineering, electronic engineering, telecommunications and design. It took many different engineers to make mobile phones happen. It's important to remember that you don't have to become an electrical engineer just because you studied electrical engineering. Your skills could be useful for something you'd never even dreamt of while studying!

Engineering careers involve learning to work with all different types of people. Careers in engineering today are flexible because so many big technologies are merging. We don't just watch shows on televisions anymore, we watch them on our phones, too, so it is valuable to have knowledge and experience across a variety of industries.

For me, being able to combine my love of music and technology has been a highlight. When I launched my album in 2017, I played the piano with my haptic gloves on. The gloves recorded the movement of my fingers as I played, and stored the data in a database. This was to show how my skill could be stored in the IoS and be downloaded and used to help someone learn to play the piano. The data could even direct special rigid gloves to play the piece with the learner's hands inside. It's an experience I will never forget.

FACT FILE

Most fun thing about your job: Knowing that the wireless technology I design is invisible yet indispensable.

CAREER HIGHLIGHTS

1. Starting my creative career aged 14 with a disastrous piano performance. This made me start writing my own music so nobody would realise if I made a mistake!

2. Becoming an entrepreneur and co-founding Worldsensing.

3. Playing piano in the world's first 5G concert.

"Learn to learn! Knowing how to learn is key. There are so many new and exciting things coming up at a fast pace, which few of us have seen before. We shouldn't be afraid to find out more, and we should be open to adapting and readapting."

Professor Mischa Dohler

Staying Connected

Have you ever wondered how electronic messages travel from one place to another? It's all thanks to a complex system of more than 400 undersea cables, around five million telecoms towers and thousands of satellites that orbit the planet at around 36,000 kilometres above the surface. Each of these things transports vast amounts of data, allowing us to ping messages to each other in seconds – no matter the distance between us. Satellite technology allows telephone calls, internet data and TV broadcasts to reach a much wider area, including remote parts of the world that aren't connected to other communication networks.

LOW EARTH ORBIT SATELLITES Despite progress in communication technology, it's estimated that nearly three billion people (more than a third of the world's population) have never been online. Many of them live in places that are unable to receive internet signals. A solution to this issue could lie in satellites, specifically low Earth orbit (LEO) satellites. Orbiting at less than 2,000 kilometres from Earth's surface, LEO satellites provide a better connection and internet speed than satellites that are further away. They also work together in a constantly moving network, whereas higher satellites stay fixed over one part of Earth. This can provide a better connection no matter where you are in the world.

LEO satellites form a blanket around Earth that offers quicker connectivity than other available options.

INTRODUCING LI-FI (LIGHT FIDELITY) There are now a range of wireless technologies available that send signals using radio waves, including 5G and Wi-Fi networks. But there are other technologies emerging, such as Li-Fi, a type of wireless technology that sends signals using pulses of light. Visible light travels at a different frequency to radio waves, so this technology could be useful in places such as hospitals and aeroplanes where there are many other radio signals in use. Visible light travels at an extremely high speed, so Li-Fi could deliver internet speeds about a hundred times faster than Wi-Fi.

SpinLaunch has a 91.4 metre vacuum chamber with an arm inside that can spin around at nearly 500 miles per hour and fling rockets into space.

SLINGSHOTS TO SPACE! NASA has teamed up with a company called SpinLaunch to trial a slingshot system, which uses a giant spinning arm to launch LEO satellites into space! This should be a lower cost, more environmentally friendly alternative to using a rocket booster launch system, as it requires much less fuel.

Li-Fi uses existing networks that power our lights to transmit data. Any device with a Li-Fi sensor that is under the Li-Fi light can access the internet.

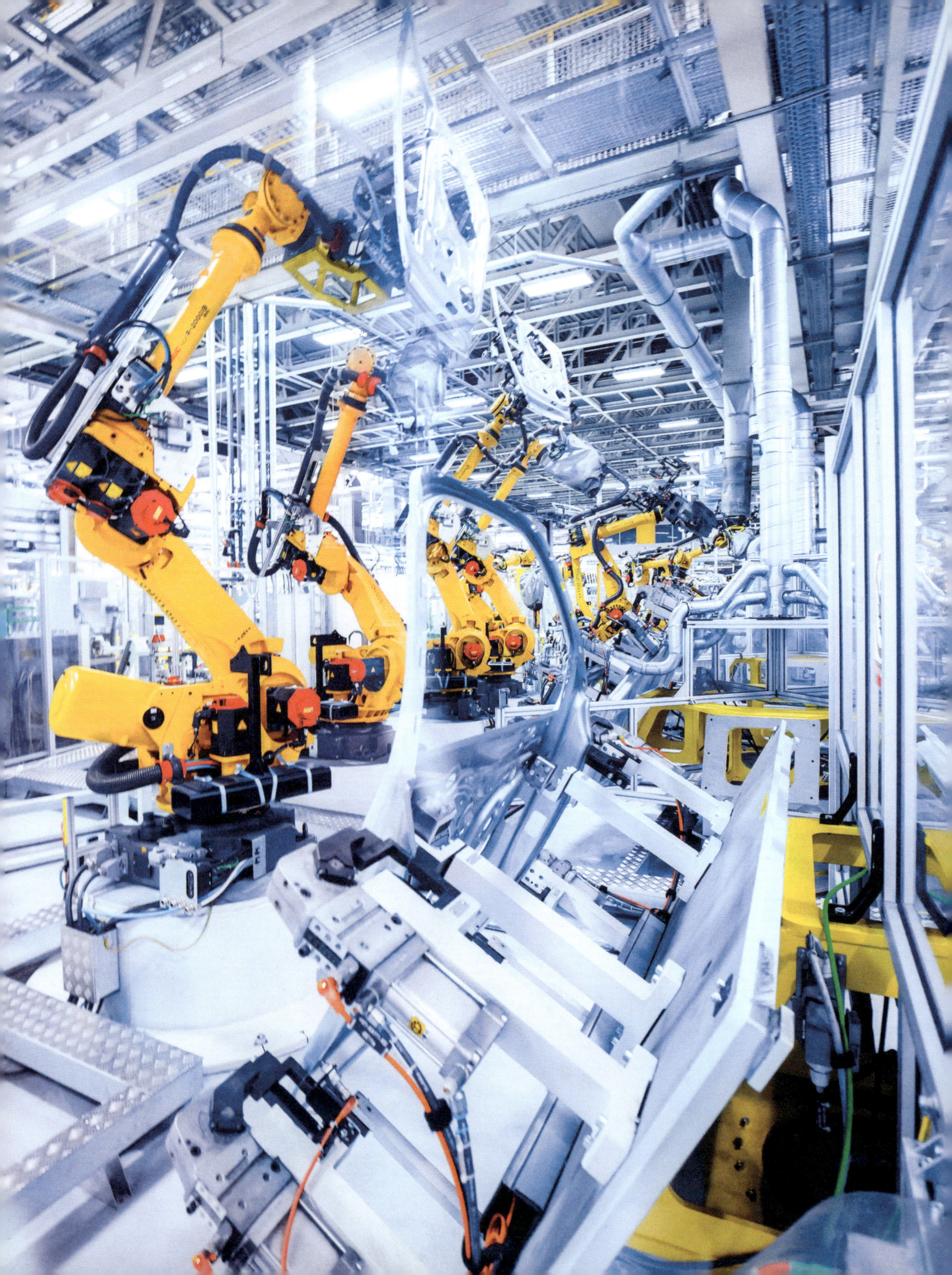

CHAPTER 8

SMART MANUFACTURING

To manufacture something means to make it from raw materials, either by hand or with machinery. When machines are involved, things can be manufactured on a much larger scale. During the First Industrial Revolution, which started in the 1700s in the UK, machinery was powered by steam. This meant that powerful engines could be built for use in many industries, such as coal mining and making textiles. A Second Industrial Revolution happened two centuries later and was powered by electricity. Assembly lines were created to mass-produce products at speed.

The Third Industrial Revolution happened in the 1970s, and this was when manufacturing became increasingly automated. Machines could be connected to each other, controlled and monitored with computers. Today, we are in the midst of a Fourth Industrial Revolution, also known as Industry 4.0, where robotics, 3D printing, AI and the Internet of Things (IoT) are being used to fully automate most manufacturing processes.

Now that manfacturing is becoming almost entirely digital, products can be made more efficiently, sustainably and accurately. In this chapter, we meet some of the engineers making a difference in this highly innovative industry and see exactly how their work is contributing to making things in a smarter way.

LEFT: The Škoda car factory in the Czech Republic uses AI to check for defects in the machinery that makes the car parts. When a defect is located, maintenance can be performed to stop the machinery from breaking down. This makes the factory more productive and less prone to stoppages.

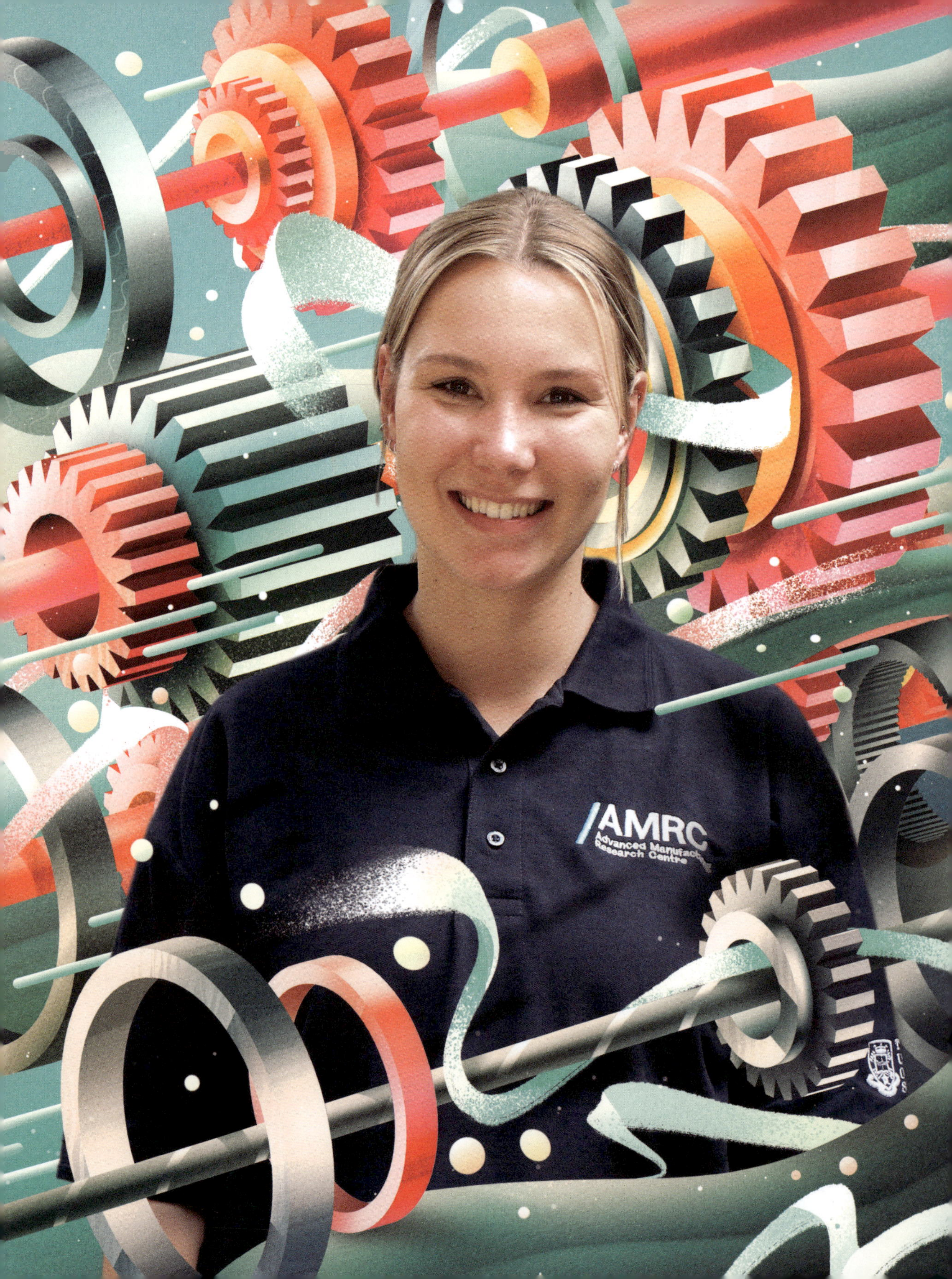
AMRC
Advanced Manufac
Research Centre

Bethany Cousins

MANUFACTURING ENGINEER

MANUFACTURING SMART PRODUCTION SOLUTIONS

At the University of Sheffield Advanced Manufacturing Research Centre (AMRC), engineers are involved in pioneering research into advanced machining, manufacturing and materials. They work with many different types of companies, such as aerospace, transport, construction and healthcare, to help them improve their current manufacturing processes. The AMRC develops new techniques for these companies, which can be immediately put into practice in already functioning production lines. This means that production doesn't need to stop while the research and development is happening – saving companies time and money.

The AMRC aims to strengthen the UK manufacturing industry by helping companies to become more productive, sustainable and competitive. All this helps support manufacturers to grow and thrive. Bethany Cousins started her engineering journey as an apprentice at the AMRC.

WHAT DOES YOUR ROLE AT THE AMRC INVOLVE?

My job at the AMRC is really varied. I often work on projects that require improvements to be made to the manufacturing process or where we need to come up with a new way to manufacture something in the most efficient and cost-effective way. To do this we use computer-aided design (CAD) software and computer-aided manufacturing (CAM) to design a solution to the problem. We always need to be innovative and creative. All our designing is digital, and we can even test the designs digitally by creating virtual simulations of collisions, forces and vibrations that happen during the manufacturing processes. It is a very cost-effective process because no materials, time or machines are wasted.

Once a solution has been found digitally, we can physically make a prototype. We test the prototype and collect data along the way, which we analyse and write up as a report for the client.

Collaboration, creativity and communication are essential in my job, and I love the team of brilliant people I get to work with. Everyone has different skills and expertise, but we are all passionate about finding solutions.

"At the AMRC, we get to be the agents of change in UK manufacturing. I find that really exciting."

Bethany Cousins

The cutting tool moves up and down within the gear. The blades of the tool cut into the inside of the gear to make the teeth.

1.

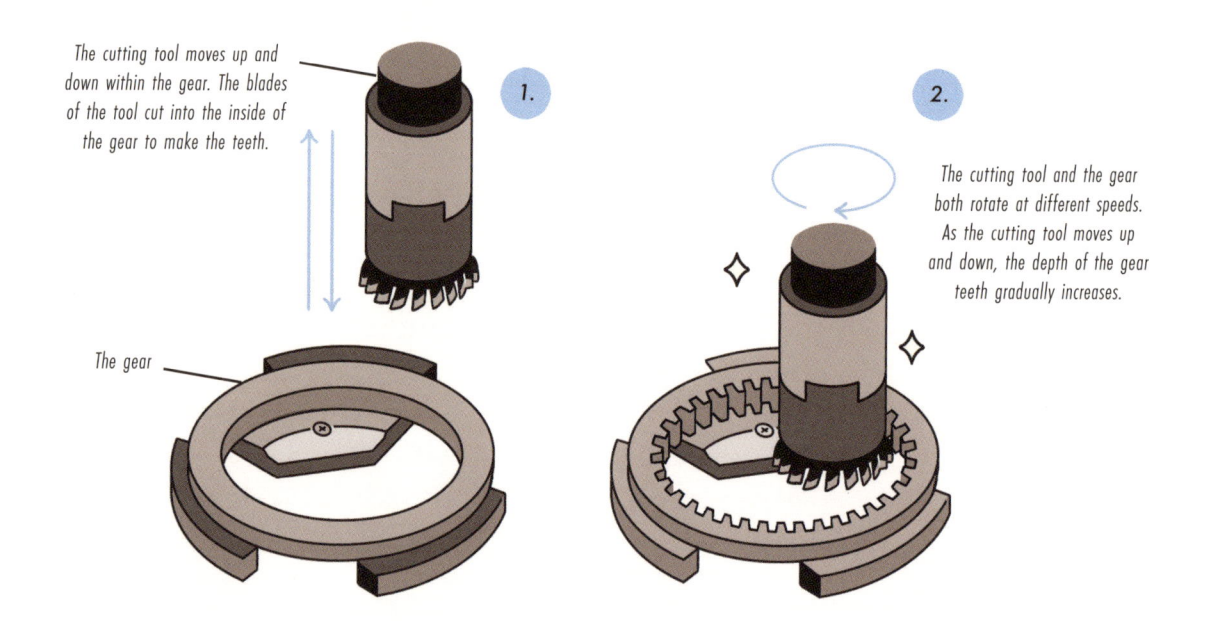

2.

The cutting tool and the gear both rotate at different speeds. As the cutting tool moves up and down, the depth of the gear teeth gradually increases.

The gear

Cutting an internal gear using the efficient power skiving method.

IN WHAT WAYS HAS MANUFACTURING BECOME 'SMART'?

One way is by becoming more digital. Traditional machines are paired with digital tools to make work more efficient and sustainable. By trialling everything on a computer screen first, we can investigate options before we commit to a process. We also find it more cost-effective to use multi-purpose machines, which can do more than one job, for example drilling and cutting. Machines that can only make certain items are not the best use of space on the shop floor (which is what we call the area in which the production actually happens) and are often very expensive too.

Sustainability is one of the big themes that runs through our company. One of our objectives is to make parts more lightweight, especially if they are for the aerospace industry. Lighter components in aircraft require less fuel to carry them, which overall is better for the environment.

Doing things differently should be encouraged in manufacturing, which is why we need more young people to join the industry. When I started my apprenticeship, I had never seen any of the manufacturing processes before and so I found it easy to think of new ways to do things. Occasionally I have had resistance to my new ideas, but it has been important to keep pushing them because they could be the shift that contributes to a smarter manufacturing future.

WHEN AND WHY DID YOU DECIDE TO BECOME AN ENGINEER?

I had a great insight into what an engineering career would be like because my family is in engineering. I have found that engineering welcomes everyone, regardless of academic achievements, background and skills. And manufacturing in particular is very broad.

At school I really enjoyed maths and physics, but didn't enjoy being at school. I wanted to use my skills rather than just learn. Engineers use maths and physics to answer questions and find useful solutions, and I love this approach, which is why I was well-suited to an apprenticeship. I wouldn't have been able to get both practical and theoretical experience in any other way.

It's been so important to study what truly interests me. Working five days a week, and then studying at university outside of these times, has been possible because I love my job. I also love watching the industry advance. The technology evolves at such a rapid pace that the most effective way of being at the cutting edge of the industry is to be right in the heart of it.

I really enjoyed meeting other apprentices at university, especially those who are based in other companies. Learning about how they are applying the theory and perhaps even doing things a little differently is great.

WHAT DO YOU FIND MOST CHALLENGING ABOUT THE MANUFACTURING INDUSTRY?

Changing traditional industry practices is challenging. Often manufacturing has been done a certain way for many years and it still works, just not as well as it could. Change can often be met with a lot of resistance from people who don't want to change things. I believe change is needed to restore UK manufacturing to the leading position it once had during the First Industrial Revolution.

WHAT ADVICE WOULD YOU GIVE TO ANYONE WANTING TO FOLLOW IN YOUR FOOTSTEPS?

Research all areas of engineering. See what options are available and remember that no matter which route you take into your career, you don't have to commit to it for the rest of your life. Enjoy experiencing different things because it is all part of the jigsaw puzzle that builds up your career. No experience is a wasted experience.

FACT FILE

Most fun thing about your job: Every project is new and completely different to the one before, and has the potential to make a difference to the industry.

CAREER HIGHLIGHTS

1. Leaving formal full-time education for an apprenticeship that shaped my career.

2. Gaining a job at the AMRC and having access to cutting-edge technologies.

3. Getting a first class degree from the University of Sheffield.

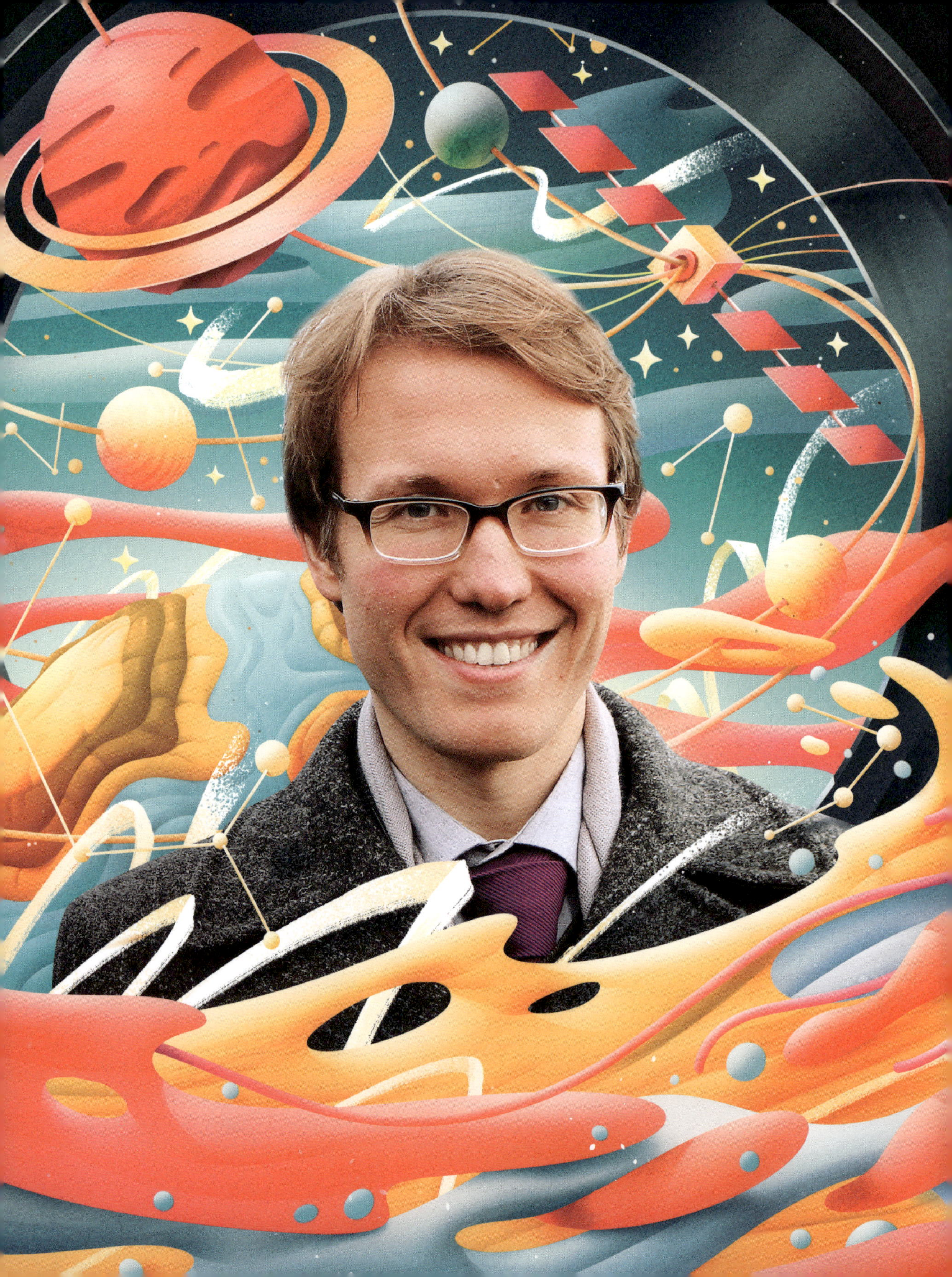

Dr Matjaz Vidmar

SYSTEMS ENGINEER
MAKING PEOPLE AND MACHINES WORK BETTER TOGETHER

Since the First Industrial Revolution, manufacturing has become more automated, with many processes now controlled by computers. This means that there are lots of different systems that need to be co-ordinated and managed so that they run smoothly – this crucial role is done by a systems engineer. Like many other industries, manufacturing has gone virtual and a systems engineer is also in charge of integrating old analogue and new digital technologies.

Dr Matjaz Vidmar has many varied interests but is an expert in physics, engineering, social science and philosophy. His broad technical knowledge and interest in bringing different fields together make him perfectly suited to systems engineering. He is skilled at integrating, co-ordinating and managing old and new systems and helping to create a much smarter industry.

HOW IS MANUFACTURING BECOMING SMARTER?

Manufacturing is increasingly driven by software engineering, where physical objects are created at the end of a largely virtual process. This means that less material is used and waste materials can be reused and recycled, especially during the design and testing stages. For example, 3D printers are replacing slower and more cumbersome traditional manufacturing processes, paricularly at the prototype stage. Manufacturing is becoming more environmentally conscious, less wasteful and therefore more cost-effective for the manufacturer and, ultimately, the customer.

WHAT DOES YOUR WORK INVOLVE?

I design processes to develop new products and services and this requires improving manufacturing systems overall. I work with start-ups who are much more willing to adopt the latest digital manufacturing processes than those with tried and tested ways of doing things.

I also look at building new products by adjusting, modifying and combining pre-existing designs and templates, rather than designing products from scratch – which can save time and money too. I am currently leading an initiative to design a new space station that uses parts of old satellites. This project is called Gateway Earth and we hope that it will help astronauts and cargo travel further into space. Throughout all my projects, I work with engineers, designers, businesses and future users to improve how things are engineered. I aim to bring everybody closer together in order to get the best results possible for a project.

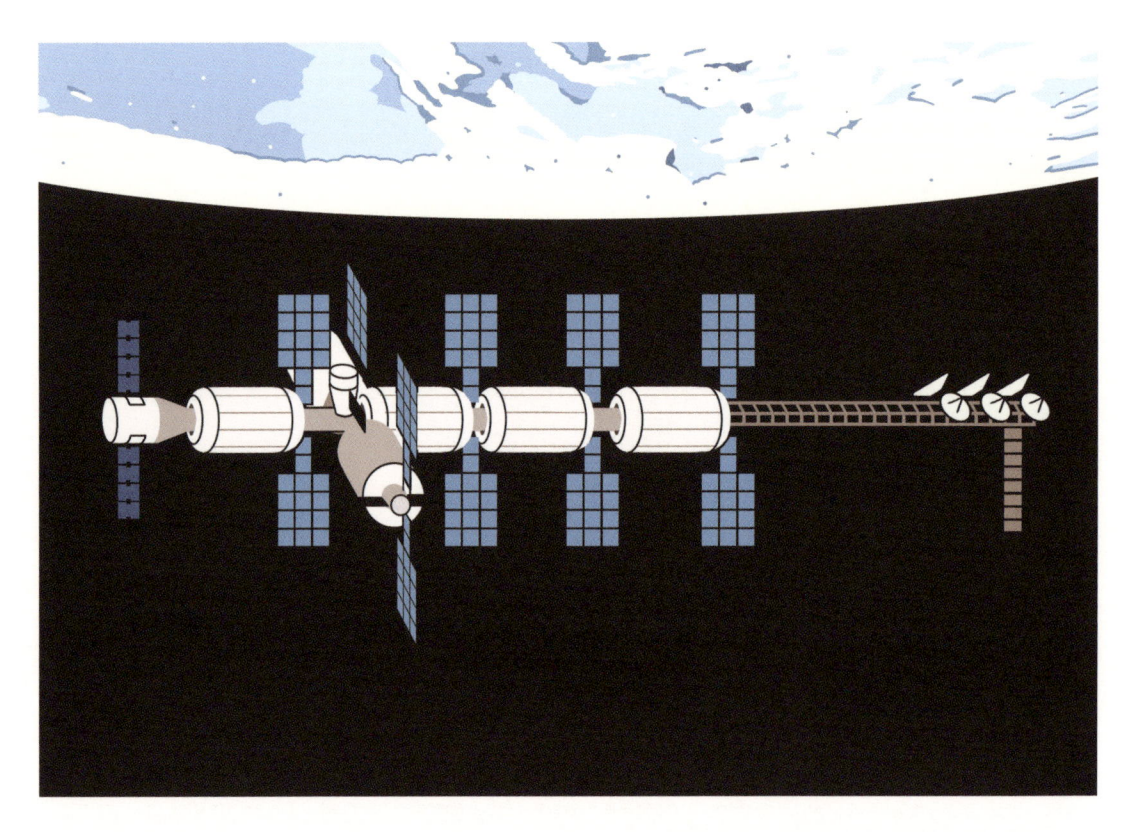

Gateway Earth is planned to be a new space station that is located in low Earth orbit. It will be used for research and also as a space hotel for tourists to stay in. It will be in an ideal location for spacecraft to dock as they depart for, or return from, missions further out in the solar system. By docking these vehicles at Gateway Earth, they can avoid having to travel through Earth's atmosphere, which can cause damage to the craft.

AS A KID, WAS IT OBVIOUS THAT YOU WOULD END UP IN ENGINEERING?

I was always very interested in stripping things down to fundamental problems, which is the basis of systems engineering design, though I didn't know that as a kid. I would look at how something worked, create a little diagram and then figure out how it could be made better. At school, I was really curious about the basic principles of everything. I did a Physics degree, which I found had elements of philosophy included in it because I was always questioning everything! Philosophy taught me how to ask questions and physics helped me answer those questions.

HOW DID YOUR STUDIES IN PHYSICS LEAD YOU INTO ENGINEERING?

I found physics really exciting, but I was bad at the maths that was involved. I love lab work, coding and data analysis, but struggled with quantum physics (the study of matter and energy) and thermodynamics (the part of science that looks at the relationship between heat and energy) and any topics that required a lot of complicated equations!

What continued to interest me most was developing systems. My final project for my undergraduate degree involved building a small solar observatory, which still exists today on top of the Physics building at the University of Edinburgh. Looking back, this project was more of an engineering project than a physics one, because it involved connecting different existing systems (such as the telescope itself, a camera and a spectrometer, which is a device that measures wavelengths of light) and working out how to use them well together.

As with most engineers, I had to teach myself what I needed to learn. To make the observatory work, I needed to become an expert in optical fibres, and I taught myself how to write code to programme the camera to capture the correct images. I also had to work out the best way to test this system. This project brought together so many of my passions and interests across physics, engineering and astronomy and led me to realising that my interests lie in engineering and innovation.

WHAT TRAITS HAVE BEEN MOST USEFUL TO YOU AS AN ENGINEER?

The need to work things out has been most useful to me. I am a problem-solver. My joy is found in the moment when everything fits, works and is useful to others! It's also extremely nice when people find value in what I do. The purpose of my work is to help make the world a better place – as cliché as that sounds. I want engineering systems to be as efficient and sustainable as possible. In my opinion, making clever advanced engineering is less about being brilliant at maths and physics but more about bringing a unique kind of technical creativity and beauty into the world.

FACT FILE

Most fun thing about your job: When connecting people and machines, you get to meet many different and exciting humans and devices.

CAREER HIGHLIGHTS

1. Getting to meet young engineers through STEM outreach in schools and communities.

2. Being inspired by a poster to start an MSc degree.

3. Having the opportunity to learn together with my university students.

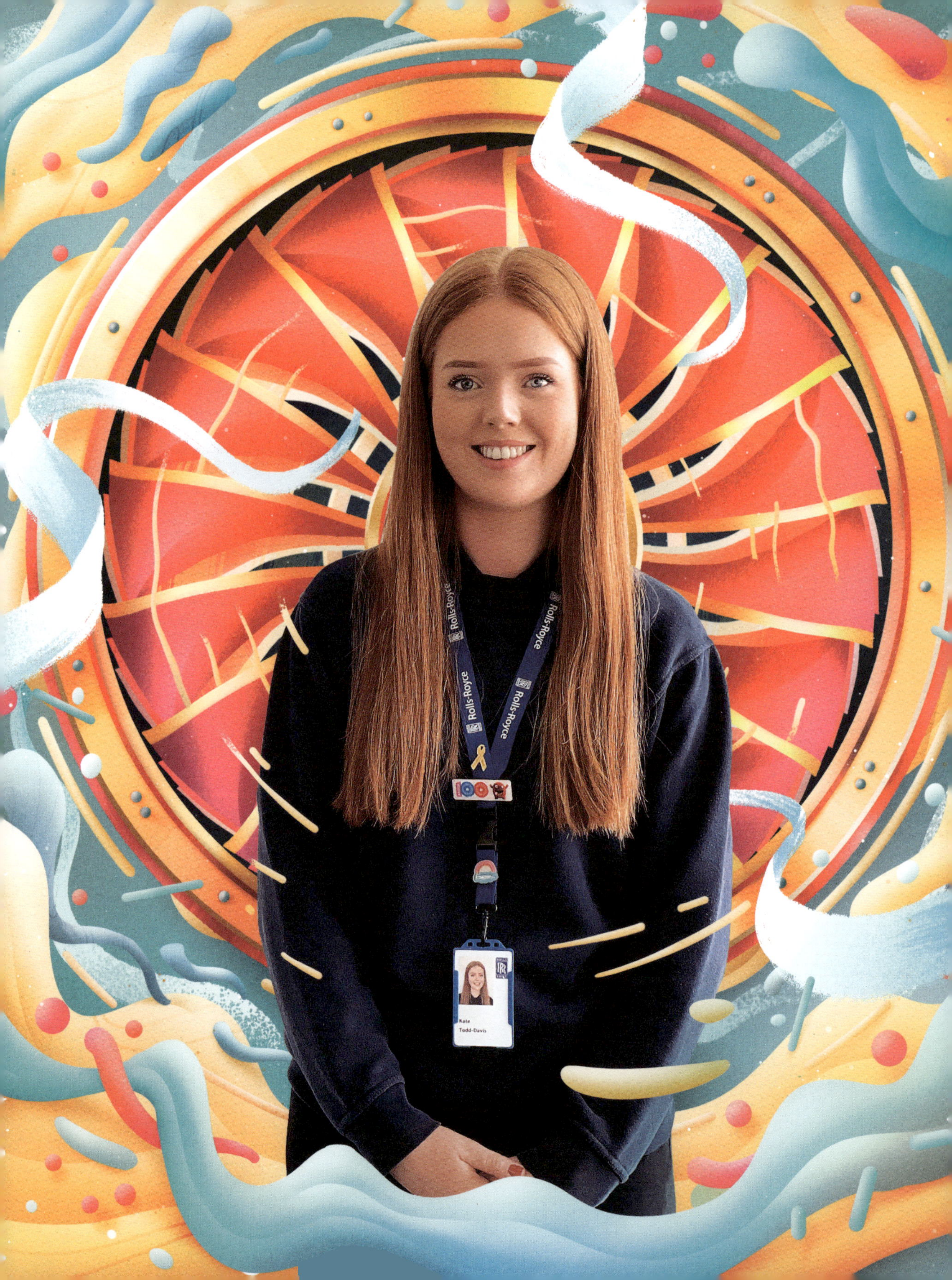
Rolls-Royce

Kate Todd-Davis

MANUFACTURING ENGINEER

MANUFACTURING PARTS TO MAKE PLANES FLY

It's an exciting time to be in the manufacturing industry and even more exciting to be an apprentice working in it. Kate Todd-Davis is an engineering apprentice working at Rolls-Royce aerospace making parts for jet engines. The processes that Kate uses day-to-day are a perfect mix of old and new technologies.

WHAT IS IT LIKE WORKING AT ROLLS-ROYCE AS AN APPRENTICE?

Working at Rolls-Royce is incredible. My work is really fascinating and I much prefer the hands-on approach to learning. The company has been really supportive and my colleagues are all encouraging. At Rolls-Royce the mindset is that apprentices are the future of the company, so we are always being taught new things and are given room to be creative too.

WHAT DO YOU DO AT WORK?

I focus on the critical rotating components within a jet engine – basically anything that turns. If you look at the front of a jet engine, you will see the fan blades and the disc that holds them all in place. We make these discs and they might seem simple, but they are very important. If a disc breaks, the broken pieces need to be contained – if they're not, it could cause the plane to be grounded. It's a huge responsibility, which is why I need to make sure that every part I make is perfect. It's great that everyone in my team is there to help so I can always ask questions if needed. Everything we do in our jobs is so critical to the overall safety of an aircraft.

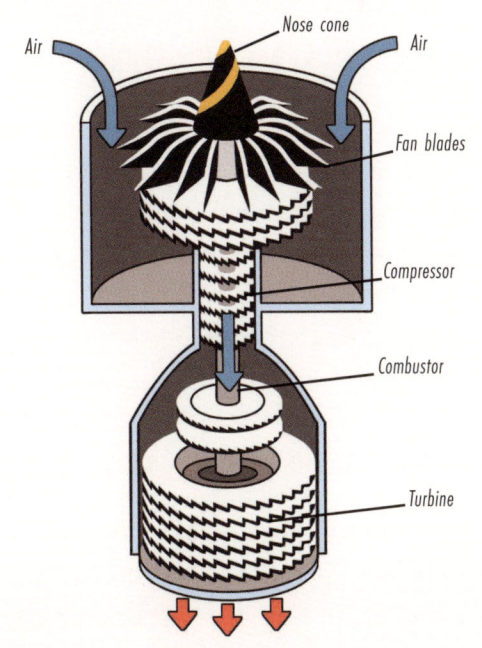

The arrows on this diagram of a jet engine show how the air flows through it. Air is sucked in the front, compressed, sprayed with fuel that is ignited and then blown out the back.

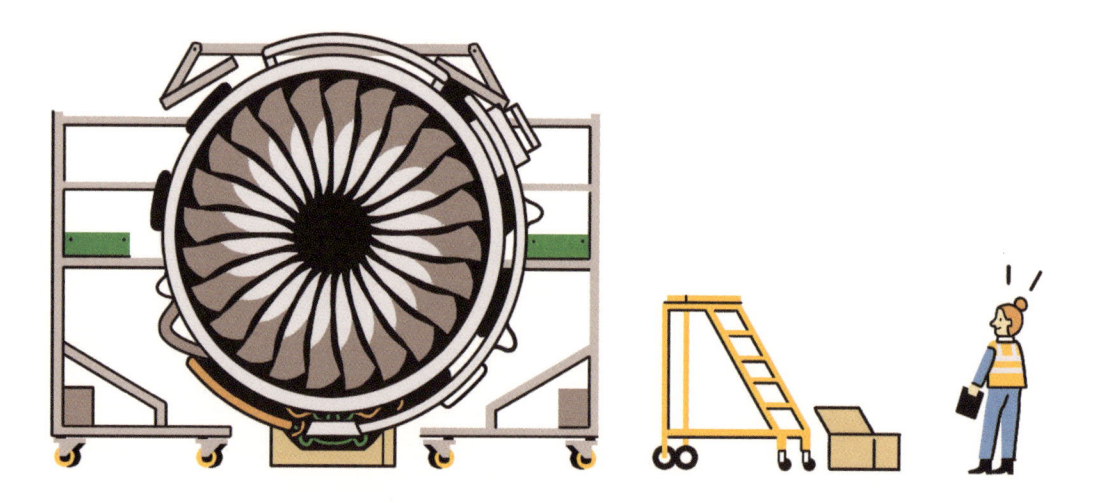

The size of a jet engine in comparison to a person!

I regularly make CAD models and instruct the machine operators on how parts should be made. It's wonderful seeing models turn into reality. After my apprenticeship, I will be working in the New Product Introduction team, which I think is the most interesting part of the business. This is where you get to work on products from the intial ideas right through to the end products.

WHY DID YOU CHOOSE ENGINEERING?

I have always been academically strong in maths and science and my mum always said I would become an engineer – although it took me a while to agree with her! I enjoyed everything science-related and liked watching programmes that explained how things worked. I have also always loved cars and remember the day when I realised that engineering could be for me. I went to watch the drag racing at Santa Pod in Bedfordshire with my dad and uncle, and we went down into the pit to look at the cars. There was a big Rolls-Royce jet engine on display there – I thought it was so cool! Now I can only ever see myself working in the aerospace or automotive industries.

WHAT DOES MANUFACTURING MEAN TO YOU?

To me, it means turning a big lump of metal into something useful! You put the lump of metal through many different processes and machines and use chemicals and tools on it in order to make a functional bit of metal that, in my case, makes a plane fly. Creating this shiny, intricate and perfectly manufactured part is definitely something to be proud of.

HOW DO YOU USE SMART ENGINEERING IN YOUR DAY-TO-DAY JOB?

For us, a big part of the smart engineering that we use is down to digitisation. For example, we can digitally track parts on the shop floor. Even though parts are so big, they have to go through so many processes that it can be very easy to lose them! We can also use computers to monitor the machines and check if they are ever inactive and why, and know what changes to make to increase productivity and make the processes as slick as possible.

WHAT IS THE STRUCTURE OF YOUR APPRENTICESHIP?

Apprenticeships are certainly not for the fainthearted. Balancing work and studying has required really strong time-management skills. I spent my first year learning traditional manufacturing methods, such as milling and turning – techniques that cut objects into particular shapes, either by rotating a cutting tool against the object (milling) or vice versa (turning). This was so helpful, as these are the processes that I now use in my job! It is essential to learn traditional manufacturing techniques in order to be able to innovate new ones.

WOULD YOU RECOMMEND ENGINEERING TO OTHERS?

I would 100 per cent recommend getting into and staying in manufacturing engineering if you have an interest in how things are made, how things work and have a good understanding and interest in science and maths.

It's really important that you choose the right apprenticeship at the right time for you. Some apprentices have joined later on in their lives, usually because they want a career change, and they have been warmly welcomed.

Everyone brings a wealth of experience and talent to the company, no matter whether they're from a more academic or practical background. Whichever route you choose to enter the industry, time and money will be invested into training you. It's so important to have diverse teams from a variety of backgrounds because this is what will drive innovation, which is exactly what our industry needs.

FACT FILE

Most fun thing about your job: Collaborating with everyone in my team to solve problems.

CAREER HIGHLIGHTS

1. Achieving a first in my degree.

2. Completing my first work-based project.

3. Being named AMRC Training Centre Apprentice of the Year.

"I try and go into work every day and soak up as much as I can. And I'm always asking 'why?'."

Kate Todd-Davis

Neil Glover

MECHANICAL ENGINEER

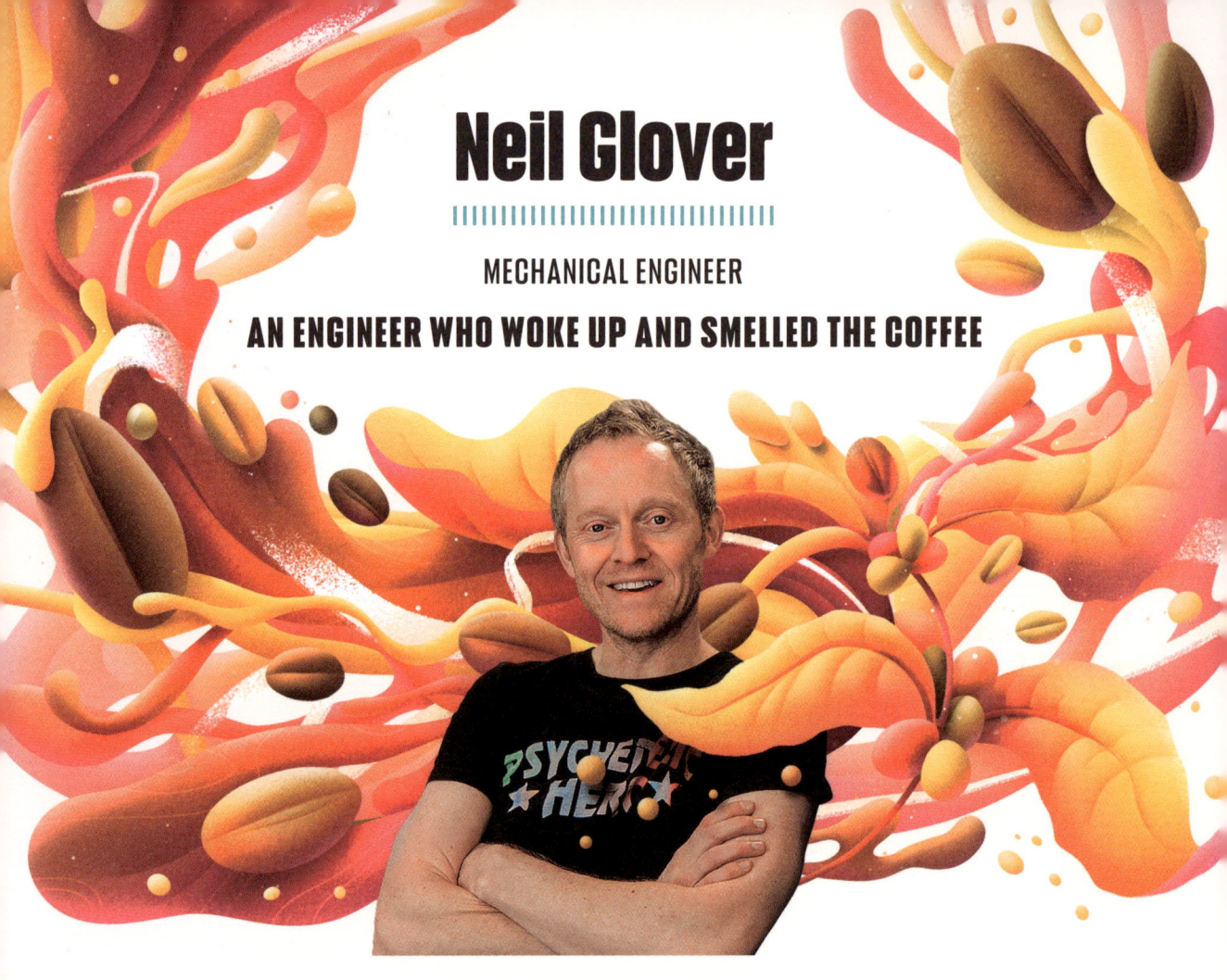

AN ENGINEER WHO WOKE UP AND SMELLED THE COFFEE

Engineers are true problem-solvers, using their creativity and imagination to design and build solutions – no matter how diverse. Neil Glover is one such engineer. Having worked in the oil and gas industry for most of his career, he then turned his engineering skills to coffee.

WHY DID YOU CHOOSE TO BECOME AN ENGINEER?

My dad and big brother are Electrical Engineers – so it's in my DNA. However, unlike them, I struggled to imagine invisible electrons flowing around a circuit. I am more visual and hands-on, so I studied mechanical engineering instead.

I completed a degree in Engineering with Business Management and European Studies at the University of Strathclyde in Glasgow. And because I wanted to study more than pure engineering, I then went on to spend a year at the University of Padova in Italy (one of the oldest universities in the world and where Galileo taught), learn Italian and further develop my communication skills. During this time I also earned a Master's degree.

WHAT WAS YOUR FIRST JOB?

Despite these international experiences, my first job was in manufacturing engineering at a company just 20 minutes away from my home in Ayr, Scotland. There I learnt to use CAD and CNC (computer numerical control) machines, such as welders or laser cutters that are controlled by a computer, to make tools.

I then transferred these skills to working in the oil and gas sector and travelled the world for 20 years. I learnt that there was a real need for a specific product that could seal the gap between the pipes carrying oil and gas out of the ground and the wellbore (the hole drilled into the ground to accommodate the pipe). So, I started my own business called Swell X in 2012 to make just that!

Our 'swellable packers' can be sent down a well, where they absorb fluid. This causes the packer to swell up and seal the well. It's a simple concept but very complex in terms of chemical engineering. I designed, built, tested, qualified and introduced Swell X packers with just a small team of industry experts. Selling our first packer was an incredible moment after all that hard work.

WHY DID YOU START TO ENGINEER COFFEE?

During my travels, I became quite a coffee connoisseur! One day in Dallas, USA, I got to visit a speciality coffee roastery, and from that day on wanted to start my own in Aberdeen so people there could have delicious coffee too. This was the beginning of Figment Coffee. The manufacturing of coffee beans is a highly technical engineering process. We monitor moisture levels and analyse bean density before accurately roasting the coffee beans using special software. The software helps us build specific roast profiles for every bean and to control temperatures and airflow rates, which in turn control the chemical reactions occurring inside the coffee beans. All this to make the perfect cup of coffee!

FACT FILE

Most fun thing about your job: The creative process of making each new coffee taste perfect.

CAREER HIGHLIGHTS

1. Getting my Master's degree from the University of Strathclyde was a really proud moment.

2. The sale and successful run of the very first Swell X packers.

3. The first time I sat in a busy Figment coffee shop, surrounded by happy customers, drinking a delicious coffee that I had roasted.

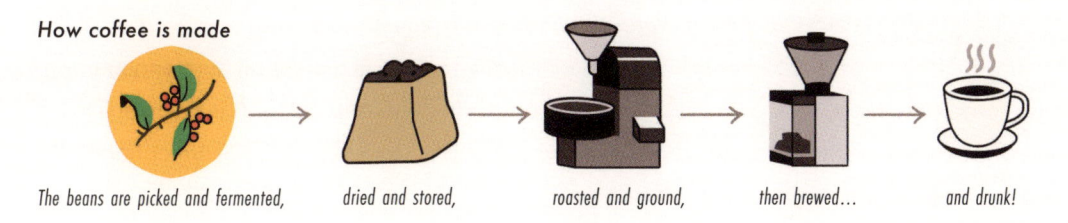

How coffee is made

The beans are picked and fermented, → dried and stored, → roasted and ground, → then brewed... → and drunk!

Factories of the Future

Smart technology is already being used in factories around the world, but it's a fast-paced, ever-evolving industry. Great Britain led the way during the First Industrial Revolution, but to become world leaders during Industry 4.0, our engineers must stay at the cutting edge of digital development in manufacturing. The cornerstone of these developments is the Internet of Things. Having machines connected to the internet makes processes quicker and more efficient and allows lots of information to be gathered and analysed.

CHALLENGES AHEAD Having so many things connected to the internet, along with the collection of huge amounts of valuable data, inevitably leads to concerns around cyber security and data protection. This is another fast-moving area of engineering, but it's vital that manufacturing industries keep up to date to ensure they have the best possible security systems in place.

POWERED BY PEOPLE It may sound like the rise of smart factories means fewer jobs for humans, and it's certainly true that it leads to a decrease in manual work on factory floors and production lines. However, Industry 4.0 does mean an increase in the need for employees with skills in IT, data science, electronics and mechatronics (a combination of mechanical, computer and electrical engineering). One thing's for sure – engineers working in manufacturing need to be flexible, adaptable and bursting with ideas for new ways of doing things!

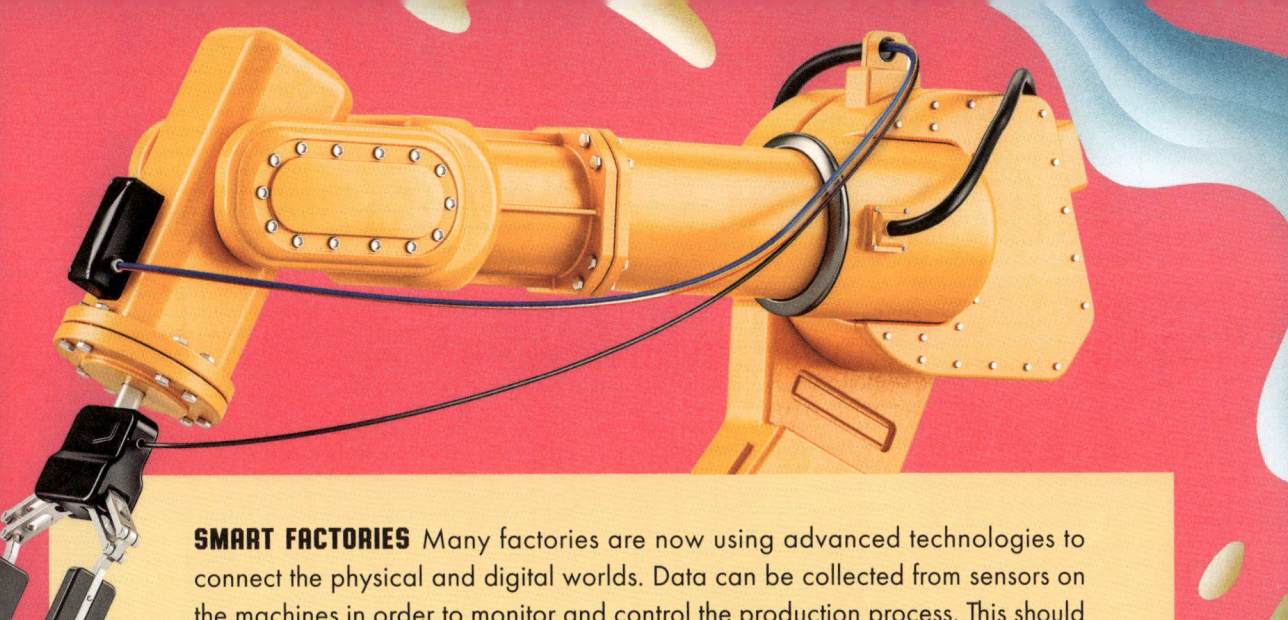

SMART FACTORIES Many factories are now using advanced technologies to connect the physical and digital worlds. Data can be collected from sensors on the machines in order to monitor and control the production process. This should lead to fewer shutdowns and therefore increase productivity.

1. The whole factory floor can be autonomous, with little or no human intervention. Conveyor belts and vehicles can be guided by laser scanners and sensors.

2. Machines with the ability to spot patterns can automatically make the adjustments needed to produce the best possible products.

3. AI robots can be programmed to make decisions and communicate with other areas of the factory in response to last-minute changes.

4. 3D simulations can be built and run without any waste.

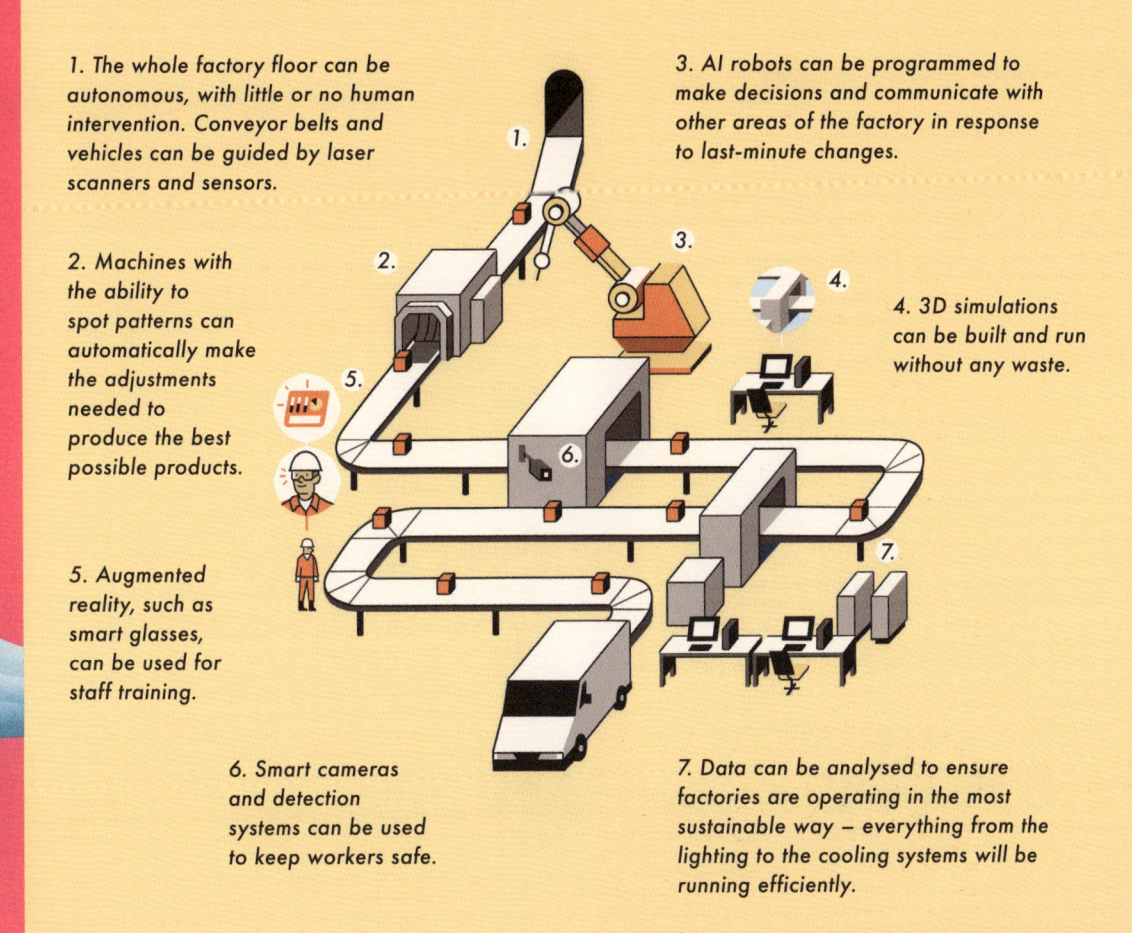

5. Augmented reality, such as smart glasses, can be used for staff training.

6. Smart cameras and detection systems can be used to keep workers safe.

7. Data can be analysed to ensure factories are operating in the most sustainable way – everything from the lighting to the cooling systems will be running efficiently.

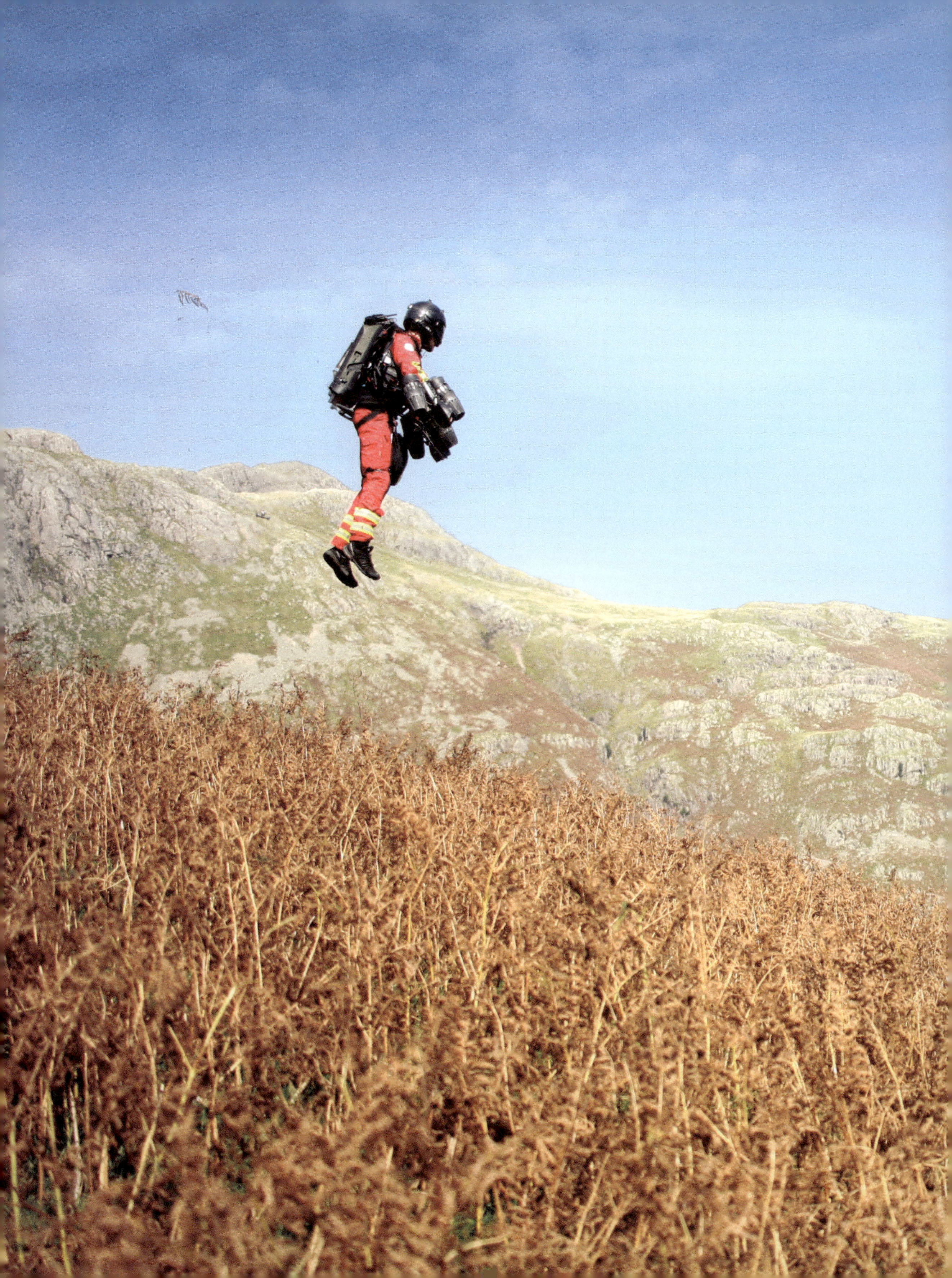

CHAPTER 9

TRANSPORTATION

Engineers work on many things that help to get us from A to B – everything from cars and trains to scooters, ships and aeroplanes. But there is also engineering for transportation infrastructure – all the necessary parts of the transportation industry that do not travel, including roads, fuelling and charging stations, ticket barriers and baggage-claim conveyor belts. Transportation requires many moving parts and the sky really is not the limit!

Some advanced technologies used for transportation have been adapted from innovations initally developed for space travel. Global Positioning Systems (GPS) and satellite navigation, electric vehicle batteries and sensors for weather, temperature and speed are just a few such examples that we benefit from today. Humans aim to travel further and faster and look for inspiration everywhere.

We have come a very long way since the wheel was invented more than 5,500 years ago, and the engineers in this chapter are playing their part in keeping us moving forwards. But it's not just about movement but also *how* we move, with many engineers focusing on ways to do so in a more sustainable and efficient way.

LEFT: Pioneering jet suit technology has been tested by paramedics to reach people who encounter trouble while hiking in hard-to-reach areas. This could reduce response time from 25 minutes if the paramedic had to climb, to just 90 seconds if they were travelling by jet suit.

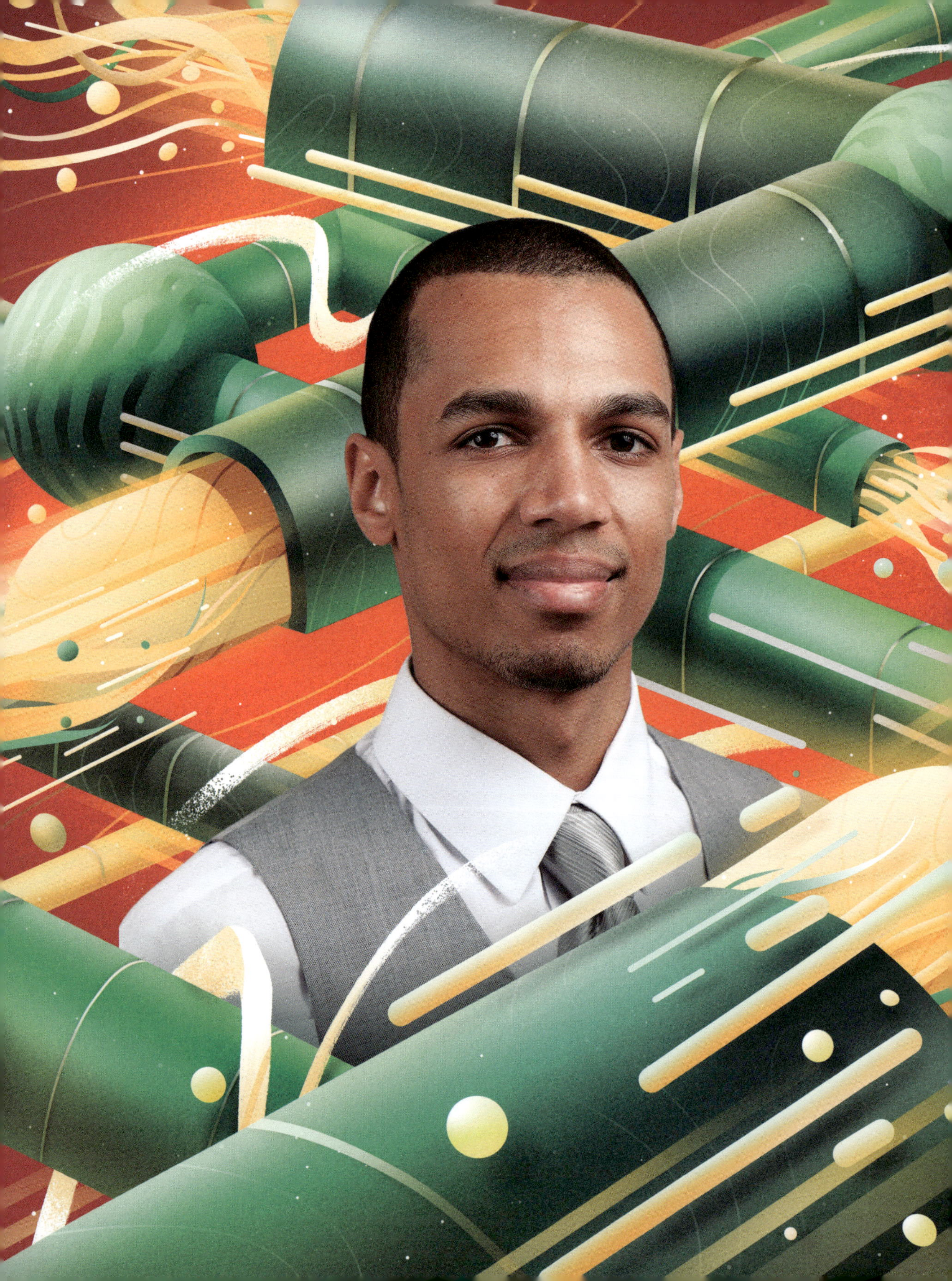

Sonny Kombo

CIVIL ENGINEER
KEEPING LONDON MOVING

Cities have vast numbers of people flowing through them every day and many methods of transportation to choose from. London, for example, offers overground and underground railway networks, buses and bicycles, river boats, scooters and taxis.

All of these systems operate in and amongst the complex network of buildings and other infrastructure, including utilities such as electricity, water, gas and telecommunication. These services need to be maintained, which can often be a complex job that needs to be done without shutting anything down. But they also need to be carefully monitored to make sure that they can't be damaged by any other works that are happening in the busy city.

Sonny Kombo is a Civil Engineer working for Transport for London (TfL) who ensures that the lives of commuters are unaffected by the maintenance work required on these transport systems.

WHAT DOES YOUR JOB INVOLVE?

When a construction job comes up anywhere in London, I have to take a look at which TfL assets, such as trains or lines, might be nearby. I also check if any of our networks, operations or staff are close to the job, in order to ensure their protection during construction.

The TfL network is so vast that most external construction work affects us in many different ways. I am in charge of identifying those ways and helping projects to be built in a manner that is safe for TfL.

"I love learning, and what I do today in engineering feels like I have a brand-new job every single day."

Sonny Kombo

If a train was forced to stop working due to external construction, it becomes very expensive for everyone involved. Also, the Tube has a daily ridership of at least 2 million people, which means that if a train was forced to stop working, it would affect a lot of people! So, it's in our best interests to keep our operations moving, despite what may be happening around us.

HOW DID YOU GET INTO CIVIL ENGINEERING?

I grew up in Kenya, where things are built differently to the UK. Back then I had very little idea of what engineers did. In fact, I thought they laid bricks and had very labour-intensive jobs. I was good at maths and physics but didn't want to study them at university. So, I went on Google and literally typed 'good at maths, good at physics, but don't want to study them. What should I do?'. An engineering page popped up from this search that really interested me.

As a result, I looked into doing a general engineering degree at university. I wanted to keep things general because I was still unclear about what engineering was. To my delight, I was accepted into the University of Warwick to do an Integrated Engineering Master's degree for four years.

Two years into this degree, I knew that I wanted to specialise in Civil Engineering because I hoped that one day I could return to Kenya and help with infrastructure there. So, I switched to Civil Engineering, joined TfL's graduate scheme and did a few jobs that led me into infrastructure protection.

WHAT'S THE BEST THING ABOUT YOUR JOB?

There is so much variety in what I do today. I never really know what I will face when I wake up in the morning. Overnight works can often lead to a cascade of problems, which I have to immediately address to avoid jams during the morning commute.

On a site visit recently, I was looking down at our railway lines from a crane to inspect how the lines may have been affected by construction work happening around them. On other days, I have gone into our Underground or Crossrail tunnels to ensure that any further drilling into the ground does not cause vibrations that could move nearby escalators very slightly and knock them out of alignment. It takes only millimetres to grind them to a halt!

At the moment, I have a massive building development close to the train platform at Liverpool Street Station, where a demolition is happening and a new building is being erected directly over an open section of the Tube line.

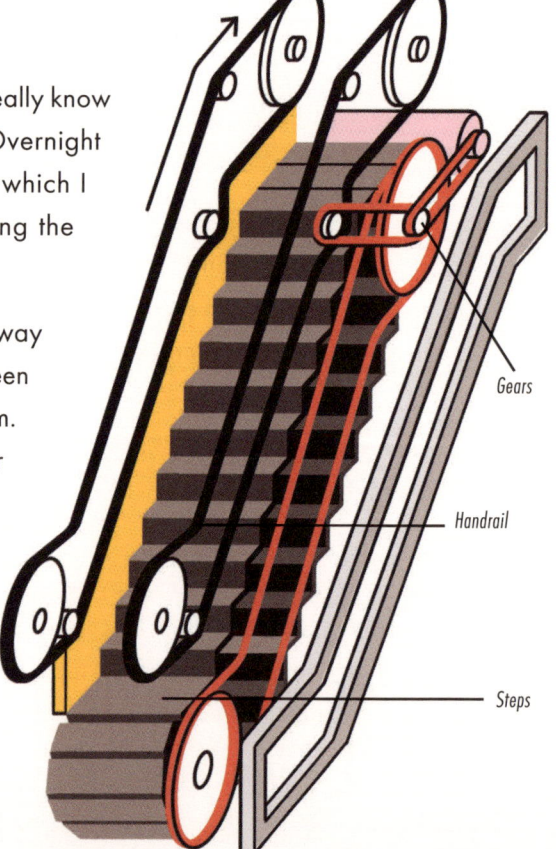

In a standard escalator, the handrail and steps are controlled by a set of gears and chains so they move at the same speed.

It becomes extremely complex to have such a busy station stay fully operational when construction is going on in the background. It's really interesting work.

WHAT HAS BEEN YOUR FAVOURITE PROJECT?

I think my favourite project has to be my first ever one, which resulted in a little cycle-hire stand being constructed outside of Fulham Broadway Tube station. I loved this job because it was a brand new experience and it had a strong sustainability and wellbeing focus. Even though the job looked simple, there were many utilities in the surrounding area, such as water, gas, electricity and communication lines, which could not be paused. They all had to be diverted for construction to happen around them. The job was difficult in terms of minimising disruption to the locals, but it was evident that I was doing my job well because people seemed to be carrying on with their daily lives just fine. The job was next to Chelsea FC's football stadium, which is the team I follow, so that was also really fun!

Another favourite job was again at Liverpool Street. This time we had to shut the station for a weekend to replace an old escalator. We had to dig out the filler between the old cast-iron escalator shaft, which had to be handled with care because any excess pressure could cause it to crack. We used a robotic arm because other tools would have caused too much vibration. The escalator was replaced on time and added eight years to its life. On the following Monday morning my phone didn't ring, so I knew that what we had done had worked!

WHAT ENGINEERING TOOLS ARE ESSENTIAL TO YOUR JOB?

I use a Geographic Information System a lot, which is essentially an interactive map where work can be plotted and recorded. When a new job comes in, I can go on to this map and look at what surrounding assets are affected. All reports and information are uploaded to this software system so that everyone involved in the project has access to the data.

Depending on the site and the project, I might get to play with 'toys', such as boring machines (that make holes in the ground) and cranes. I help to plan how these machines operate. Half of the time I am reviewing drawings, documents, calculations and models at my desk, but I much prefer going out onsite and seeing the projects for real.

FACT FILE

Most fun thing about your job: Seeing people go about their daily lives with no idea that engineering is going on all around them — it means I am doing my job well.

CAREER HIGHLIGHTS

1. Finding out what engineering is and that I might enjoy it.

2. Switching from design to find a part of engineering that I love.

3. Mentoring university graduates and college students and seeing the engineering world through their eyes.

Krystina Pearson-Rampeearee

AEROSPACE ENGINEER
MANAGING SYSTEMS THAT FLY

Aerospace engineering involves designing and building flying machines. Each machine contains millions of different parts, all working in unison. The parts are organised into systems, such as the fuel system, hydraulic system (that controls things such as the brakes or landing gear) or flight control systems (which are used to control the direction that an aircraft is flying in). As a Senior Flight Systems Engineer, Krystina Pearson-Rampeearee supports the research, design and development of the systems used to control the direction and speed of an aircraft. She's been with BAE Systems for over eight years, working on lots of different projects. Currently, she's working on the next generation fighter jet system, Tempest.

WHAT DOES YOUR JOB INVOLVE?

I work as part of the team researching actuators. Actuators convert energy into motion, and they're used in all kinds of manufacturing and industrial engineering applications. On an aircraft, they're used to operate things like tail rudders, wing flaps and doors.

HOW DID YOU GET INTO FLIGHT SYSTEMS ENGINEERING?

At school, I really enjoyed maths and mechanics, so I assumed I'd take mechanical engineering at university. But when I was 15 years old, I heard the roar of passing jets at an airshow and I got hooked on the aerospace industry. A degree was expected of me and there was no talk of apprenticeships. Looking back, that would have been a great option for me. Eventually I came out of university with a Master's degree in Aerospace Systems Engineering, but it took me a little while to get my first job because I didn't have much work experience. I was pleased to accept a job at MGR Foamtex Ltd in Oxfordshire, where I designed luxury suites for first- and business-class aircraft. At MGR we would design things such as the foam that goes in the seats and panelling that goes on the walls – everything in a plane has been engineered! I was a Technical Design Engineer there for almost three years before moving to BAE Systems as a Flight Systems Engineer. I now help to develop complex, cuting-edge systems, some of which will be going into the new Tempest fighter jet.

WHAT ADVICE WOULD YOU GIVE TO ANYONE WISHING TO PURSUE A CAREER IN ENGINEERING?

Learn about the industry through people and companies and find a mentor. There are many different sectors in engineering, so it is important you find something that really interests you. No engineer is limited to one role – there are many possibilities to apply your skills and knowledge to different roles in the future. Say yes to opportunities and stretch your comfort zone, but also be aware of not taking on too much, as mental and physical wellbeing should be priorities too.

FACT FILE

Most fun thing about your job: Every day is different, I never get bored and I'm always learning new things!

CAREER HIGHLIGHTS

1. Becoming a Chartered Engineer.

2. Being selected for the Top 50 Women in Engineering Award in 2022.

3. Completing a Master's degree in Aerospace Systems Engineering.

Tempest fighter jet concept model

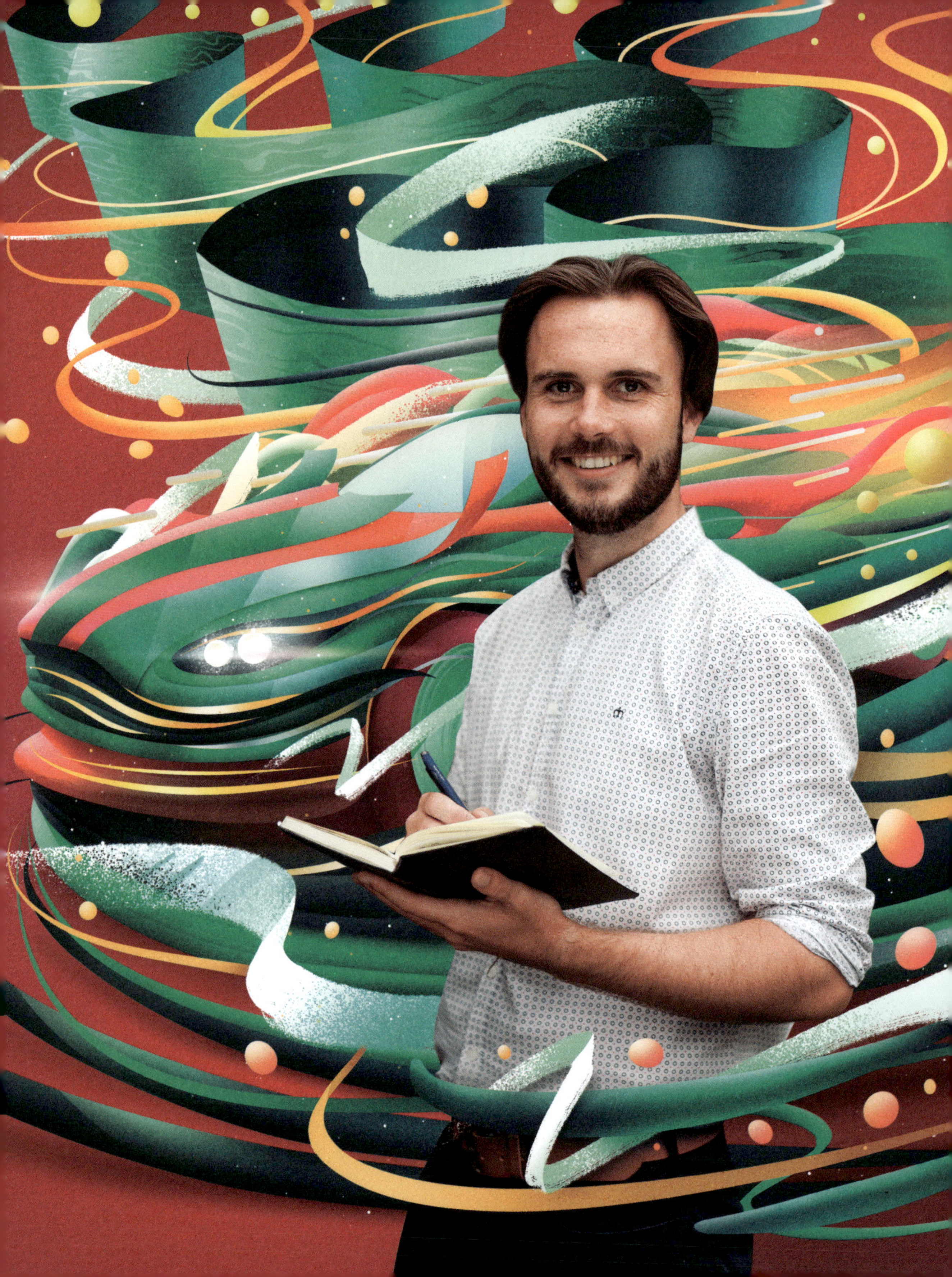

Todd Downs

SENIOR QUALITY ENGINEER
PROVIDING QUALITY THROUGH ENGINEERING

Since the first car was built in 1885, much has changed in the automotive industry. There are now hundreds of different cars to choose from – from electric cars to luxury sports cars and everything in between. Cars are built for many different purposes, but every piece, from bonnet to bumpers, has been specifically engineered by someone who likes life in the fast lane.

Todd Downs has a passion for luxury supercars and found his way to an apprenticeship at Aston Martin through a conversation he had at a car fair. His educational path has not been conventional, but his enthusiasm and willingness have always been a major driver of his career.

HOW DID YOU END UP WORKING FOR ASTON MARTIN?

When I was 14 years old, I met an Aston Martin engineer at a car fair. Their job really excited me and they helped me secure a week's work experience at Aston Martin's manufacturing facility during my summer holidays. During that week, I was given a grand tour of the entire site, introduced to every aspect of the business from concept to design, was shown how to use CAD software and met lots of people, from repair specialists to designers. I even got to help to dismantle and rebuild a DB9, which was a car that I really liked. I also spent some time with the new university graduate intakes, who told me about the pros and cons of university and how it compares to apprenticeships. This experience fired up my interest in the industry and despite my choice to do art, drama and music at GCSE, I still had enough of an education to enrol on an apprenticeship scheme at the age of 16.

WHAT WERE THE HIGHLIGHTS OF YOUR APPRENTICESHIP?

Working with the team from the very inception of an idea, designing it virtually and then eventually building it part by part – making changes and adjustments along the way – has been the best experience. I have worked on my dream cars and driven one all the way from the UK to Paris, which was amazing. For a guy like me, who only came close to cars like this growing up when they would overtake us on the motorway, it is pretty surreal.

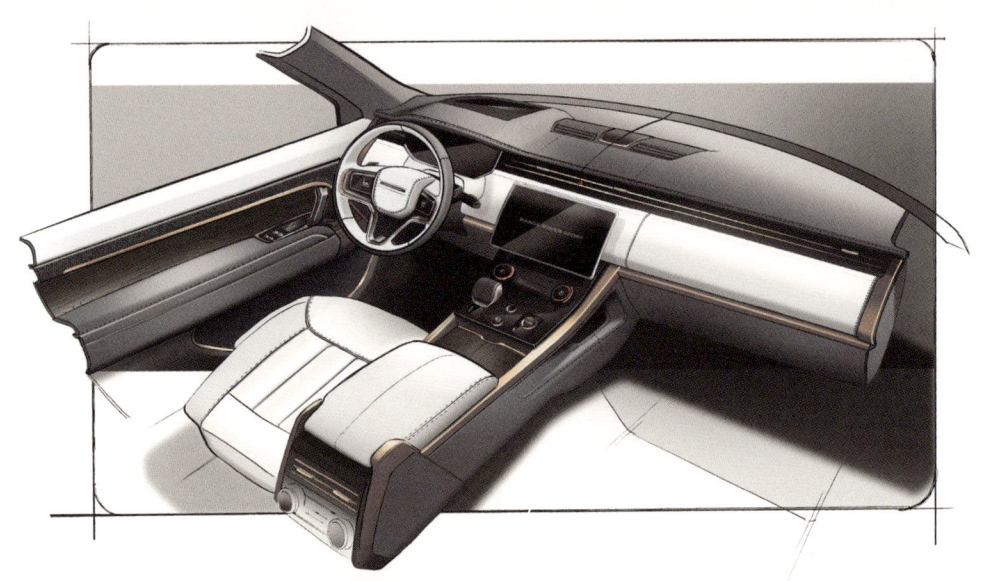

Engineers and designers work together to create detailed plans for all of the features in a car. They ensure that each feature is the correct shape and size for its function, as well as being easy and safe for the driver to use.

Practical learning is much more suitable for me than learning the theory, and I loved getting paid while doing it. Even though apprentices are not highly paid, it was still better than having my two part-time jobs in a kitchen washing pots! After saving up, I was able to buy my own car (not an Aston Martin) and rent my own place to live at the age of 18 years old, which was well before my friends. It gave me a head start in life, matured me, taught me how to manage time and showed me the importance of determination and positivity.

WHAT MAKES YOU A GOOD ENGINEER?

Having a genuine passion and interest for the industry is key. I loved watching shows such as *Top Gear* on TV and have always been deeply fascinated by how things have come to be and how they work. My communication and people skills have been most valuable to me throughout my career. I also get a real kick out of solving problems, getting creative, designing things that never existed before and learning from mistakes.

HOW DID YOU GET TO WHERE YOU ARE NOW?

I finished my apprenticeship at 20 years old and then went into quality engineering, where I was responsible for the quality of the car body construction, vehicle attributes (such as performance and comfort) and interior and exterior trim. You'll be surprised by how the way that a car is sealed influences the ride experience. For three years in this job, I visited suppliers to ensure quality was maintained.

I then left Aston Martin to move into quality engineering for interior and exterior trim full-time, where I was working with Aston Martin, Jaguar Land Rover and Bentley. Today, I am a Lead Engineer for Jaguar Land Rover.

WHAT'S NEXT FOR YOU?

My team management skills have always been more of a weakness than my engineering work, so I have enrolled in a management degree. I'm very proud of my Engineering apprenticeship qualifications from Aston Martin, but I would like to lead my own team one day. Eighty per cent of managers in the UK don't have management degrees and I don't want to be part of that statistic.

WITH HINDSIGHT, WOULD YOU DO ANYTHING DIFFERENTLY WITH YOUR CAREER?

No! Life is good. I'm happy with the decisions I have made and the things I have done over the years because it has led me to where I am now. Engineering is certainly a challenging career, but it's these challenges that make my job so rewarding. At the beginning of my engineering journey, I often questioned if I was clever enough to be working for Aston Martin, but I don't think that now. I have learnt and achieved a massive amount over the years and now have so much more self-belief.

It's important to be comfortable in yourself and know what is best for you. The decision you are making about your career isn't somebody else's decision – it's yours.

FACT FILE

Most fun thing about your job: Diagnosing issues with cars – I enjoy investigating the problem from start to finish, often taking the car apart and putting it back together again multiple times in the process!

CAREER HIGHLIGHTS

1. Winning Apprentice of the Year in 2018.

2. Leading my team to win an IMechE Apprenticeship Competition.

3. Leading a team of technicians and engineers in the USA during my time at Aston Martin.

"It is good to consider the views of our parents, grandparents and friends; however, it's you who will be doing the job, not them. It's crucial to listen to your gut instincts and follow what you genuinely find fascinating."

Todd Downs

Battery-Powered Transport

In a bid to reduce harmful carbon emissions from vehicles, many governments have plans to phase out petrol and diesel vehicles. Currently, most people are still driving petrol or diesel cars, but others have moved to hybrid or fully electric vehicles. Hybrid vehicles have an internal combustion engine (the kind that is powered by petrol or diesel) but can switch to an electric motor. New electric vehicles will need to be affordable, quick to charge, able to travel long distances and reach high speeds. Battery technology is likely to be the key to achieving this.

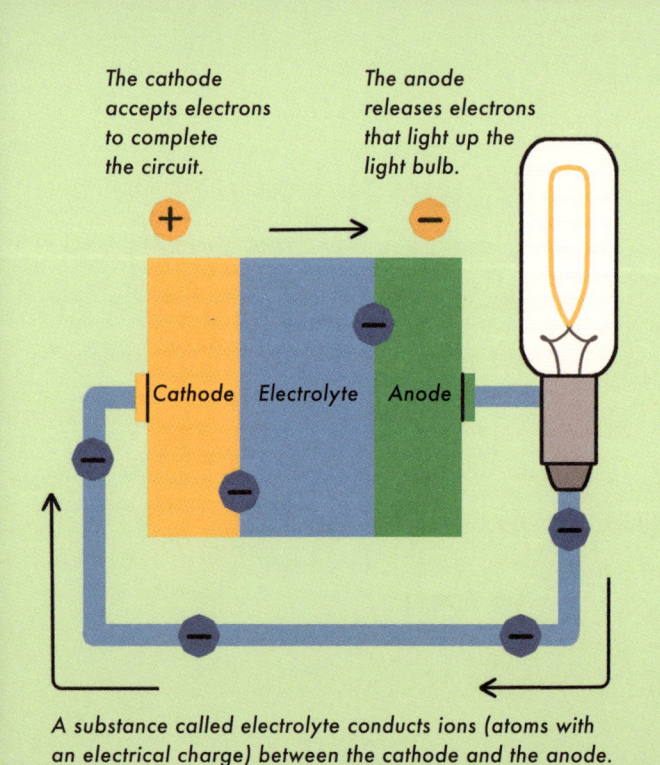

The cathode accepts electrons to complete the circuit.

The anode releases electrons that light up the light bulb.

Cathode | Electrolyte | Anode

A substance called electrolyte conducts ions (atoms with an electrical charge) between the cathode and the anode.

HOW A BATTERY WORKS

A battery stores chemical energy and converts it into electrical energy. There are many different types of battery, but they fall into two main categories: primary and secondary. Primary batteries can only be used until they have discharged all their energy. Secondary batteries can be recharged. The most common secondary battery is Lithium-ion, which can last around 12 years. In an electric car, thousands of battery cells are bundled together to make one giant Lithium-ion battery.

Electric car charging points have been built in many places so that the cars still offer the same freedom as a traditional vehicle. Some electric cars can charge for a 270 kilometre journey in just 15 minutes.

THE RACE IS ON Researching, testing and making new technology is time-consuming and expensive. In the time it takes to develop new batteries for electric vehicles, other sustainable power options could become more popular. It could be that we end up with a range of options to sustainably power our vehicles. One thing's for sure, the engineers working in this industry will need to move at top speed to develop the electric vehicles of the future!

DEVELOPING BETTER BATTERIES Here are some exciting developments in battery technology that could be beneficial to electric vehicles:

THE POWERWALL This is a large battery designed to store solar power for days when it's not sunny. Powerwalls could be used to charge electric cars, which would help to ease demand on the electric grid – this is the system of wires that supplies buildings with electricity.

SOLID-STATE BATTERIES Producing the batteries for electric cars can create high carbon emissions. However, a new type of solid-state battery could change this by using a ceramic material instead of liquid electrolyte to carry the electricity. This makes them lighter and faster to charge and able to hold more energy. The materials used could drastically reduce the carbon footprint of an electric vehicle battery.

GRAPHENE This material is a great electrical conductor and if used in batteries, it could offer fast charging times and help to prevent overheating. Production costs of graphene can be high, but a new, lower-cost form of graphene has been developed that could help to super-charge batteries.

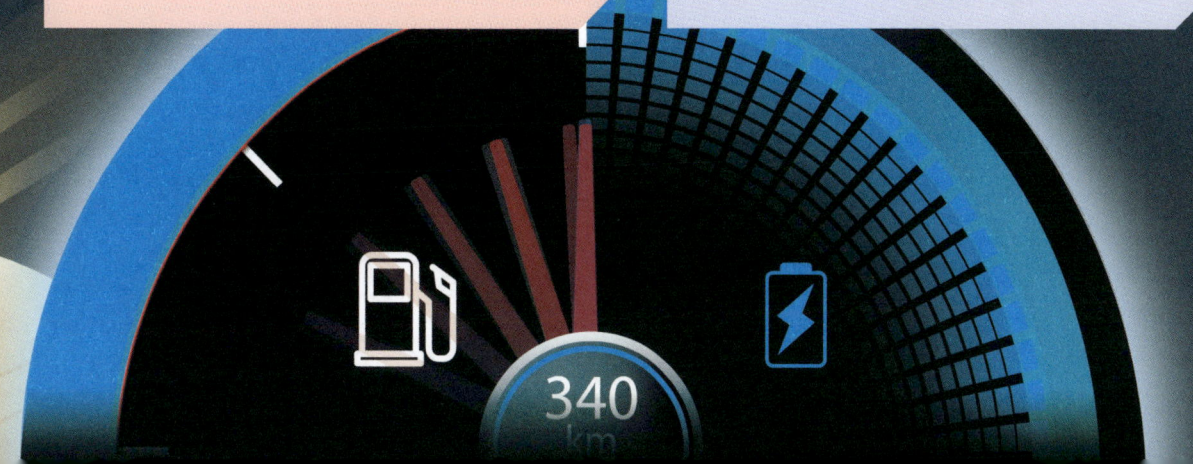

340 km

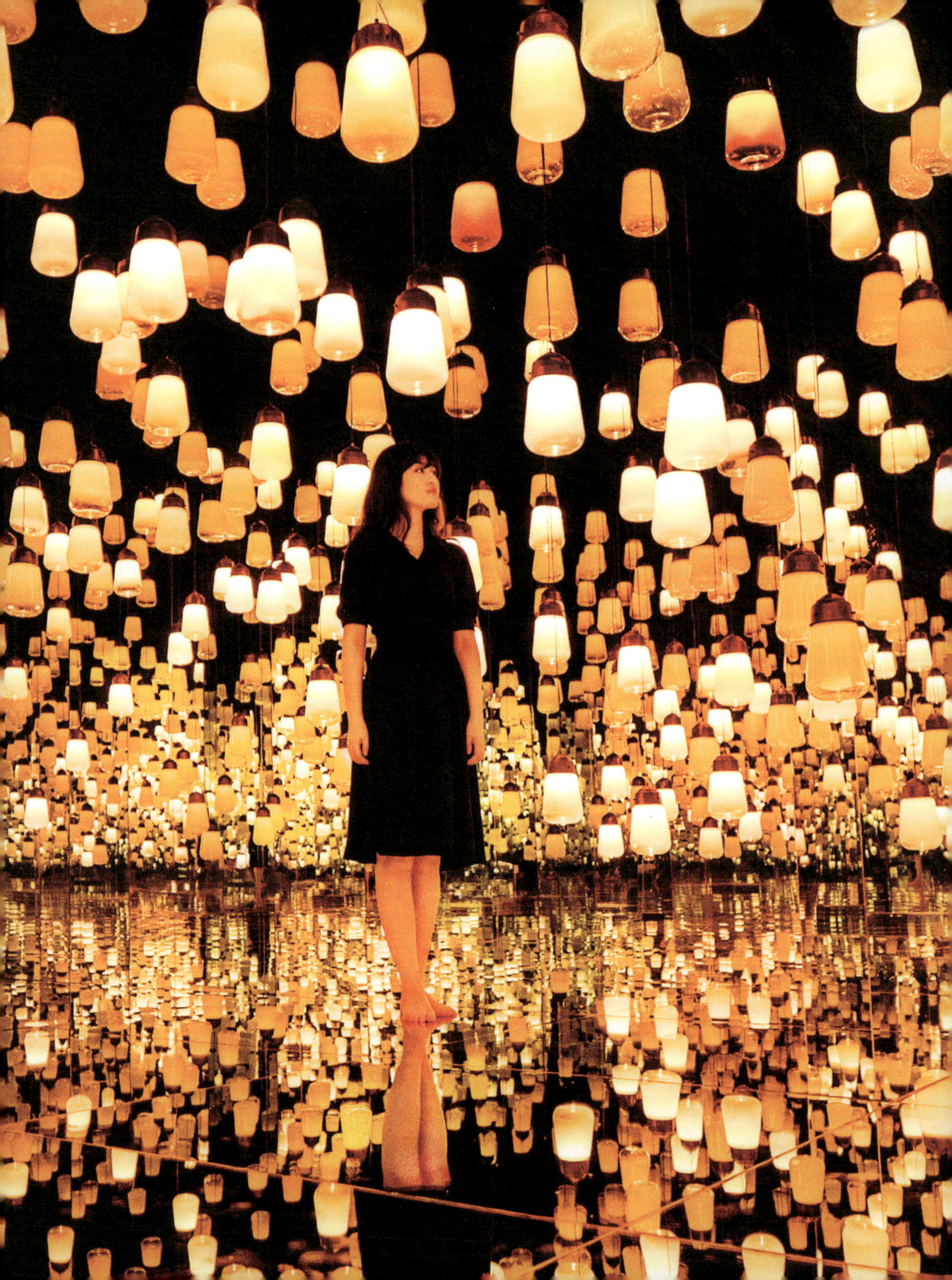

CHAPTER 10

ENTERTAINMENT

Engineers play a huge part in providing us with entertainment of all types, from sports, online gaming and music streaming to social media, concerts and much more. Engineers help to shape our spaces and the way that we interact with them, whether in the virtual or real world. Entertainment technology is evolving at a rapid pace, and augmented and extended reality are deepening our experiences.

Entertainment is largely digital these days, so an interest in coding, computing, simulation and other digital solutions will be really useful to the engineers of the future. We now have a range of devices that we can use for entertainment that allow us to watch films, listen to music and podcasts or connect with one another on social media in an instant.

The engineers in this chapter work in a broad range of industries and are contributing very different skills to their particular sector of entertainment. But they all share one thing in common – each of them has started their career in a traditional form of engineering. They demonstrate that no matter what training you have had, you can use your knowledge, experience and interests to launch yourself into a completely new field. They have each followed their passions to develop a career that suits them and provides fun and enjoyment for others.

LEFT: Forest of Resonating Lamps – in this immersive art installation, lamps have been strategically placed within a room. When a person stands still close to a lamp, it shines brightly and makes a sound. The light and sound then spread to nearby lamps, creating a path of light around the room. The artwork was created to express the beauty of continuity.

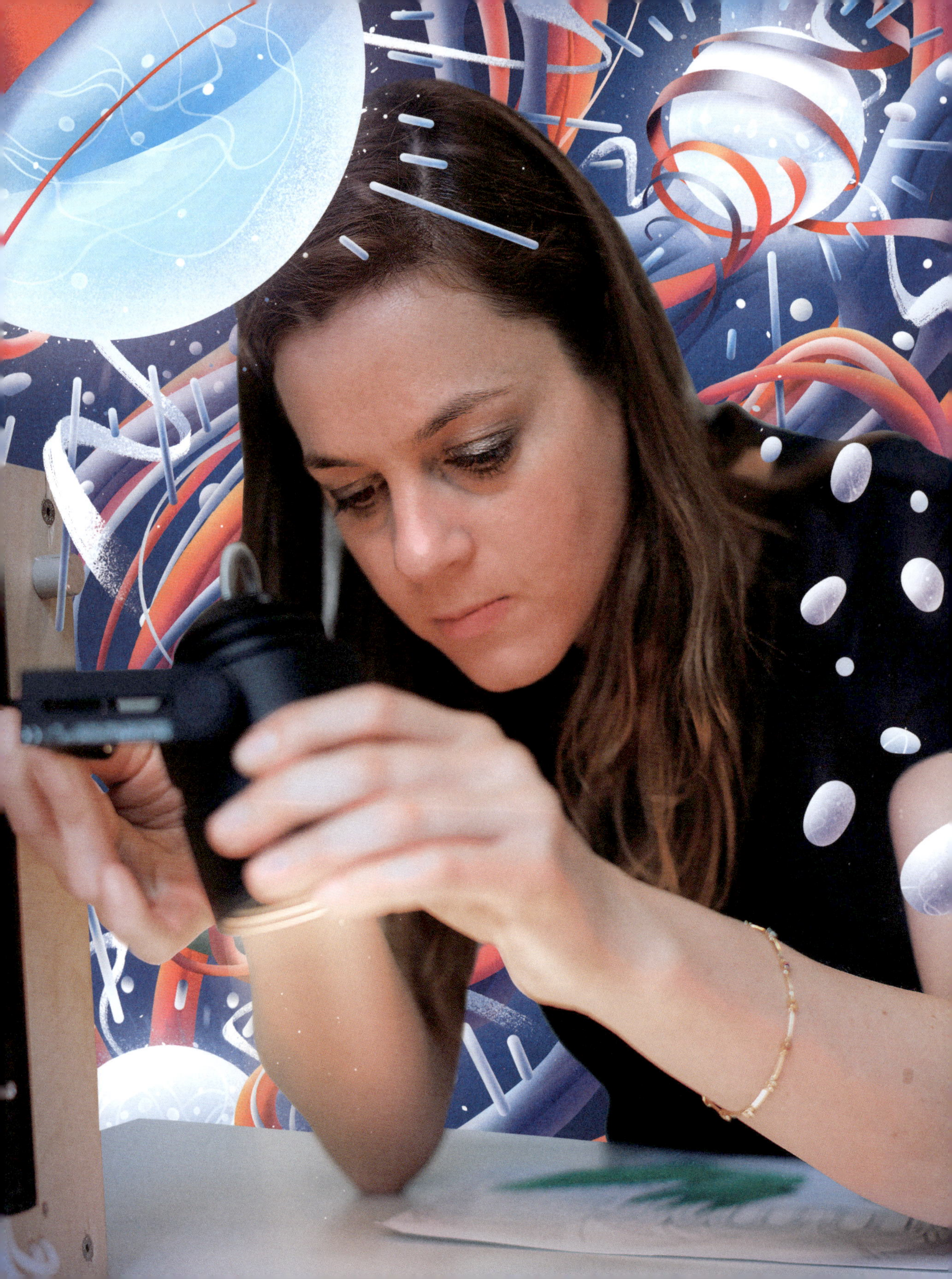

Pavlina Akritas

ELECTRICAL ENGINEER
USING LIGHT TO CURATE EXPERIENCES

Light is a fascinating thing. Natural light affects our sleep and our moods and even helps our body to make vitamins that we need. Red light makes us sleepy, while blue light makes us feel more energised. Light can even influence our enjoyment of a space or event.

Many of our spaces are now lit with artificial light, which has often been carefully engineered. Lots of engineering goes into illuminating dark spaces, from developing the lightbulb to supplying the electricity. In recent times, advanced engineering, such as AI and the IoT, has been used to control light, allowing it to be manipulated in new and exciting ways. Pavlina Akritas is one engineer with a passion for lighting design whose work exists in the space where art and science meet.

HOW AND WHY DID YOU END UP IN LIGHTING DESIGN?

My dad is an engineer, so I was exposed to the career from a very young age. I was born and raised in Cyprus, which meant that at the time I didn't have access to the type of STEM programmes I now see for children in the UK that introduce young people to engineering. Most of us at a young age needed a little push into a career path and that little push came from my father.

I went to an English school in Cyprus and did GCSEs and A-levels in English. I was very good in school and I really loved maths, seeing it almost as a hobby. I knew my career would involve maths in some way, but I had no idea at that age what job I wanted to do for the rest of my life. So, I chose my first degree in Electrical Engineering at the University of Illinois in the USA, purely because I wanted to play tennis for the university!

I really loved being an athlete and was very disciplined and dedicated to it. I recently had my first child and staying fit and healthy is still a priority.

After my first degree, I went on to do a Master's in Light and Lighting at the Bartlett School of Architecture at UCL in London. This is where I fell in love with the discipline and got my first job working in lighting design after I graduated.

WHAT DOES LIGHTING DESIGN INVOLVE?

It involves designing lighting solutions for clients to fit certain spaces, for example museums, offices, universities or fashion shows. But it could be for any space, really – I even designed the lighting for the London Aquatic Centre for the 2012 Olympics. My job involves thinking about what lighting options are available and then translating them onto a computer.

I use lighting modelling software, which recreates how light will look in a space. I then do mock-ups either in the Arup Light Lab (where I work) or onsite where I play with real lights to recreate the computer simulations. This is an important part of my job because simulations can only take you so far. My work involves calculations, writing computer code, building scale models and going into spaces to install mini test cases so that I can make tweaks and adjustments.

I work closely together with the client and other members of the design team to ensure that expectations are being met. On some jobs, such as in museums or galleries, I need to be mindful of how light can affect fragile and precious artefacts. In fashion shows I need to consider how light is used to illuminate the models and their garments and how the audience will respond to the light. There is a lot to consider, but I really enjoy having the power to change people's experiences through light.

WHAT HAS BEEN YOUR FAVOURITE PROJECT?

The project I am most proud of is the Gagosian Gallery at Grosvenor Hill in London. I was tasked with 'bringing the outside inside' by creating a real-time daylight experience. This meant that the client wanted the light outside to be copied inside – at the same time!

"I usually ask 'How can I do something?', rather than 'Can I do something?'. There is always a solution to every problem."

Pavlina Akritas

As there were no skylights to help with this, my solution was to write a code that worked with an exterior sensor to take measurements of outside weather conditions. The code then used the information from the sensor to control a series of different coloured light-emitting diodes (LEDs) to shine at different intensities and colours to match the conditions outside.

This solution tested all my engineering skills to the limit, but, after a lot of hard graft, it worked! We switched on the system on a day that was partly cloudy. Through the windows we could see a cloud passing over the building and it triggered the control system to dim the lights and turn them slightly blue. When the cloud passed, the lights changed to a brighter, warmer light. It was a surreal and satisfying experience to see the technology I had designed come alive.

THE GAGOSIAN GALLERY

The lighting program that Pavlina designed for the Gagosian Gallery space mimicked the natural light outside the building. The client didn't want the wall near the windows to feel different in colour, otherwise the art would look different too, so it was crucial that the electric lighting matched the daylight.

WHAT WOULD BE YOUR TOP TIPS FOR ANYONE EMBARKING ON A CAREER IN ENGINEERING?

Engineering has helped me to think outside the box and not be afraid of complexity. I am always keen to tackle new projects by turning concepts into reality and pushing ideas to their limits. But I couldn't do any of this if I didn't have a passion for what I do – it's the key to success in any job.

Find out what you're passionate about first and then find an area of engineering that fits your passion. Engineering is the broadest industry I know, so I guarantee you will find something. You don't necessarily need to be great at maths and science, but you do need to have a willingness to learn and an interest in your area of expertise.

These days, so much of the work we do is computer-based, so take advantage of that by travelling and working remotely and gain as much experience as you can. This will help you discover what you like and don't like. Unconventional perspectives and different backgrounds bring so much value to engineering teams.

FACT FILE

Most fun thing about your job: Seeing the impact it has on people.

CAREER HIGHLIGHTS

1. Lighting fashion shows for Paris Fashion Week.

2. Helping to deliver the lighting and controls for a major tech giant's store on 5th Avenue, New York, USA.

3. Helping to create the skylights that filter natural light in the Broad Museum, Los Angeles, USA, and seeing the influence that our work has on the architectural design.

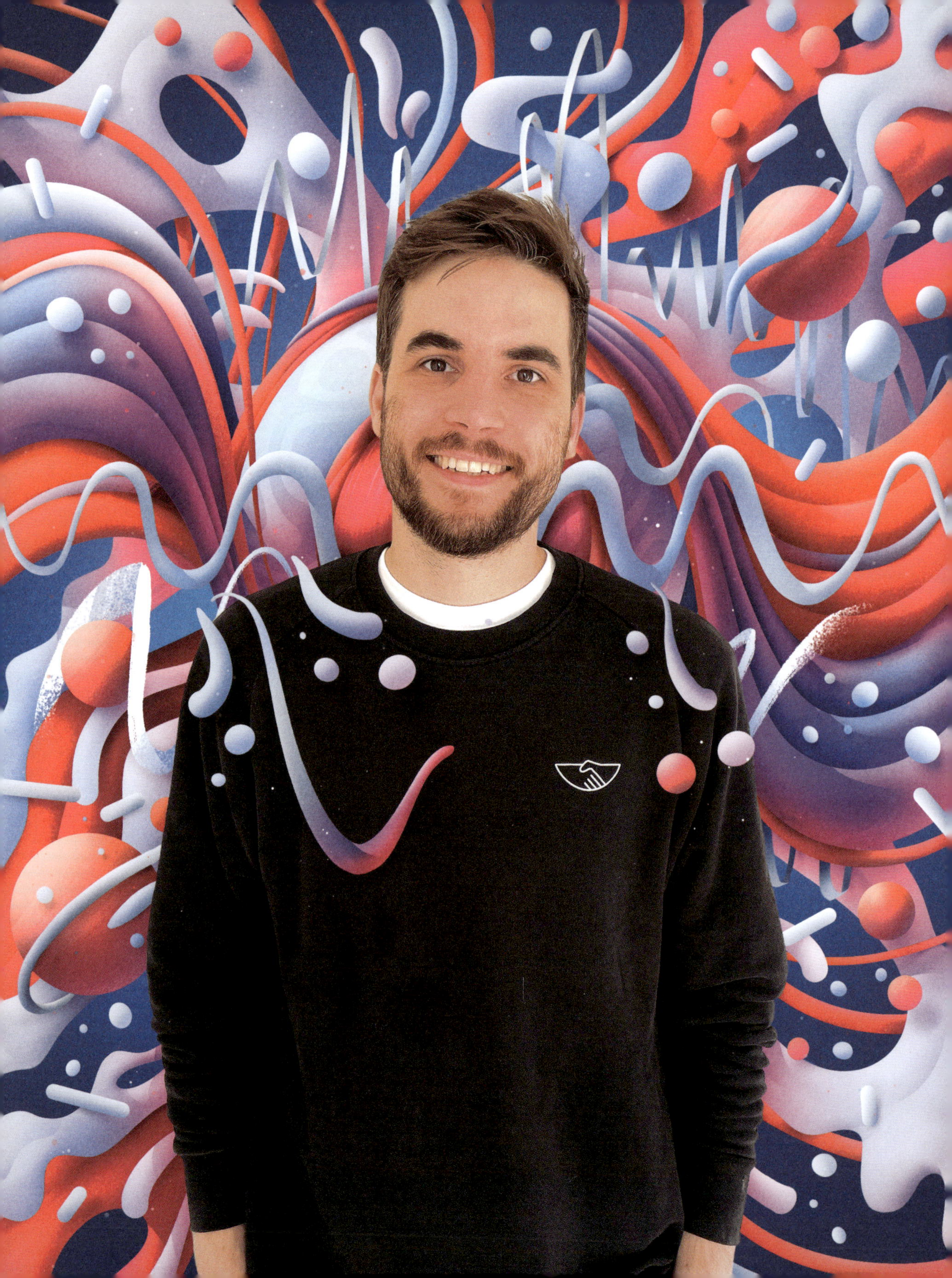

Dr David Trevelyan

SOFTWARE ENGINEER

ENHANCING INTERACTIVITY FOR ONLINE CONTENT CREATORS

Many budding engineers are both creative and logical and that can be difficult when choosing a career path at a young age. Schools like to make things simple by encouraging you to choose either the sciences or the arts, but what if you have a passion for both? That was the dilemma for Dr David Trevelyan, who created his own career path in entertainment by combining his passions. He has always loved music, but was great at maths and coding, so he combined these two disciplines and ended up working at TikTok enhancing their audio effects.

WHY AND HOW DID YOU GET INTO ENGINEERING?

My dad is a Professor of Engineering at Durham University. He believed I would love a career in engineering, and he was right in the end. But as a teenager, I wanted to find my own path, without being influenced by others. So, I visited lots of universities to see what medicine, maths, music and engineering offered. Music and maths seemed tough, competitive and difficult to pursue as a career and I certainly didn't have the personality type for medicine, despite being good at science. I related to the engineers the most and could see myself hanging out with them.

> "The work I do in engineering is so interesting, challenging and rewarding. And because it's on a topic that's so close to my heart, it never really feels like 'work'."
>
> **Dr David Trevelyan**

I chose to do Mechanical Engineering at Imperial College London because it is a really broad degree and I wanted to keep my career options open. Imperial has a great reputation and I also wanted to be in London, where I could develop my music-producing skills part-time.

At Imperial we covered interesting topics such as electronics, mechanics and maths, but after my Master's, I did not feel ready to enter the world of work. So, I pursued a PhD in Physics, programming computers to predict how molecules flow when in a fluid.

DID YOU STILL HAVE AN INTEREST IN MUSIC TOO?

Very much so. After my PhD, I continued to work as a postgraduate researcher at Imperial College London for one more year. During this time, I also developed my knowledge and experience of creating virtual instruments – computer applications that sound like real instruments. I fell in love with this sort of challenge and decided that I wanted to make a career out of it. So, I began a search of which companies I could work for. Many of the companies were based in Los Angeles and Berlin, which made it difficult for me to connect with them and impossible to get an internship.

But then, in my mid-twenties, I discovered that a company near London were hiring software engineers to develop the same musical tools that I had been experimenting with at home. So, I applied to work for them. I was so excited for this opportunity to do what I love, but my application got rejected because I did not have enough music technology experience. This rejection was a major turning point for me and motivated me to create my own music technology portfolio to demonstrate what I could do in this industry.

The software development skills that I learnt during my PhD were really useful in helping me to create my music technology portfolio, which I then presented to a small start-up based in London called Jukedeck. To my delight, they offered me my first job.

When David is working in his home studio, he will often switch between typing code and playing a MIDI keyboard so that he can test the code that he is writing.

Jukedeck specialised in developing artificially intelligent software for generating music. By hiring me they took a chance on me, because my physics and engineering background wasn't a perfect fit. Nevertheless, they seemed to like my vision and enthusiasm despite not having much music technology experience. Jukedeck users could make music by deciding on the length of a track and when the musical climax would occur. These inputs would then go back to the Jukedeck servers, which would compose a musical piece, delivering it back to the user within seconds. I worked for Jukedeck for three and a half years.

WHAT DO YOU DO ON A DAY-TO-DAY BASIS AT TIKTOK?

I now work in Research and Development at TikTok, with more emphasis on development. I lead a project with a few engineers who are developing a musical Software Development Kit (SDK).

You might be familiar with visual filters that are often used in entertainment platform apps – they can change the look of a photo in hundreds of different ways. They might make your photos look more sunny or add spectacles to your selfie. Visual filters are similar to audio filters, which is what I work on. Audio filters can make you sound as though you are underwater or in an echoey room, for example. What we do is really nerdy, but so cool. My team and I contribute to making entertainment platforms more musical and more fun.

WHAT ADVICE DO YOU HAVE FOR ANYONE DECIDING ON THEIR CAREER?

Getting to where I am today was a combination of luck and hard work. My advice to any young person figuring out their own career path is to try to recognise and pursue what you enjoy. Our work consumes a huge amount of our daily lives so you should do something that you love! I sometimes like asking this question: 'Do you want to enjoy your life for five days or only two days of the week?' And my answer is: 'If you can, why not go for all seven!'

FACT FILE

Most fun thing about your job: Seeing other people create music or other art with the musical tools that I have built.

CAREER HIGHLIGHTS

1. Getting a place on the Master's and PhD programmes at Imperial College London.

2. Getting my first music tech job at Jukedeck.

3. Joining TikTok and working on more musical engineering projects that I'm really interested in.

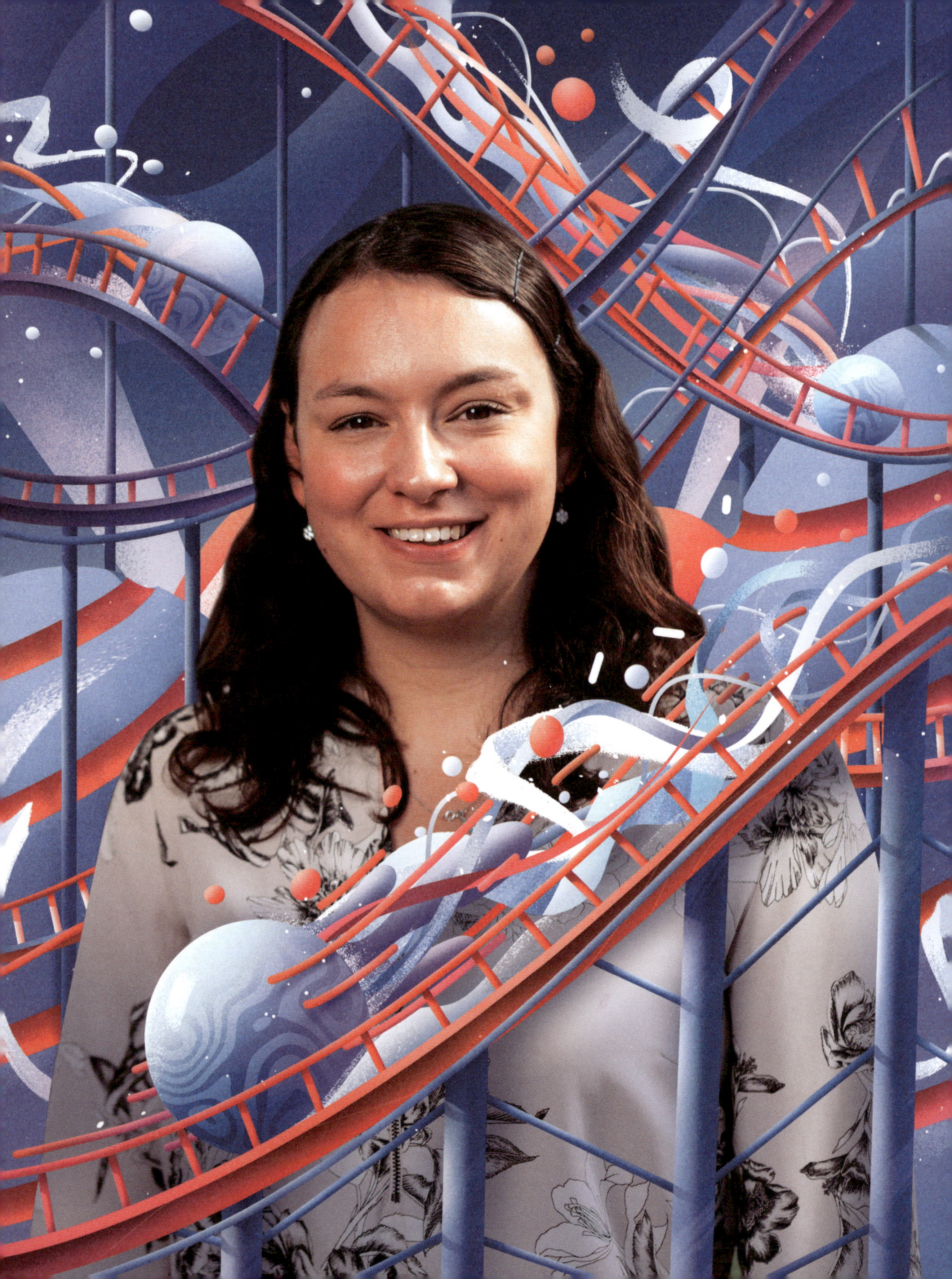

Michelle Hicks

CEO AND CIVIL ENGINEER

CREATING MEMORABLE EXPERIENCES THROUGH ENGINEERING

Michelle Hicks studied Civil Engineering in order to fulfil a childhood dream of one day designing and building theme park rides. Through various civil engineering jobs, she went on to co-found her own theme park design consultancy business called Firefly Creations. Her dream had come true. Designing giant roller coasters with twisting tracks and massive drop towers is not dissimilar to designing civil engineering infrastructure such as railways, roads and bridges. At Firefly Creations, the team use their knowledge of classic engineering to bring cutting-edge experiences to their guests. Michelle's career journey proves that lifelong passions and smart career choices can lead to the job of your dreams.

HOW IS FIREFLY CREATIONS MAKING A DIFFERENCE TO PEOPLE'S LIVES?

Firefly Creations' rides give people a space to escape from daily life and have fun – I believe theme parks are so important for our wellbeing. I always loved visiting them when I was younger and would go at least once a year with family and friends. I would count the days until our next trip – I just couldn't get enough! Initially my parents thought 'It's just a phase', but here I am 20 years later, with my 'phase' going stronger than ever.

Through engineering and technology, I want our visitors to have experiences they will never forget. And for this to continue once they've returned home, too, through the apps we have designed and built with AI, augmented reality (AR) and virtual reality (VR). Our projects are found all over the world and continue to be more sophisticated thanks to advancements in technology. I hope that the work we do is helping to make the world a happier place.

WHAT WAS THE TURNING POINT IN GETTING INTO YOUR INDUSTRY?

My childhood passion for theme parks influenced the decisions I made about my education and career. At the age of 14, I attended a lecture at the University of Reading on roller coaster design, which influenced me to pick A-level subjects that would allow me to study civil engineering. This lecture made me realise that what I loved doing most could become a career through engineering.

From that moment on, I did everything to immerse myself in the industry, including working in a restaurant at Chessington World of Adventures Resort at the age of 16. This job opened my eyes to the complex operational process behind every theme park, because they really are impressive, well-oiled machines.

I chose to study at the University of Surrey because they had a great Civil Engineering course and I was fortunate enough to be offered a scholarship through a sponsoring company. I worked for my company sponsor during the summer breaks and in a placement year halfway through my five-year degree. By the time I had finished my Master's, I had clocked up two years of industrial work experience, which put me ahead of other graduates in getting my first job. I still highly recommend work experience, whether voluntary or paid, for getting into industry as soon as possible.

WHAT DID YOU DO AFTER YOU GRADUATED?

My first official job after graduation was with my sponsoring company, WSP, an engineering consultancy for railways, bridges, highways and other types of infrastructure. I had a very technical engineering role, which gave me a strong understanding of the engineering design process. I also co-ordinated large teams of structural designers, hydraulic engineers and mechanical and electrical systems engineers, which eventually led me into a project management role.

Through these work experiences, it was clear that project management was the best fit for me. I loved looking at projects from a bird's eye view, while also contributing my in-depth engineering

Kraken Cove Drop Tower – one of the rides that Michelle and her team have worked on.

knowledge to certain aspects of the project. One day, a project management role at Merlin Entertainments for Chessington World of Adventures Resort became available. This was a great opportunity to combine my engineering and project management knowledge with my love of theme parks, and of course I jumped at it! I transferred my skills in infrastructure to theme parks and this is where my journey in theme park design officially began.

WHAT HAS BEEN YOUR MOST REWARDING PROJECT?

It is really difficult to pick just one, but what comes to mind is the habitat we created for tigers at Chessington World of Adventures Resort. Our main focus was to create the best place for these endangered animals to thrive. At the same time, it was crucial to educate guests about the importance of conservation efforts to protect their habitats in the wild. The project took us several years to finish, but when the tigers arrived onsite for the first time, they looked so happy – and still do. We won an award for our work and I'm so proud of what we achieved.

WHAT DOES YOUR JOB INVOLVE TODAY?

Our main focus at Firefly Creations today is bringing stories to life. We use technologies involving set design, live streaming, props, audio, lighting, special effects and AI to take our visitors on a compelling, educational and unforgettable journey.

We are using AI and AR more and more to enhance sensory experiences – what you see, hear and even smell. Theme park experiences have come a long way since I was growing up, and every day I'm amazed that our work helps to push boundaries and take the experiences of our guests to new levels. Our work with mechatronics (technology that combines electronics and mechanics), coding and computing is not just pushing frontiers in entertainment but also in other industries, such as healthcare, too, where AR and VR can be used in surgery.

WHAT ADVICE DO YOU HAVE FOR ANYONE WANTING TO FOLLOW IN YOUR FOOTSTEPS?

You don't have to follow a defined career path: you can find a route into whatever you're passionate about, just like I did. I constantly sidestepped to get where I am today and have never looked back. Work hard, enjoy learning, push yourself and I promise your career will be incredibly rewarding.

FACT FILE

Most fun thing about your job: Experiencing the rides I have worked on with friends and family.

CAREER HIGHLIGHTS

1. Opening the first attraction I worked on, The Gruffalo River Ride Adventure at Chessington World of Adventures Resort.

2. Co-founding my own company, Firefly Creations.

3. Achieving the status of Chartered Engineer.

Extending Our Reality

AUGMENTED REALITY (AR) enhances the real world with interactive elements. For example, it could make it look as if there is an animal in front of you when viewed through your smartphone camera. Smart glasses are expected to become more popular in the future and the technology is being developed to enable data to be projected onto car mirrors and windscreens.

VIRTUAL REALITY (VR) fully immerses you in a simulated digital environment, which you can interact with using a headset. VR tricks your senses into thinking you are really in the artificial world, such as on the Moon or riding a roller coaster.

MIXED REALITY (MR) is similar to augmented reality in that it can overlay digital elements on the real world. But the difference is that it allows you to interact with those elements. MR can have many practical uses, such as teaching pilots how to fly planes or allowing surgeons to safely try out new procedures.

MR devices allow users to interact with digital elements. Here an engineer is using a holographic blueprint to help him design an electric motor.

Extended reality (XR) is a broad term for all the different types of technology that enhance or simulate real-world experiences. The entertainment industry, particularly gaming, has driven some of the big developments in this area. Here are just some of the ways our reality can be extended with this incredible technology:

DEALING WITH THE DATA XR technology generates large amounts of data, which can be costly to store. The development of computer chips with the capacity to store more data will be one of the keys to unlocking the huge potential of XR in the future.

XR allows people to experience things that they would not usually be able to and can allow for a deeper understanding of a situation.

STROLLING INTO THE FUTURE? It's hoped that XR could be useful in encouraging 'less scrolling and more strolling'. There are lots of exciting ways this technology could be used to encourage people to get outdoors and discover more about the world around them, from learning about local landmarks to finding out about the trees and plants in their local area.

USING XR TO SAVE THE WORLD XR could also help people to engage with big issues such as climate change. For example, it could allow us to experience simulations of different scenarios for the future, depending on the actions taken now. In 2016, Professor Jeremy Bailenson and his team found that using VR to show the effects of climate change from the point of view of sea coral led to an increase in the empathy people felt for ocean life.

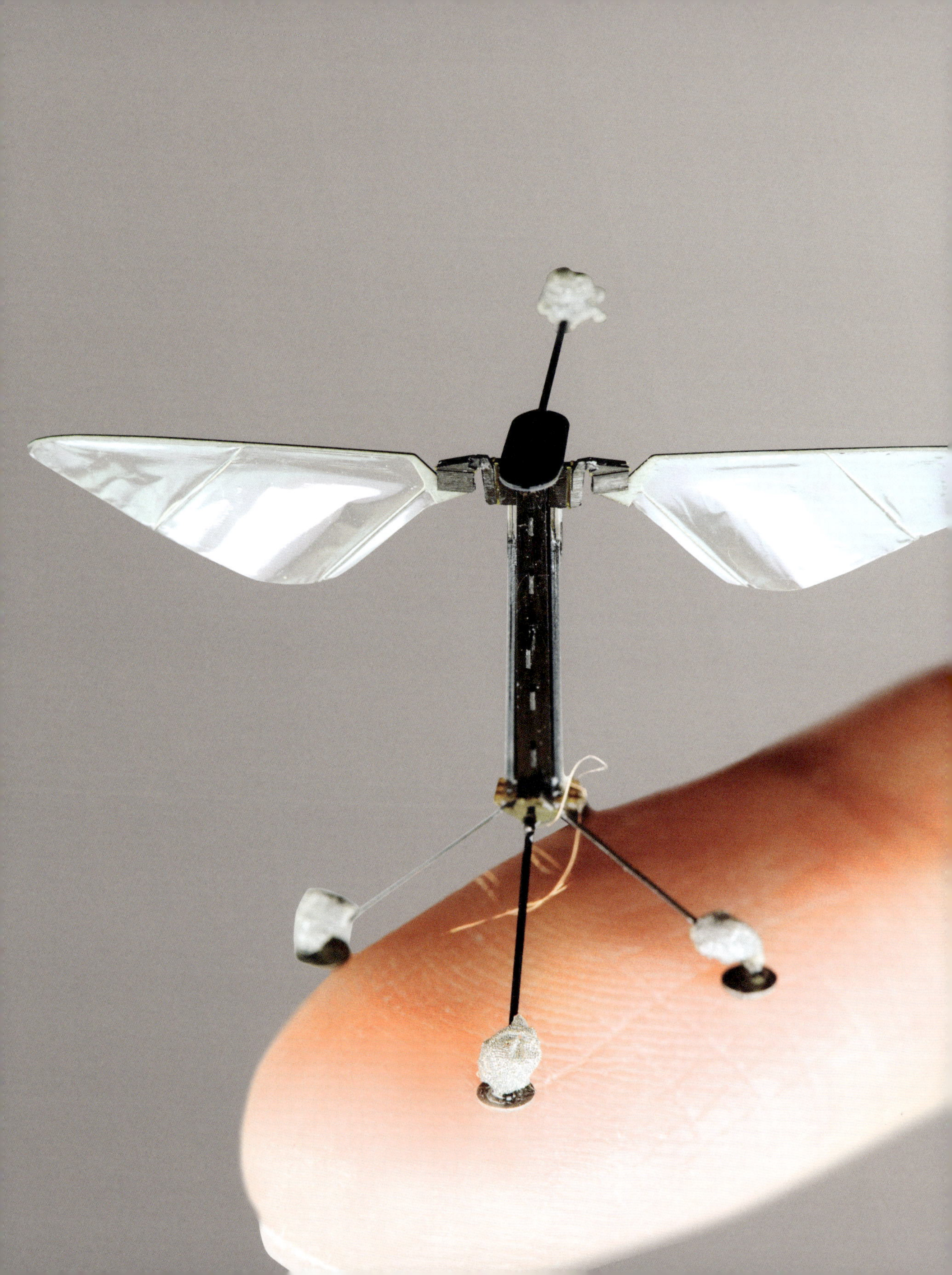

CHAPTER 11

ROBOTICS AND ARTIFICIAL INTELLIGENCE

Robots are often designed to do tasks that would be difficult, dangerous or repetitive for humans. They are especially useful in certain industries such as manufacturing, where they can increase efficiency, or farming, where they can harvest crops. However, robotics technology is useful for so much more than making things. Advances in mechanical, materials and communications engineering, and developments in 5G, augmented reality and AI, are giving robotics a life of its own.

Robots are being incorporated into more and more aspects of our lives, from robotic surgery to restaurants and shops run by robots. Robots containing cameras and sensors are able to react to their environments and interact with humans. In some cases, robots are even able to control themselves by making their own decisions and learning from their experiences.

In chapter eight, we learnt about Industry 4.0, where robots are playing a leading role in making the manufacturing industry more digital – allowing humans to perform the more creative and innovative jobs. In this chapter, we meet some engineers who are using robotics and AI in unusual and groundbreaking ways. Their work is helping to build a future that blends robotics technology into all our lives, improving the quality of our human experiences.

LEFT: This tiny robot was inspired by the biology of a bee. It is about half the size of a paperclip and has wings that flap when an electric current is applied to them. Some RoboBees can also swim underwater and use static electricity to perch on surfaces. Small robots such as this one could be used to pollinate crops, help in search and rescue missions and monitor the weather and climate.

Silas Adekunle

ROBOTICS ENGINEER
CREATING ROBOTIC LAB ASSISTANTS

Robotics combines engineering, computer programming and the study of living organisms in fascinating ways. Silas Adekunle is one individual who has followed his interest in living things to develop a variety of robots that are helping make a difference in the world.

WHAT MADE YOU WANT TO WORK WITH ROBOTS?

When I was young, I was fascinated by wildlife and thought I was going to become a biologist. I grew up in Nigeria, and then at the age of 12 moved to the UK, where I joined an after-school robotics club. This is where I fell in love with robotics. I went on to do a Robotics degree at the University of West England, and then I started my own robotics company called Reach Robotics, designing a robot to use with video games.

WHAT DO YOU DO NOW?

I now have two other businesses. One is called Awarri, which focuses on the development of new technology to help people across Africa. For example, we send robotics kits to schools in Africa to help introduce kids to STEM subjects. My other company, which I co-founded, is called Reach Industries. At Reach Industries we have built an AI system that helps scientists to work more efficiently by automating many of their repetitive tasks. Our system is called Lumi and can act as the eyes and ears of a lab by capturing video, sound and data from experiments and analysing them. Lumi also learns from the process so it can improve how it works. This innovative process can take over some of the admin tasks in a lab and free up scientists to do other, more complex tasks.

IS THERE ANYTHING THAT YOU WOULD HAVE DONE DIFFERENTLY IN YOUR CAREER?

I don't think so! My route into engineering wasn't very traditional, but that's a good thing. Following non-traditional paths can lead to new, innovative ideas, helping us find completely new solutions to problems. Along the way, I have learnt Japanese and also developed my skills in art, which have helped me with my creative design process and broadened my perspectives. My diverse skill set has also helped me with fundraising, business management, marketing and sales.

WHAT DO YOU LOVE ABOUT ENGINEERING?

I love the fact that I get to contribute to a better world by engineering solutions that can help people and advance science. I love dreaming something up and then bringing it to life. Passion, hard work, being okay with failing and empathy have all been key.

FACT FILE

Most fun thing about your job: I get to make Sci-Fi a reality by thinking of innovative products that have never existed and bringing them to life.

CAREER HIGHLIGHTS

1. Seeing a classroom of students looking in awe at the movement of our robots.

2. When a father told me about a meaningful interaction that his child had with one of our products.

3. When a scientist told me that they couldn't imagine working without our technology!

"Always remember that you have the right to be an engineer just like anybody else. Your worldview is unique to you and valuable to the industry. Never compare yourself to others — by doing that you overlook your own uniqueness."

Silas Adekunle

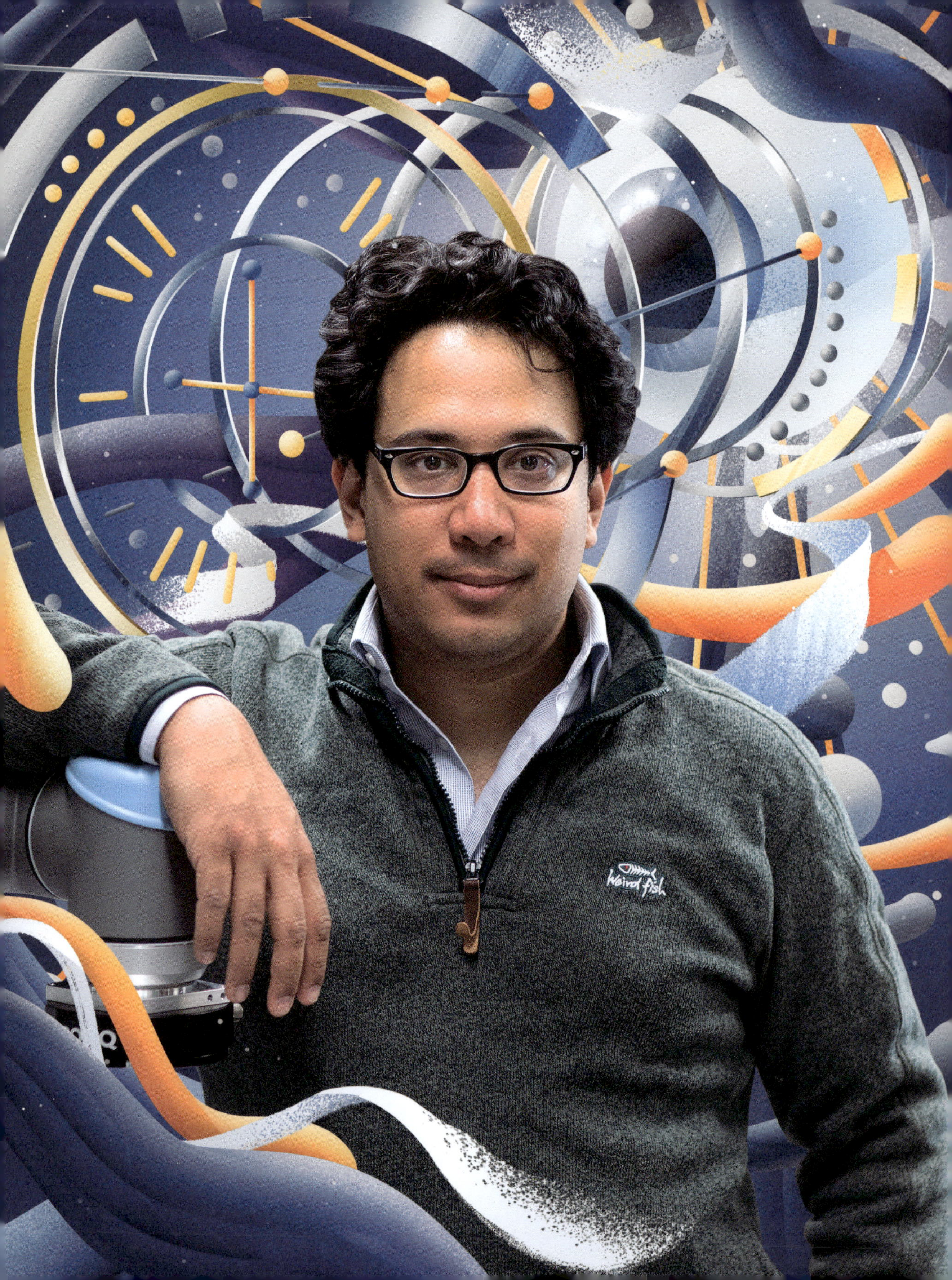
weird fish

Professor Aldo Faisal

PROFESSOR OF AI AND NEUROSCIENCE
MAKING COMPUTERS MORE HUMAN

Professor Aldo Faisal is leading an AI research group at Imperial College London in a field called reinforcement learning. He is fascinated by the interaction between humans and machines, and how interactivity between them can be used in computers to influence our behaviour and help us make decisions.

WHAT IS AN EXAMPLE OF REINFORCEMENT LEARNING?

In reinforcement learning, AI discovers the world around it in much the same way that humans do, by trying things and learning from the result. This sort of information gathering allows AI to make good decisions in complex and often changing environments.

For example, reinforcement learning could be used in self-driving cars. The car collects data about various things in the world around it, such as how to overtake other cars safely, change lanes, stay on the road and when to take side streets. This changes and influences the decisions that the algorithm controlling the car makes. Continuously updated data helps the algorithm to learn. This is a form of AI that can be used in other applications, such as manufacturing robotics and healthcare too. In hospitals, data is obtained from all patients and can help to speed up decisions made by doctors. The doctors would not be able to process such huge quantities of data the way AI can, so it can help them to make better decisions as well as quicker ones.

"People with perfect grades are not necessarily the greatest engineers or researchers. To be a good engineer, it is important to try things and make mistakes."

Professor Aldo Faisal

WHAT REINFORCEMENT LEARNING HAVE YOU CREATED IN YOUR LAB?

The AI we are building helps us to better understand humans. We create a type of digital 'genius butler' who can work out what their human wants to do before the human knows themselves. This technology is almost like human augmentation!

AI can help people with mobility issues to move again by using data to try and work out the intended action of that person. The technologies we have built gather data on eye movements. Based on extensive studies and research, eye movements reveal patterns that can tell us what a person's intended actions are, based on what they pay attention to.

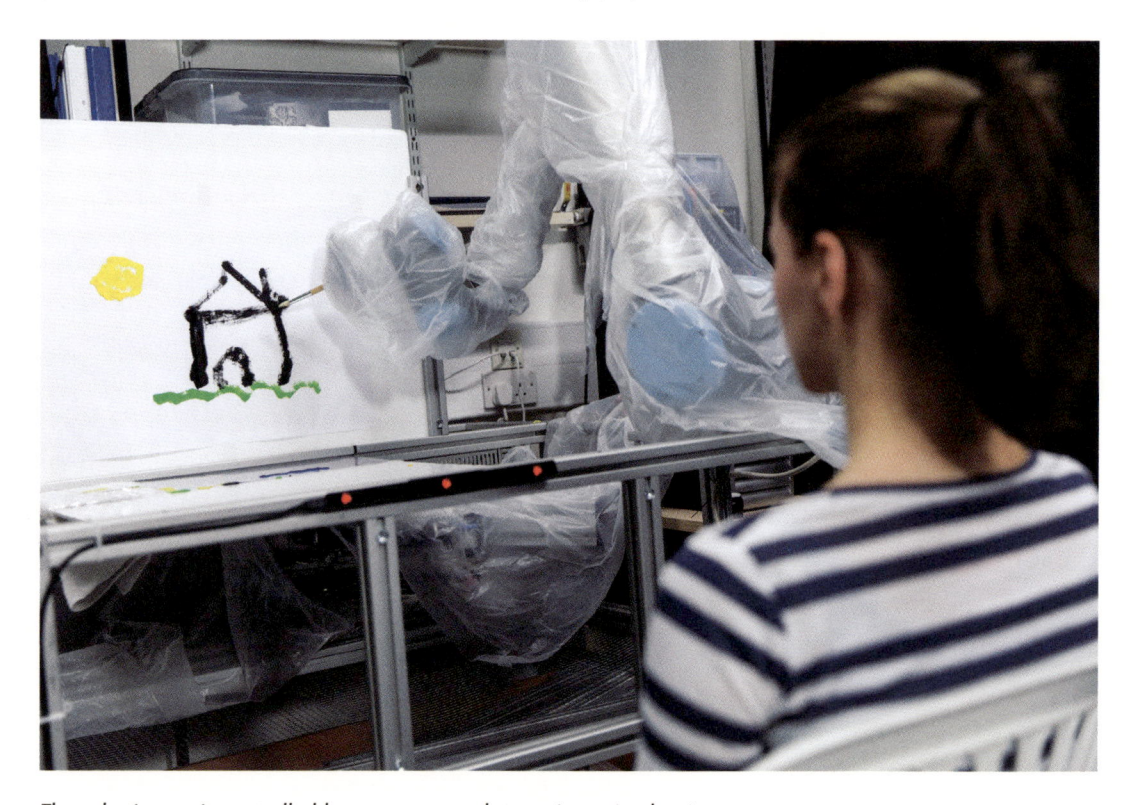

The robotic arm is controlled by eye commands to paint a simple picture.

We are using this knowledge to answer the question: what is this person intending to do, based on where they are looking? From this research, we have built robotic bodysuits and self-driving wheelchairs that are controlled by a person's gaze.

WHAT GOT YOU INTERESTED IN AI?

I read a book when I was 16 years old that described how people learn. The author had studied how the human brain functions and used this knowledge to build more intelligent computer systems. The idea of human brains inspiring AI really struck a chord with me. Coincidentally, the professor and author of this book lived in my local town in Germany. So, I went to meet him, which led me to study Computer Science at university. He eventually became my supervisor when I was completing my Master's research.

At this point, I hadn't learnt much about the biology of the brain, so I went to study for a PhD in Neuroscience at the University of Cambridge. My research there was on the movement of animals and insects, viewing them as robotic systems built by nature. This was the beginning of my work in reinforcement machine learning and human interaction.

After my PhD, I researched how our brains control movement, to find out how we learn and whether there are mathematical equations to describe how the brain moves the body.

I then received an offer from Imperial College London that I couldn't refuse! They wanted me to help set up a laboratory that crossed over with two other departments: the Department of Bioengineering and the Department of Computing. This laboratory would be entirely unique and an amazing opportunity for me to do all the things I really enjoy with a practical and hands-on approach.

DO YOU NEED A DEGREE TO LEARN AI?

Not at all, you can start learning the basics of AI at any time. There is loads of material on the internet to get started with the basic principles. Learning about AI is all about being creative – curiosity and playfulness are really important for innovation. I always played with LEGO when I was little and now I'm just playing with bigger toys!

WHAT DOES AN AI-LED FUTURE LOOK LIKE?

AI is already being incorporated into our daily lives. Some supermarket chains now have shops where you just walk in and pick up what you want and leave, without visiting the checkout. AI technology is transforming most daily life processes – the downside being that when it stops working, we will notice.

Everything that affects us needs to be built by engineers. We apply scientific knowledge in a way that is useful for society. We shape the future and change the world for the better. I know now that I wouldn't want to be doing anything else!

FACT FILE

Most fun thing about your job: My team and I get to play with and build incredible 'toys' every day, and what we build is helpful for other people.

CAREER HIGHLIGHTS

1. Restoring the ability of a fully paralysed person to reach and grasp again with their own hands.

2. Founding a centre that now has more than 70 researchers working on AI for healthcare.

3. Being awarded a UKRI Turing AI Fellowship to work on reinforcement learning for the next five years.

Jennifer Olsen

BIOMEDICAL ENGINEER

MAKING PROSTHETICS BETTER

Prosthetics are mechanical devices that can take the place of body parts. They can be an essential part of life for many people. Today, advanced prosthetics include sensors, motors, batteries and flexible materials to allow them to be more adaptable. As a Biomedical Engineer, Jennifer Olsen conducts research to make robotic prosthetics that function more like human hands.

Most robotic prosthetic arms are controlled using muscle activity, which are electrical signals that naturally occur within the body. Sensors are embedded into the sockets to detect these signals and move the prosthetic. Jennifer specifically works on improving the design of the sockets so that they better transmit the signals.

WHAT MADE YOU INTERESTED IN BIOMEDICAL ENGINEERING?

As a child, I loved discovering how things worked, but had a difficult time at school due to bullying. From the age of ten I was home-educated and loved learning things my own way. I sat my GCSEs a year early and went to sixth form college at 15 years old.

The STEM outreach officer at my college suggested I enter the National Engineering Competition for Girls, which was run by Talent 2030. I ended up winning my category with my design of a prosthetic elbow. This competition opened my eyes to the world of engineering and healthcare and inspired me to pursue biomedical engineering.

I went to Newcastle University to study Mechanical Engineering, where I completed my final year project in magnetic spinal rods, which are placed in a person's back to support the structure of their spine. This project helped me to secure a PhD position researching upper-limb prosthetics, which is where I am today.

WHAT IS THE FOCUS OF YOUR CURRENT RESEARCH?

I work on prosthetic sockets, which are the parts of prosthetic limbs that are in contact with the person's arm. Current designs of prosthetic sockets do not always transmit the control signals from the muscles very well, so the arms are often unreliable. My research focuses on making better socket designs to transmit these signals effectively, and also making them more comfortable in the process.

I've had to learn lots of new practical skills to make these prosthetics. I have learnt to code in Python, which is important for turning signals from the muscles into instructions for the prosthetic, and also how to use 3D printers to prototype my designs. I've even been lucky enough to spend time learning alongside trainee prosthetists in clinics. I really want to help bridge the gap between engineering research and what actually happens in prosthetics clinics because it can be easy for an engineer to create something without keeping the patients at the centre of their focus.

FACT FILE

Most fun thing about your job: Getting to work with amputees and develop new designs of prosthetics with them.

CAREER HIGHLIGHTS

1. Being named as one of the Top 50 Women In Engineering in the UK in 2021.

2. Winning the Talent 2030 National Engineering Competition for Girls in 2016.

3. Presenting my research to MPs in UK Parliament.

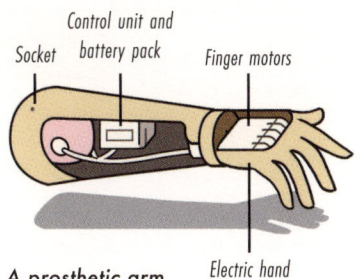

A prosthetic arm — Socket, Control unit and battery pack, Finger motors, Electric hand

Joshua Schofield

RESEARCH ENGINEER
USING ROBOTICS FOR WORK AND FUN

Robotics and AI are now being used across most industries. This means that more engineers and physicists are needed to keep up with coding and maintenance, especially as machines become more advanced. Joshua Schofield completed a four-year Engineering apprenticeship at the National Physical Laboratory (NPL) and is now discovering where his true interests and passions lie.

WHAT HAS BEEN YOUR ENGINEERING JOURNEY TO THIS POINT?

I did my GCSEs at a grammar school and then spent a year at a university technical college (UTC) before I opted for an apprenticeship – despite most of my school friends choosing to go to university. I wanted a more hands-on and practical approach to learning, so it was absolutely the best fit for me. UTCs generally have strong connections with various different engineering companies and mine helped me to find the National Physical Laboratory apprenticeship programme. I was interested in it because it offered a job with a great blend of science and engineering.

WHAT HAVE YOU ENJOYED MOST ABOUT YOUR APPRENTICESHIP?

The best thing was being able to experience a variety of engineering areas. At the start of my apprenticeship, I was given the chance to build a heavyweight robot for a BBC show called *Robot Wars*. Building this large machine sparked a passion for robotics in me — especially in how robots can be used to solve complex problems. The experience I gained during this helped me to contribute to building an emergency low-cost ventilator during the COVID-19 pandemic. With input from experts, we were able to build something quickly and cheaply, which was so crucial at the time.

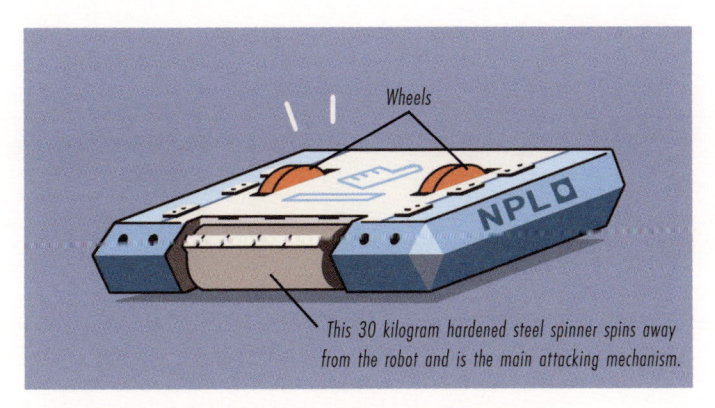

Wheels

NPL

This 30 kilogram hardened steel spinner spins away from the robot and is the main attacking mechanism.

The robot that Joshua helped to build for Robot Wars was called NoProbLemo (which uses the letters NPL for the National Physical Laboratory).

WHAT ARE YOU DOING NOW?

Today, I am completing my Master's in Renewable Energy and will be studying different renewable energy technologies (for example, solar, wind and tidal energy). I will be researching what makes them suitable for different locations and needs. I'll be focusing my research on solar panels and how we can improve their efficiency to get as much power out of them as possible. In particular, I'm going to be using automated robotic systems to carry out very precise, very accurate light measurements on solar panels — something that robots are very good at! I've always been interested in environmental issues, so it's going to be great to try something new.

FACT FILE

Most fun thing about your job: Solving brand new problems in the lab every day.

CAREER HIGHLIGHTS

1. Building and testing a new ventilator in response to COVID-19 and receiving a Pandemic Service award from the Royal Academy of Engineering — one of my proudest moments.

2. Taking part in the STEM competition, 'F1 in Schools'. We travelled to Malaysia to compete in the World Finals, finished 7th and won the Research and Development award!

3. Building a cryogenic radiometer — an instrument used to measure the power of a laser. I had to solder wires thinner than a human hair!

Machines with Brains

AI and robotics technologies are advancing every day. Using robots in place of humans can be useful for repetitive tasks and those that require accuracy – robots don't get tired or distracted the way humans can. This has not only changed the type of jobs humans do but, with everything being controlled remotely, the team working on a project can also be scattered across the globe. However, this is only the beginning – there are many exciting possibilities for the ways that humans and machines can work together.

DIGITAL TWINS Virtual representation of a real-life thing is called a digital twin. It can help engineers test building designs, rocket launches and also treatments for health conditions. Researchers at a company called Neurotwin are working on a project that's attempting to replicate the human brain. The team hopes that the model will be able to help to predict how individual patients will respond to treatment for conditions such as epilepsy and Alzheimer's disease. The aim is for all humans to have their own digital twin from birth to help to predict and protect them against diseases.

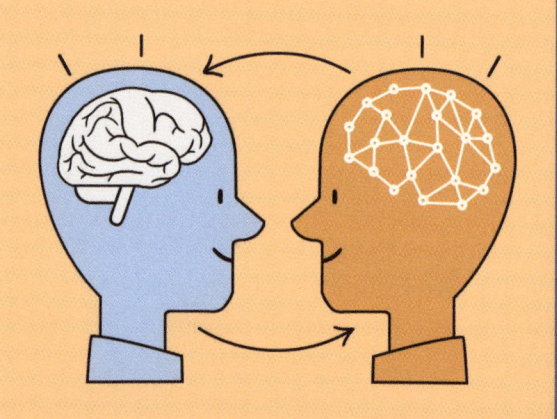

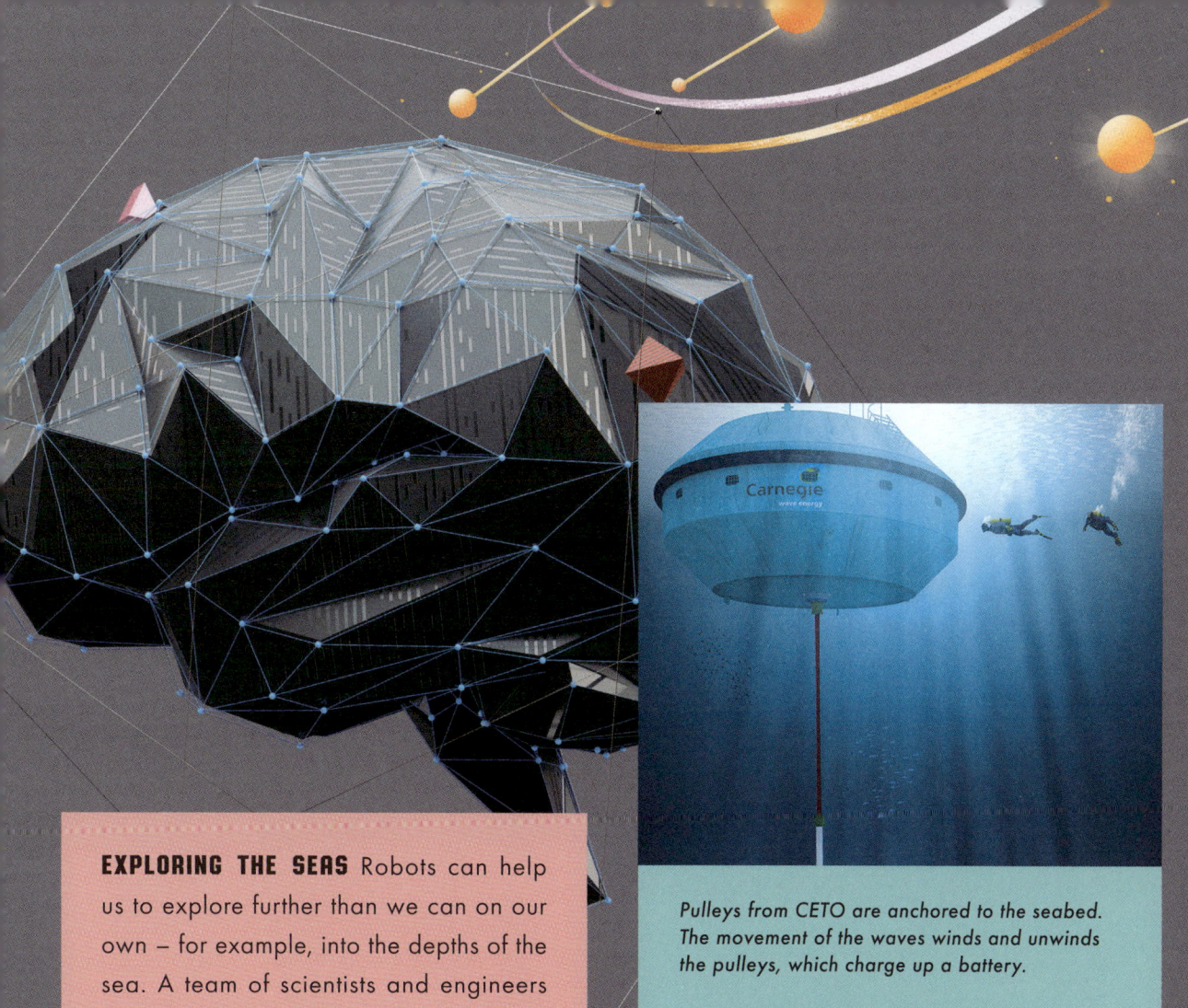

EXPLORING THE SEAS Robots can help us to explore further than we can on our own – for example, into the depths of the sea. A team of scientists and engineers from the Woods Hole Oceanographic Institution in Massachusetts, USA, have built an advanced underwater vehicle called Orpheus, which uses AI technology and sensors to learn about this largely unexplored environment. Orpheus uses AI to learn about the surrounding environment and can adapt in real-time to the dark and high-pressure conditions, allowing it to further unlock the secrets of the oceans. Similar technology could be used on other planets that are difficult for humans to explore.

Pulleys from CETO are anchored to the seabed. The movement of the waves winds and unwinds the pulleys, which charge up a battery.

HARNESSING WAVE POWER Reinforcement learning is being used to harness the potential of wave power. One underwater system that does this is called CETO, and it collects energy from the movement of waves. Using reinforcement learning, CETO works out the best place to position itself in the sea to make the most of the wave movement and generate the most energy. All the wave power collected is transferred to batteries on land, which is then used to power other things, such as our homes.

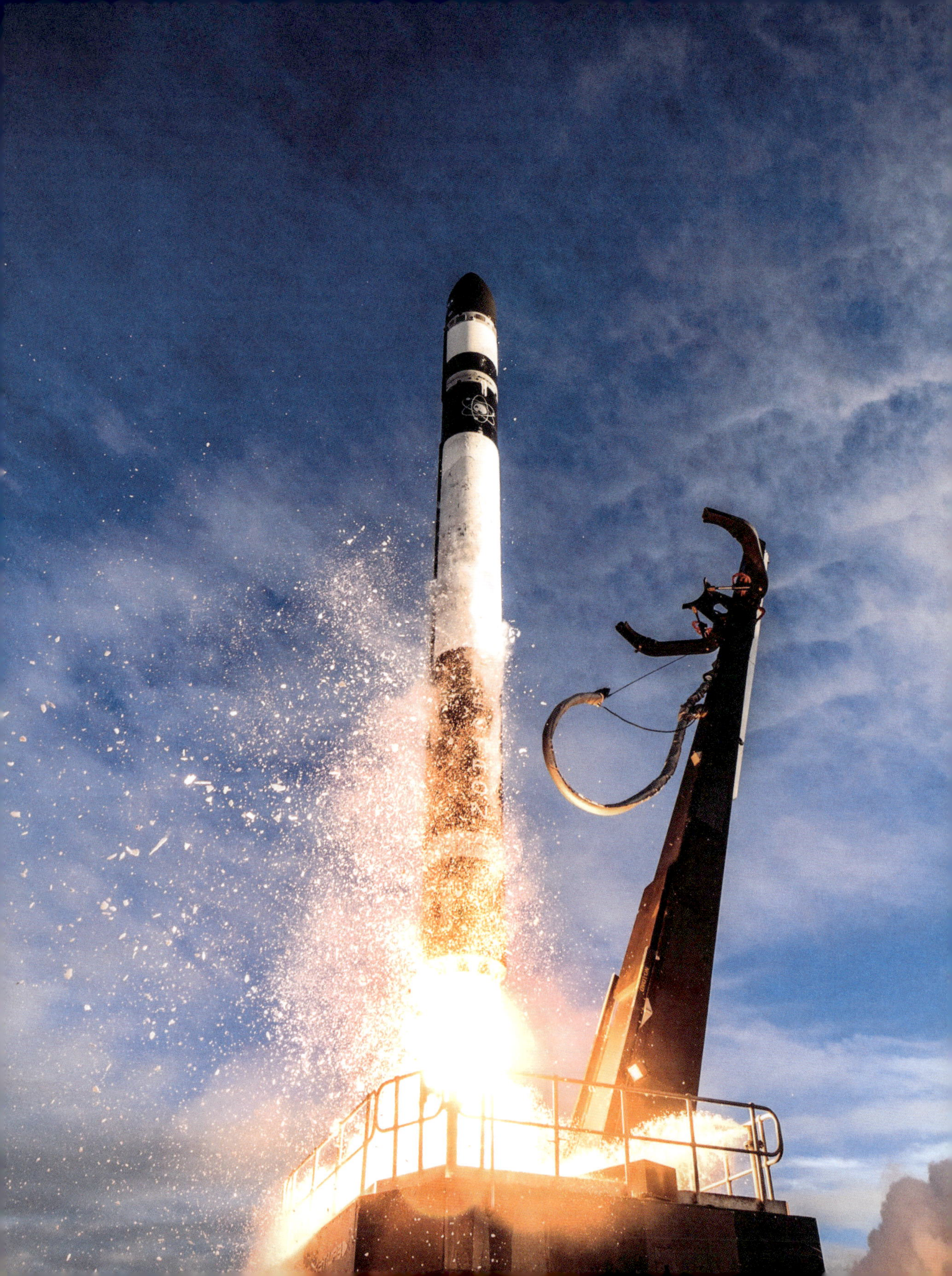

CHAPTER 12

EXPLORING BEYOND OUR PLANET

For thousands of years, humans have been looking up at the stars and wondering what lies beyond our solar system. We have engineered rockets, spacecraft and many other technologies to try and answer the question about whether life exists beyond Earth. Our discoveries have helped us in many ways, including giving us a better understanding of how life on Earth came to be and also how we can protect it for the future.

Engineers have risen to the challenges of making space exploration possible, which is not an easy task considering the extreme temperatures, lack of gravity and high levels of dangerous radiation out in space! It is especially difficult to create spacecraft and satellites to withstand these conditions because it's not always possible to test them on Earth.

There is still much more that we can learn from space and the race is on to explore further and faster. And that is where the engineers in this chapter come in. They are helping to find new ways of exploring beyond our planet, and in doing so have to let their imaginations and creativity run wild.

LEFT: Launch of the ELaNa-19 mission to send 13 CubeSats into low Earth orbit.

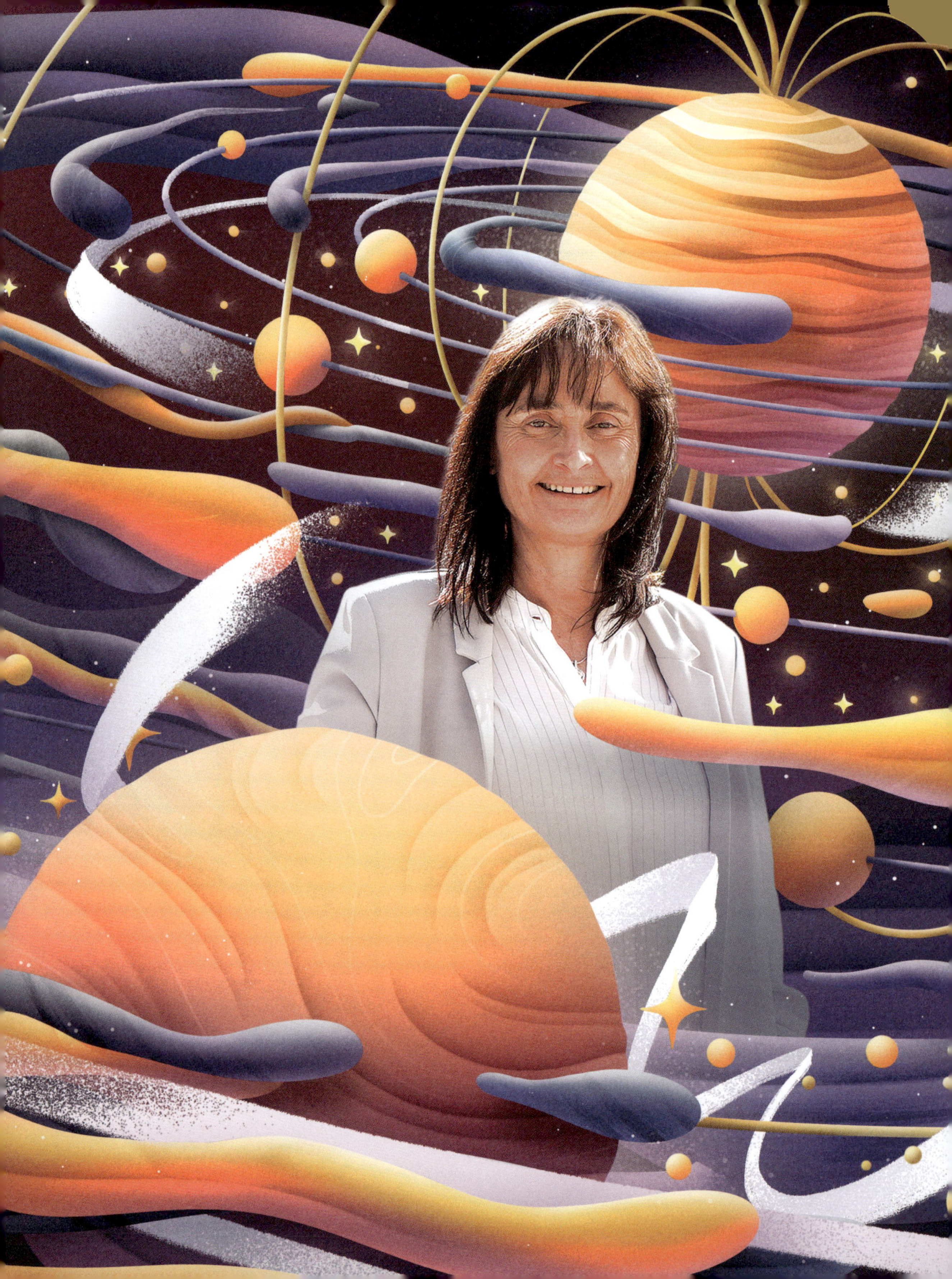

Professor Michele Dougherty

PROFESSOR OF SPACE PHYSICS

BRINGING SCIENTISTS AND ENGINEERS TOGETHER TO EXPLORE THE OCEANS OF OUTER SPACE

The furthest humans have travelled into space is to the far side of the Moon, which is a distance of 400,171 kilometres. However, uncrewed missions (ones without humans) have been able to explore much further. But these missions still need to be controlled by humans back on Earth.

Professor Michele Dougherty, a pioneering Space Physicist, has been in charge of the magnetometer (MAG), an instrument on board two spacecraft – Cassini and JUICE (the JUpiter ICy moons Explorer). JUICE will arrive at Jupiter around 2030, where it will collect data about the magnetic fields surrounding Jupiter and its moons before orbiting the moon Ganymede, a goal that no-one has achieved so far.

HOW DOES ENGINEERING AND SCIENCE CROSS OVER IN YOUR RESEARCH?

The teams that I lead are made up of both engineers and scientists. Without the engineers designing and building our instruments, we can't get the data we need to do the science. I describe to the engineers exactly what it is that I want to measure out in space, and they design and build ways to help me to do it.

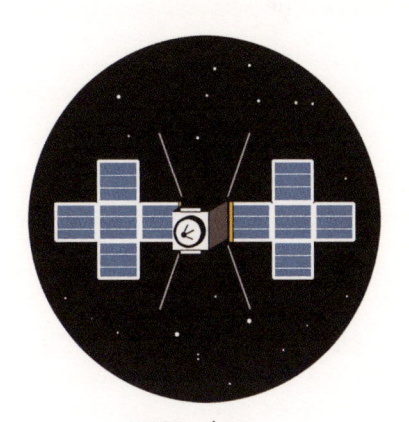

JUICE orbiter

One of the aims of the JUICE mission is to work out exactly how deep and salty the ocean is on Ganymede. To do that, we're looking for very small changes in the magnetic fields around it, which is what the magnetometer detects. This is very tricky to do as there are hundreds of other things going on that can interfere with the data we are trying to collect. Sometimes, it can feel like we're trying to find a specific needle in a haystack full of needles! At the same time, we are also collecting data on the health of the instrument itself because we constantly need to check that it is working properly.

An artist's concept image showing the JUICE spacecraft by Jupiter.

WHY DO WE WANT TO LEARN ABOUT THE OCEAN ON GANYMEDE?

Because it could provide us with clues as to how life can survive beyond Earth. The majority of life, as we understand it here on Earth, needs water in order to survive. So, by exploring other planetary bodies that have water, we might be able to find places in the solar system (and beyond) that humans could live on. We know that there are many other galaxies with solar systems besides our own in the universe, so it's likely that there is another planet out there that also has the correct conditions for organisms to survive and thrive. However, seeing as we don't yet have the technology to travel beyond our solar system, we're starting by trying to understand a space body that is a bit closer to home (relatively speaking!).

HOW DID YOU END UP IN THIS CAREER?

I went to a girls' school in South Africa where they didn't teach physics. So, I studied maths, biology, accountancy, geography and other subjects that I can't even remember now – it was so long ago! I do remember that I was really good at maths, though. My dad was an engineer who lectured at the local university, and their Physics department took a chance on me and agreed to let me do a BSc – despite the fact that I hadn't studied physics or chemistry at school.

The first year of my BSc was not fun! I found physics really difficult because of my basic lack of knowledge, and I was bad at chemistry. Thankfully, I would go home every evening and my dad would go through all the lectures with me. It took me a really long time to feel that I had caught up.

I completed my BSc, then an Honours degree and a PhD in Applied Maths. I then went to Germany to do a fellowship before I was offered a job at Imperial College London, which is where my career really flourished.

At Imperial, I was asked if I wanted to spend one day a week making a model of the magnetic field surrounding Jupiter, in order to help us understand it. I said 'Sure!', even though up until this point I had never looked at any spacecraft data in my life... I barely knew anything about the project, but the research just grabbed me and that was that – I became a planetary scientist.

Through experience and time, I see now that I'm really good at managing people and bringing talent together to solve problems. I do this by stepping back from the details and looking at the bigger picture, which can be difficult – it's easy to get caught up in the finer detail. Today, the teams I assemble span many continents. The Jupiter mission, for example, involves 250 scientists and engineers from all over the globe.

YOU ARE SUCH A TRAILBLAZER, BUT WHO INSPIRES YOU?

When I was a kid, I got my first view of Jupiter and Saturn through a telescope that my dad had built in our back garden – he was such a positive influence on my interest in space and would be thrilled with the work I get to do now.

Another source of inspiration for me is a female colleague called Margaret Kivelson from UCLA who is over 90 years old. She led a team who sent a magnetometer instrument on a spacecraft called Galileo to Jupiter over 40 years ago. Margy is the trailblazer, really.

WHAT IS THE MOST IMPORTANT PIECE OF ADVICE YOU CAN GIVE ANYONE CONSIDERING A CAREER IN SPACE ENGINEERING?

I would advise everyone to say yes to things they don't actually know they can do. I have taken many chances in my career and it's been fun proving to myself and others that I can do things that people didn't think I could. When I say yes to things, I am often both scared and excited at the same time. In these situations, I really test myself to see what I am capable of and what always gets me through these challenges is my love of science and engineering, and my willingness to work really hard.

FACT FILE

Most fun thing about your job: All the interesting people that I get to work with.

CAREER HIGHLIGHTS

1. Being involved in the Ulysses spacecraft flyby of Jupiter.

2. Discovering the release of water vapour from Saturn's moon, Enceladus.

3. Being chosen as the Principal Investigator for the JUICE magnetometer instrument.

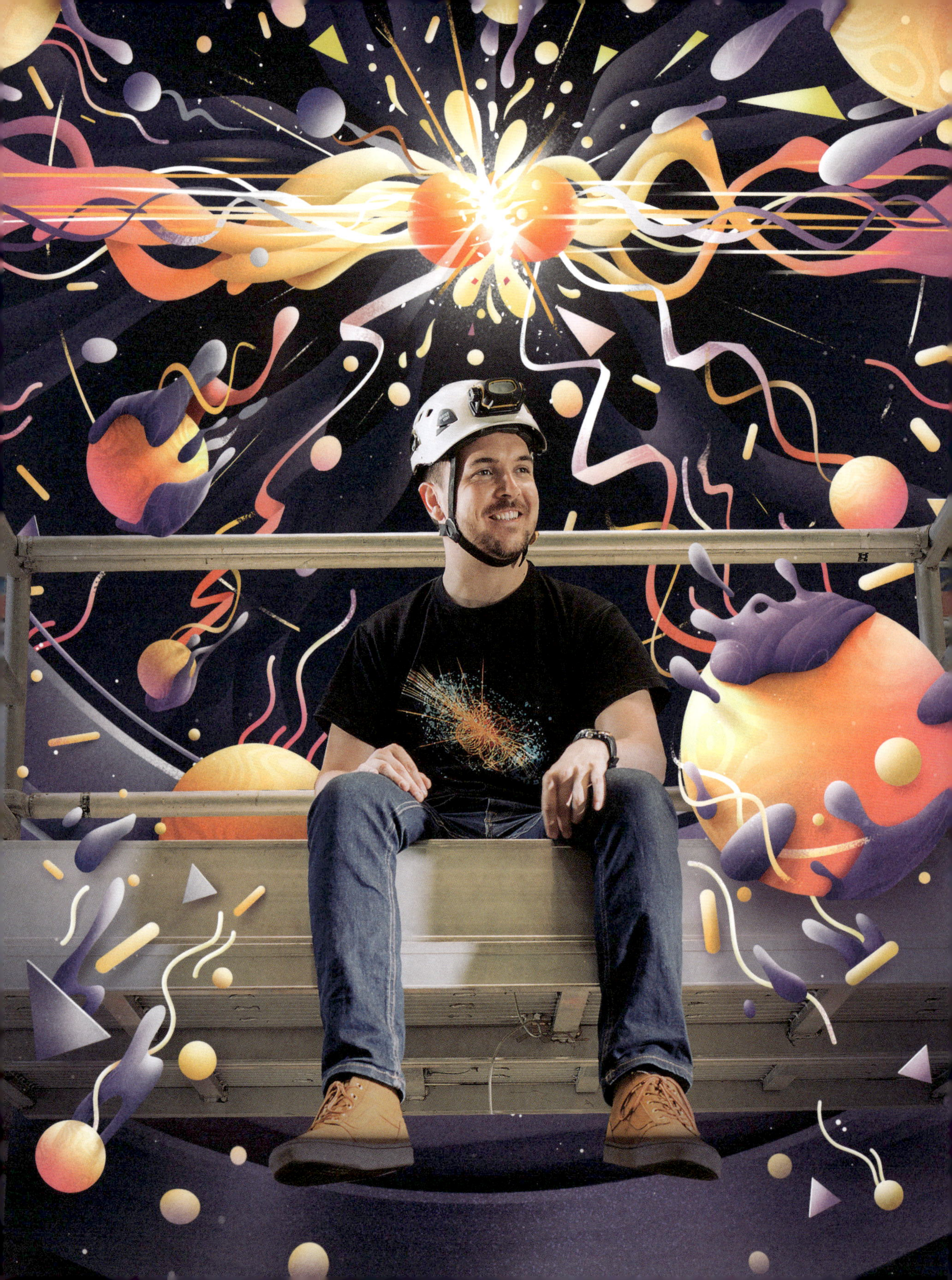

Jamie Pinnell

MECHANICAL ENGINEERING TECHNICIAN
SMASHING THROUGH THE SECRETS OF THE UNIVERSE

Scientists and engineers have come up with many different ways to explore how the universe started and how life on Earth began. One way is to try and unlock the secrets of the universe by studying its particles, which are very small pieces of energy or matter. To do this, they need some very powerful instruments, the largest and most complex of which is located at The European Organisation for Nuclear Research, also known as CERN.

CERN houses the Large Hadron Collider (LHC), a particle accelerator that is used to accelerate small particles to super-high speeds. The aim is to smash the particles together to reveal other particles that existed shortly after the Big Bang. The more powerful the accelerator, the faster the particles race and the more spectacular the collisions could be. Jamie Pinnell is one of many engineers working at CERN, building and upgrading the instruments there. He works to help collect and analyse scientific data on the fundamental particles that make up everything in our universe.

HOW DOES THE LARGE HADRON COLLIDER WORK?

The LHC is a circular track with a circumference of 27 kilometres – this gives the particles enough distance to reach high speeds. The particles travel in beams in opposite directions guided by powerful magnets and boosters. In order for the magnets to be powerful enough, they need to be kept at a super-cold temperature of −271.3°C, which is colder than outer space! The particles in the beams are squeezed together, and the beams are directed at one another with such great precision that it would be like firing two needles at each other from ten kilometres apart and having them hit point to point.

Thousands of scientists, technicians and engineers come from all over the world to use the LHC and the nine detector machines at CERN. Vast quantities of science data is produced here and shared with the rest of the world.

WHAT DOES YOUR JOB INVOLVE?

I work on the New Small Wheels, which are huge disc-shaped parts being installed to upgrade the ATLAS detector. Particles travelling at almost the speed of light in the LHC collide right in the centre of the ATLAS detector. When the particles smash together, the impact produces debris that contains brand-new particles. It's the job of ATLAS to detect and record these new particles.

My job at CERN is both amazing and challenging because of the sheer scale of everything. The experiment is situated 100 metres underground because we need a special, controlled environment. Energy from outer space that has entered our atmosphere and vibrations, noises and signals at ground level could all affect our equipment. I install, modify and improve ATLAS, which is a bit like working on the world's largest 'ship in a bottle'. Every component has to be passed down to us from ground level through a hole that is about half a tennis court wide so that we can construct it below ground. The whole ATLAS Experiment weighs as much as the metal frame of the Eiffel Tower, is half as tall as Nelson's Column and as wide as a whole tennis court. I use cranes and cherry pickers to move the large parts and construct the experiment. Precision is essential because the sensitive detectors can track individual particles across a cavern the size of a cathedral – I have to make sure everything fits together exactly.

HOW DID YOU GET TO THIS POINT IN YOUR CAREER?

I really enjoyed science and arts at school and often took things apart to understand how they worked. This trend continued through to A-level, when I took chemistry, physics and graphic design. My physics class visited the Rutherford Appleton Laboratory (RAL) in 2008 to see the newly built Diamond Light Source (DLS). DLS is a circular particle accelerator (called a synchrotron) that works like a giant microscope to study anything from fossils to jet engines, viruses and vaccines. Seeing the DLS sparked my interest in how physics labs function.

The Large Hadron Collider

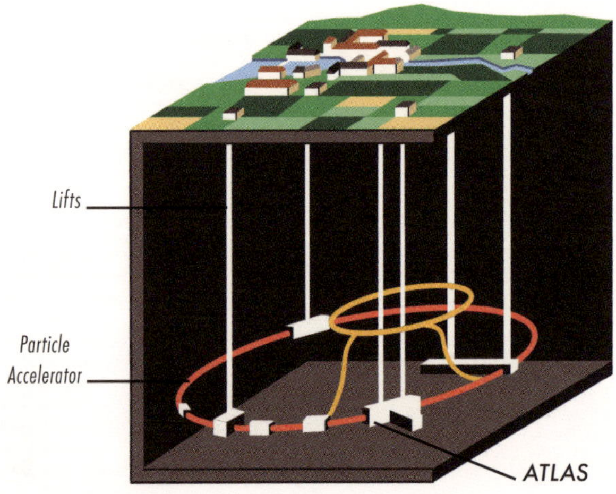

The particle accelerator

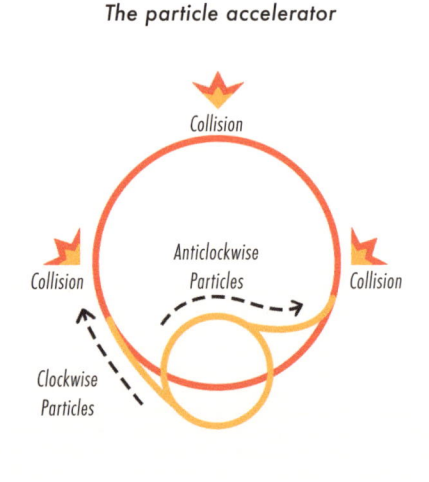

An apprenticeship opportunity came up at the laboratory in 2010 and I took a chance on a career in mechanical engineering that I knew nothing about. During my four-year apprenticeship, I tried working in a few different departments at RAL, which allowed me to find out who I really was as an engineering technician.

In my third and fourth years, I worked in Grenoble, France at the Institut Laue-Langevin (ILL) and European Synchrotron Radiation Facility (ESRF). This opened my eyes to living and working in an international environment.

WHAT GOT YOU TO THIS POINT IN YOUR CAREER?

I said yes to most things that I wasn't sure about: leaving home at 18 for an apprenticeship; presenting a show on engineering at RAL; giving a speech at the University of Oxford's Pitt Rivers Museum and leaving the UK to go to CERN. Each step has led to more opportunities, whether that is learning something new, making new contacts or helping someone else on their own career path. It's a joy to work for an organisation that is helping to expand the frontiers of human knowledge.

WHAT WOULD YOU DO DIFFERENTLY IN YOUR CAREER, WITH HINDSIGHT?

I don't think I would make any changes! I've made mistakes, I've broken tools, I've been in conflict with colleagues and I've doubted myself, like anyone in their careers. Each time was a learning experience and I came out as a stronger, better technician and person. Over ten years ago now, a senior technician once said to me 'I still haven't broken my last tap' – meaning that the mistakes he has made have not caused him to give up on his profession, and that he is still making mistakes and learning from them. This always acts as a reminder that I still have a lot of experience to gain in engineering, and that's exciting!

Jamie in front of one of the New Small Wheels.

FACT FILE

Most fun thing about your job: It's always changing – one day I'm 100 metres underground piloting giant machines, the next I'm in my office helping to design the next big thing in ATLAS.

CAREER HIGHLIGHTS

1. My first time seeing the blue glow in the nuclear reactor.

2. The first time I entered the ATLAS cavern, and the first full winter I spent working inside.

3. Watching seven years of hard work finally come together in the ATLAS cavern.

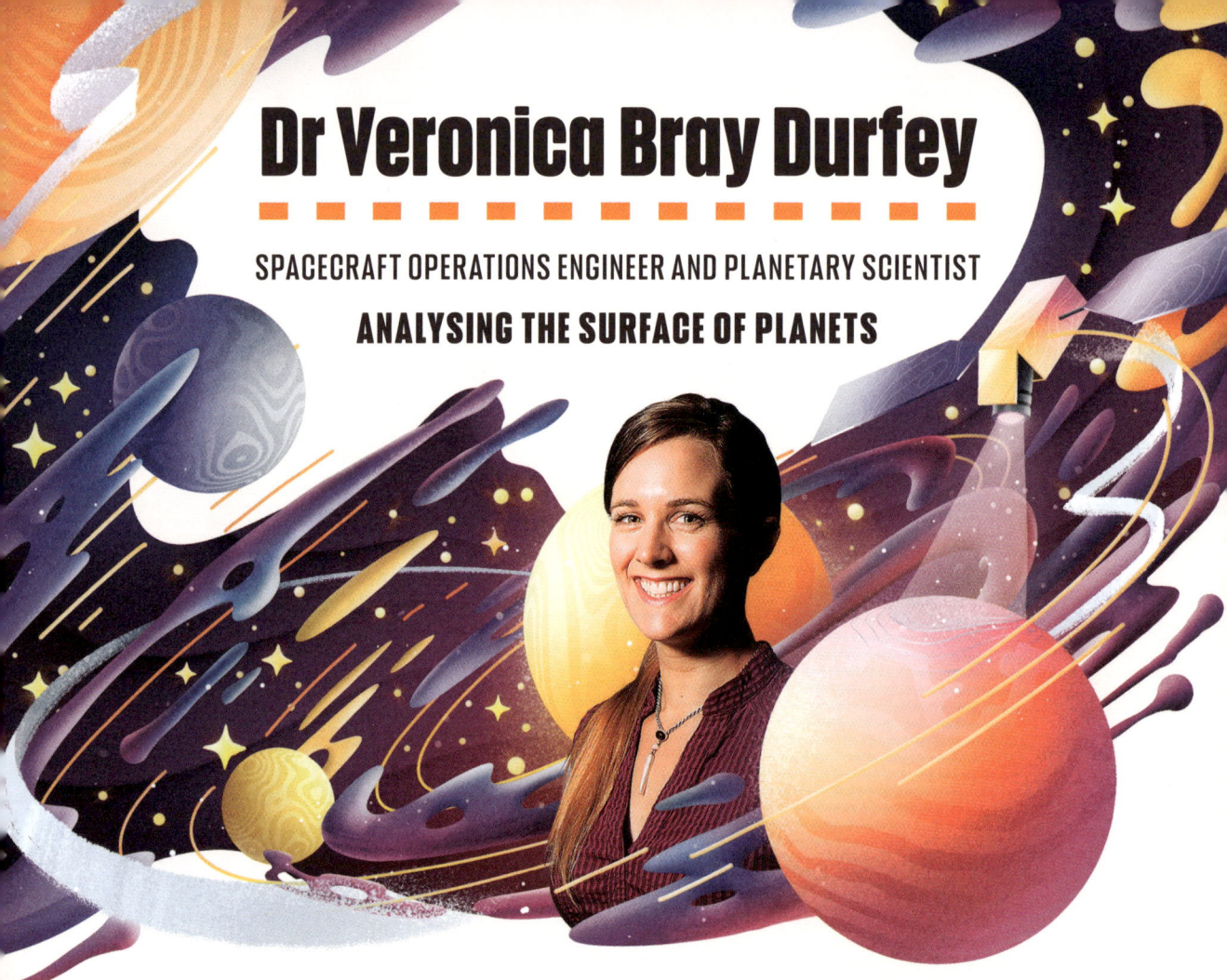

Dr Veronica Bray Durfey

SPACECRAFT OPERATIONS ENGINEER AND PLANETARY SCIENTIST
ANALYSING THE SURFACE OF PLANETS

When travelling beyond our planet, we need to know what to expect when we arrive at our far-away destination. In order for teams to know where to land, detailed images and other data are collected by spacecraft operations engineers and analysed by scientists before the journey begins. Dr Veronica Bray Durfey is one incredible person who can do both of these things.

WHAT DOES YOUR JOB INVOLVE?

I currently work as a Planetary Scientist and Spacecraft Operations Engineer with HiRISE, which is a camera on board the Mars Reconnaissance Orbiter (MRO). The MRO is a satellite orbiting Mars and it houses many instruments that record data about, and images of, the red planet. I plan what areas we want to take images of, and the images are often so detailed that we are able to see objects as small as a coffee table on the surface. They can even provide information about the minerals that can be found on Mars, all from 400 kilometres above the surface!

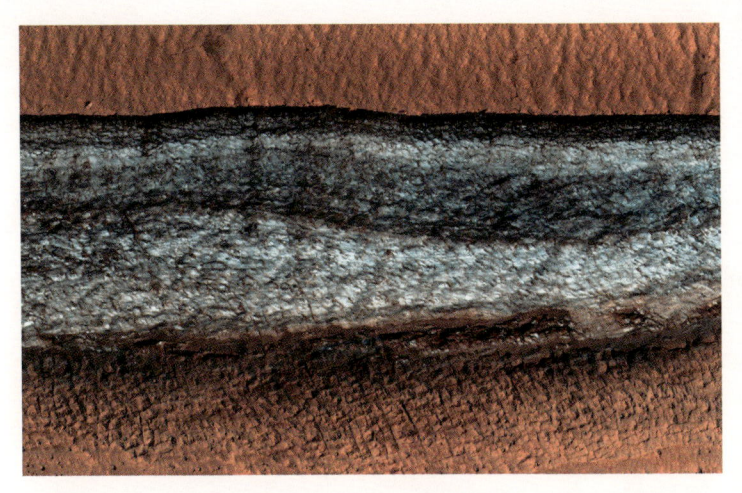

This image of Mars' surface was taken by the MRO in August 2022. It shows a cliff face that is covered in ice. There are currently a few dozen cliffs like this one that have been discovered so far on Mars.

FACT FILE

Most fun thing about your job: Seeing places on other planets and moons that no human has seen before!

CAREER HIGHLIGHTS

1. Being one of the first people to see Pluto with the New Horizons mission.

2. Discovering a new impact crater on Earth – the Nadir crater off the shore of West Africa.

3. Being bold and asking for a job role I wanted, which led to me using the HiRISE camera to photograph Mars landers!

One part of my job is to study asteroid and comet impacts that have happened on the surfaces of all different planetary bodies (not just Mars), which helps us to understand how the planets formed. I have worked with many different missions over my career, so now I'm able to spot subtle differences in a planet's surface. If I was to see a new image of Pluto, for example, I could call upon my knowledge of Mars, the Moon or Jupiter's moon, Europa, to help work out what we are seeing.

The other part of my job involves working with a team to achieve the scientific goals of a mission. This depends on the scientific instruments we choose to send to space to collect data. Our one major constraint is the weight of the instruments because we have to use as little energy as possible to get them into space. This limits the number of data storage devices and other technology that we can send. We are also challenged by extreme temperatures, radiation levels and the download speed of the data. It takes time for information from the spacecraft to reach us here on Earth and all of this needs to be taken into consideration. It is expensive to send anything to space, so the ideal solution is to find the lightest, lowest energy-consuming, smallest data-storage devices possible to be able to carry out the science once the spacecraft has reached its destination.

HOW DID YOU GET TO THIS POINT IN YOUR CAREER?

Since the age of six I've been fascinated with planets and minerals, so I love that I can work with both of these things. Today, I am so inspired by new images from the latest missions. They remind me that we haven't seen everything yet – there are always new places to explore and new questions to answer.

Watch This Space

THE ISS AND BEYOND Since 1998, the International Space Station (ISS) has been orbiting at around 408 kilometres above Earth. From Earth, the ISS looks like a star, but up close you can see that it's a feat of human engineering! Made up of different modules and powered by eight giant solar panels, the ISS is the largest orbiting laboratory ever built. Such a huge object couldn't be transported to space in one piece, so it was taken in bits and assembled there. The ISS is a brilliant example of how vehicles can not only be built in space but also upgraded and maintained there, paving the way for the possibility of other human habitats in space.

There are usually between three and seven crew members living and working aboard the ISS at all times, conducting experiments and ensuring everything is functioning correctly.

Space exploration is a fast-paced industry and, recently, huge leaps in space technology have been driven by a number of private companies, such as SpaceX, Blue Origin and Virgin Galactic. Previously, most space exploration was funded by governments. These companies have developed reusable rockets and launching components that can be assembled in space with the aim to make space travel more accessible and sustainable. The vision of humans living on other planets might not be as far away as we imagine!

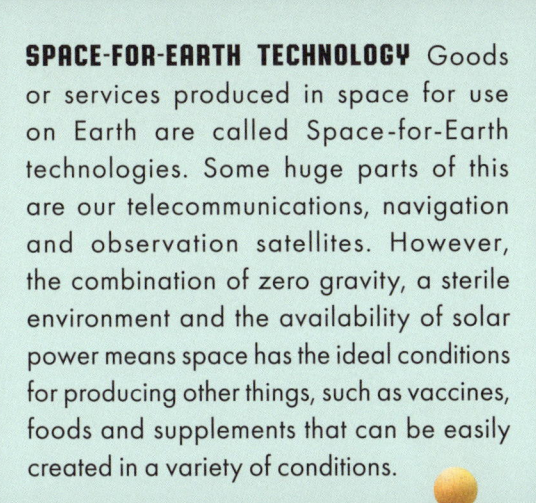

In the future, it might be possible to mine asteroids for useful resources.

MINING ASTEROIDS Of the thousands of asteroids in our solar system, many are known to contain important elements, including the precious metals platinum, iron and nickel. These are used in the production of everything from phones to cars, but there is only a limited supply here on Earth. This has led to the idea that asteroids could be mined so that the elements can be used either on Earth or in space. Any water mined from asteroids could also be used to support human life in space.

SPACE-FOR-EARTH TECHNOLOGY Goods or services produced in space for use on Earth are called Space-for-Earth technologies. Some huge parts of this are our telecommunications, navigation and observation satellites. However, the combination of zero gravity, a sterile environment and the availability of solar power means space has the ideal conditions for producing other things, such as vaccines, foods and supplements that can be easily created in a variety of conditions.

LITTER-PICKING IN SPACE Ever since humans first ventured into space, we've been leaving debris behind – everything from old satellites and parts of rockets to nuts and bolts. With more spacecraft leaving our atmosphere, it is becoming increasingly important to clear up this junk and avoid it causing a dangerous collision. Scientists and engineers are working on a range of solutions, and in 2021 launched a satellite that uses magnets to collect space junk. Another satellite with a giant litter-picking claw is currently in development.

Timeline of Engineering

Humans have been engineering useful things for millions of years. As our world changes, we continue to engineer creative solutions, but we must also aim to be more sustainable. This timeline highlights some key feats of engineering from prehistory to the present day. Each colour represents a different category as shown in the key below.

1700
Piano
Bartolomeo Cristofori invented the piano. It looked like a harpsichord, but instead of using a keyboard to activate the plucking of strings, the new instrument used a keyboard to activate hammers that hit the strings. While all harpsichord notes have the same loudness, a piano can go from quiet to loud.

3.3 MILLION YEARS AGO
The oldest stone tools
Early tools were created by using one stone to knock sharp shards off another. Each of the shards could then be used for cutting. The earliest examples were found in Kenya and date to a time before our species existed.

1608
Telescope
Although we don't know who invented the telescope, Dutch spectacle maker Hans Lippershey patented an instrument 'for seeing things far away as if they were nearby'. Galileo Galilei later improved the device and used it to observe the night sky.

TO THE DISTANT PAST — 5000 BCE — 200 BCE — 1600s

ABOUT 6500 BCE
Cement
Nabataean traders who lived in today's Syria and Jordan created waterproof cement by combining lime and silica. They used it for many things, such as to build houses and cisterns that collected rainwater in the desert.

ABOUT 3200 BCE
First wheeled vehicle
The earliest remains of a wheel that would have been used on a cart are from Slovenia and are dated to about 3200 BCE.

1738
Spinning machine
Until the 1740s, cotton thread was prepared by using a spinning wheel. Then Lewis Paul and John Wyatt patented the Roller Spinning machine and other systems to speed up fabric production.

FROM 312 BCE
Aqueducts
Over roughly a 500-year period the Roman empire built 485 miles of aqueducts. These were a series of pipes, canals and bridges that transported fresh water from mountains down to cities using gravity.

KEY TO TIMELINE COLOURS
- Human Needs
- Climate and Environment
- Powering Our Future
- Infrastructure and Construction
- Healthcare
- Advanced Materials
- Communication
- Smart Manufacturing
- Transportation
- Entertainment
- Robotics and Artificial Intelligence
- Exploring Beyond Our Planet

1769
Steam engine
Since the 17th century, people have been able to harness the power of steam and use it for jobs such as raising water from mines. In 1769, Scottish inventor James Watt greatly improved the technology and created an engine with parts that could stay at the temperature of the steam, rather than needing to be cooled and heated as previous engines did.

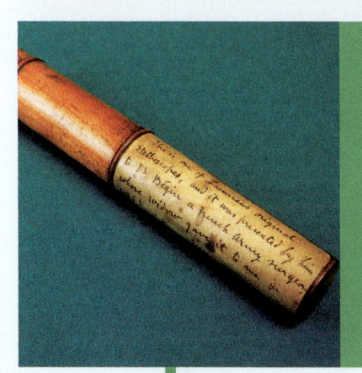

1886
First practical car
German inventor Carl Benz built the Benz Patent-Motorwagen with an internal combustion engine and wire wheels, like a bicycle's. It was fueled by petroleum ether, which drivers had to buy at a pharmacy because petrol stations did not yet exist.

1816
Stethoscope
French physician René Laënnec invented the stethoscope, a wooden tube that amplified sounds coming from a patient's lungs and heart. Previously, doctors would place their ears on patients' chests.

1876
Telephone
Scottish-born Canadian-American Alexander Graham Bell developed the first telephone by sending voice signals down a telegraph wire. He had a personal interest in sound technologies and communications because his mother and wife both had hearing loss.

1800s   **1840s**   **1880s**

1843
First computer program
Mathematician Ada Lovelace wrote the first computer program about 100 years before a computer existed. With her friend Charles Babbage, she also designed (but didn't build) a steam-powered computer called Analytical Engine.

1863
The first underground railway
This underground rail line went from Paddington to Farringdon in London and was hailed as an engineering success. It is still in use today. Initially, the trains were pulled by steam locomotives.

1783
Hot-air balloon
Invented by Joseph-Michel and Jacques-Étienne Montgolfier, the hot-air balloon was the first successful human-carrying flight technology.

1879
Electric lights for the home
Thomas Edison invented a cheap light bulb that lasted for many hours and could be used in the home. Then, he also invented a system to distribute electricity to power light bulbs and other appliances.

1887
First electricity-generating wind turbine
Professor James Blyth invented this special windmill in his garden in the UK. Since electricity generated by wind power was considered too expensive, nobody commercialised the technology until the 1980s.

1907
Plastic
Bakelite, the first fully synthetic plastic – produced with no natural substances – was invented by Belgian chemist Leo Baekeland. It could be moulded and was not expensive to make. It was advertised with the slogan 'The material of 1,000 uses' and at the time of Baekeland's death in 1944, it was used in 15,000 products.

1913
Assembly line
Henry Ford's first plant produced only 11 cars per month. So, Ford developed a moving assembly line where workers stood in one place. That sped up the line so much that a Model T car could be assembled in 90 minutes. This speed made the car so much cheaper to make that you didn't have to be rich to buy one.

1969
Moon landing
Neil Armstrong became the first human to set foot on the Moon. It tooks dozens of engineers nine years to design, build, and test the Apollo systems. Then, they watched as Apollo 11 safely travelled to the Moon, stayed in orbit while two of the astronauts took a separate lander to and from the Moon's surface and brought the three crew members home safely.

1890s — **1900s** — **1920s** — **1960s**

1903
First aeroplane
Wilbur and Orville Wright from Ohio, USA, invented the first aeroplane. In its first trial, it lifted from the ground for 12 seconds before landing with a thud 37 metres away. It then performed better and better, going further and further, launching the world into the aviation age.

1926
Television
John Logie Baird was the first to demonstrate a working television. Later, he made the first transatlantic TV transmission from the UK to the USA. The BBC began using his system for the first public television service in 1932.

1950
Tokamak
Andrei Sakharov and Igor Tamm proposed a way to generate energy from nuclear fusion, the same process that takes place inside the Sun. To do that, they suggested using a hollow doughnut-shaped reactor vessel called a tokamak.

1950
Turing test
Can a machine imitate human conversation perfectly? Can it fool people into believing it is human? This is the concept behind a test invented by Alan Turing for analysing machines' intelligence. No computer has passed it yet.

1982
Computer-aided design (CAD)
John Walker founded his company Autodesk and launched CAD software for the PC. This computer software allows users to design, in 2D and 3D, anything from a little marble to an entire city plan.

2020
Messenger RNA (mRNA) vaccines
Most vaccines include bacterial or viral proteins (or weakened bacteria or viruses), so our immune system can train against them. Instead, mRNA vaccines contain instructions for our body to create the bacterial or viral proteins. mRNA vaccines are quick to make, and work just as well as traditional vaccines. The first mRNA vaccines to be approved were used against COVID-19.

1996
Dolly the sheep
Scientists at The Roslin Institute in Scotland used a single adult cell from a sheep to produce a new sheep (named Dolly) that had the same DNA. This process is called cloning and has helped to study diseases and genetics.

2013
Lab-grown burgers
Food experts in London tasted the first lab-made beef burger created by Dutch Professor Mark Post and his team. They said it was 'close to meat, but not that juicy'. The burger was produced from cows' stem cells — cells that can develop into specialised cells. In this case, they were stimulated to develop into muscle cells. The meat we eat is animal muscle.

2016
Sophia
Developed by the Hong Kong-based company Hanson Robotics, Sophia is a social humanoid robot programmed to learn through interactions with humans. Sophia can take part in conversations and show 60 facial expressions.

1990s — **2000s** — **2020s** — **TO THE FUTURE**

1973
Mobile phone
Motorola manager Martin Cooper called his competitor Joel S. Engel, Head of Research at AT&T Bell Labs, while walking in New York City. The mobile phone he was using weighed more than one kilogram and was nearly the size of a shoebox.

1972
Landsat 1
Landsat 1 was the first satellite to focus on Earth. This type of satellite can detect changes that impact big areas of the planet — for example, the effect that bushfires in Australia have on air quality in the United States. They can also spot algae blooms in the ocean, which can be harmful to marine wildlife.

2010
Tallest building in the world
The Burj Khalifa in Dubai, UAE, was opened. At a breathtaking 828 metres tall, it holds several records, including being the building with the most floors in the world — it has 163.

2021
James Webb Space Telescope (JWST)
The JWST was launched into space. It can show us objects from further away in space than previous telescopes could and with more detail than ever before.

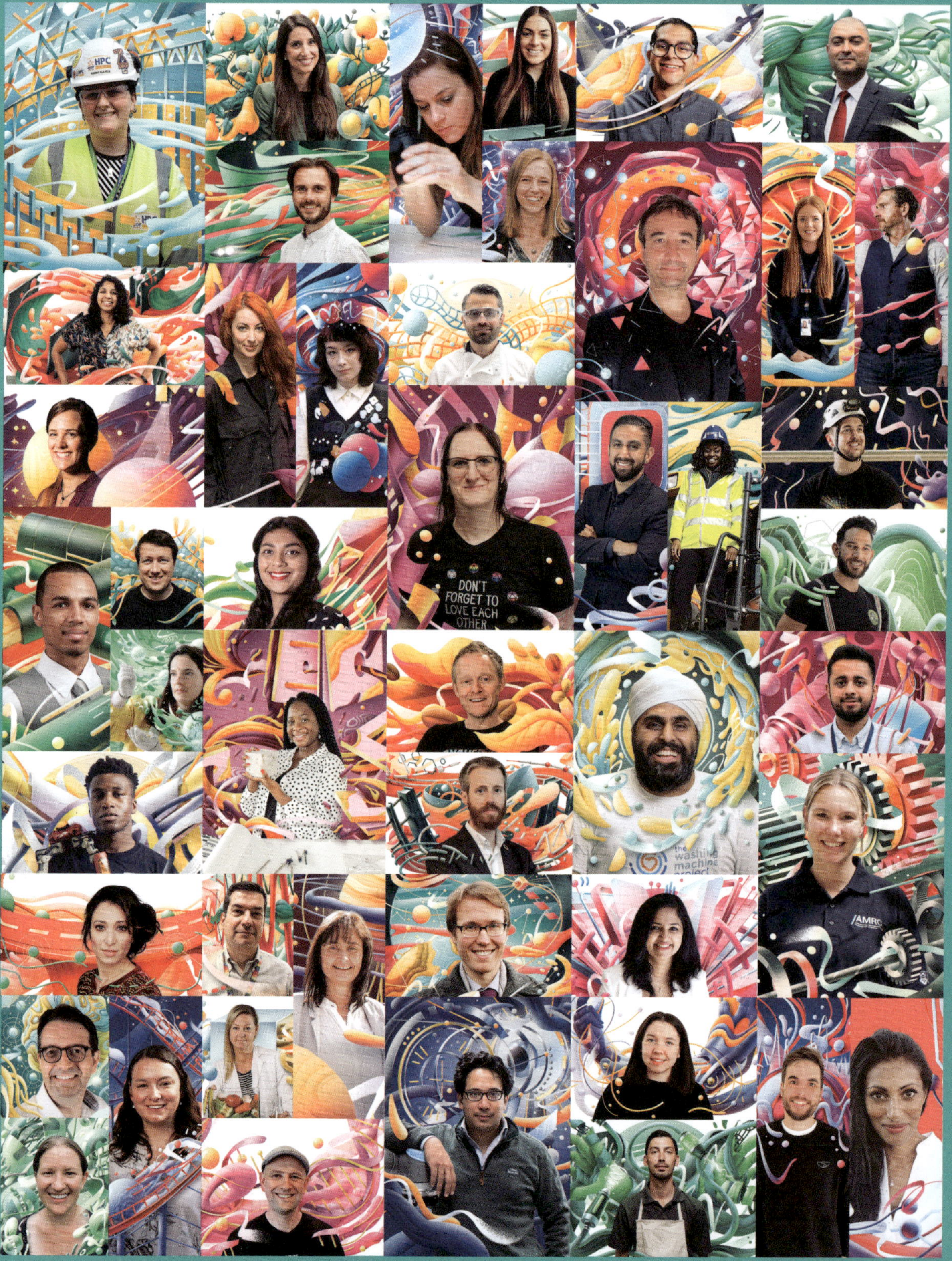
HPC
DON'T FORGET TO LOVE EACH OTHER
AMRC

A FINAL NOTE

It's been wonderful to meet engineers from all different backgrounds and walks of life. All the engineers in this book have inspired me because they have all pursued careers in areas of engineering that have been the most personally rewarding to them. It is also incredible how the work that they do has the potential to have a huge impact on the rest of the world. Engineering is all around us – and often we don't even notice it – but it really does make a difference.

In interviewing each and every engineer for this book, I was struck by their ambition and determination to develop the skills they need – even if they had to teach themselves and learn on the job. They enjoy going to work every morning because they care about what they do and it is clear that they are all proud of their work too. I continue to learn huge amounts from their innovation and creativity.

I hope I've shown you that anyone can be an engineer, no matter their background. Being good at maths and science is important, but it's not the only thing that matters. Being practical, creative and enjoying being hands-on are all signs you might love engineering. And as the field of engineering continues to evolve, it is clear that having good digital knowledge will arm you with one of the main skills needed to have a long and prosperous career.

If you are thinking about a career in this impactful profession, figure out what you are most interested in and what you are good at, and be open to the fact that things change and develop with time. Your career and your future is up to you. No one else can decide how your life will turn out. So, go, be your best self and don't let anything stand in the way of you fulfilling your greatest potential – you might just find that in engineering!

Glossary

academia The part of society that is related to studying, especially at university level.

academics Teachers or students in higher education, such as universities.

accreditation Getting approval or official recognition for reaching a certain standard.

aeronautical Relating to the design and construction of aircraft that operate within Earth's atmosphere.

aerospace Relating to the design and construction of aircraft that operate both inside and outside Earth's atmosphere.

agricultural The science and practice of farming; working with the land, growing crops and raising livestock.

algorithm A set of mathematical rules or instructions that a computer uses to make calculations or solve problems.

architect A trained professional who plans and designs buildings.

astronautical Something that is linked to the science and technology of space flight.

augmentation The process of making something larger, stronger or more effective.

autism A disability that affects how people communicate or interact with the world.

autonomous Something that is independent, for example, when a vehicle can control itself without the need of a human.

bespoke Specially made for someone and their needs.

biodegradable Something that can decompose naturally, ideally without causing any pollution.

bioenergy The energy produced from waste products of living materials, such as wood or plants. It is an example of renewable energy.

bioengineering Engineering solutions and technology for healthcare.

biological Connected to the science of biology – the study of living things.

blueprint A plan that maps out how something can be made or achieved.

capacity The maximum amount that something can hold or produce.

catalyst A person or event that acts as a trigger for change.

clinical Relating to medical treatment.

collaborate To work with someone or a group of people towards a common goal.

contractor A company or person who is hired to carry out specific work on a contract, or supply materials and people for a job.

cystic fibrosis An inherited condition that causes damage to the lungs and other organs through a build-up of sticky mucus.

decompose To decay or rot.

delegate To give out tasks and responsibility to others in order to get a job done.

demolishing The process of pulling down or completely destroying a building.

deployable Something that can be repositioned whenever and wherever it is needed.

diagnose To identify an illness or problem.

diagnostic Techniques used for identifying illnesses or problems.

digitisation To make something digital.

displacement When people are forced to leave a place where they usually live.

dispose To get rid of something, or throw it away.

durable Something that is strong and able to last a long time without much damage.

ecosystem The connected system between all living things in a certain area.

efficient Something that works very well with maximum productivity and little waste.

electromagnetic The electrical and magnetic forces or effects created by an electric current.

embankment Raised earth or stonework, which can protect against flooding.

entrepreneurship Being an entrepreneur – someone who has set up a business.

execution The way a plan is carried out.

feasibility How possible something might be to carry out.

fertiliser A product spread on land (such as manure or chemicals) to help plants grow.

fission Splitting apart atoms to create energy.

fossil fuels Substances, such as oil or gas, that were created underground out of plant and animal matter from millions of years ago. They are used to produce energy.

friction The force between two surfaces that creates tension and makes it hard for them to slide alongside each other.

fusion Joining atomic nuclei so that they fuse together and create energy.

geothermal Linked to the natural heat from within Earth.

global warming The steady rise in Earth's temperatures caused by an increase in carbon dioxide in the atmosphere.

greenhouse gases A collection of different gases, such as carbon dioxide and methane, that trap heat inside Earth's atmosphere and cause the planet to warm up.

habitable A place that is possible to live in.

hardware The physical parts of a computer or digital device, such as the wiring and machinery.

harmonious Working well together, in harmony.

high vis clothing Short for 'high visibility', protective clothing made of fluorescent material so that the wearer is seen.

hydraulic engineer A type of civil engineer who is focused on the flow of liquid, such as water or sewage.

industrially Using industrial processes to make something on a large scale.

industry A groups of businesses that create or sell similar things.

infrastructure A basic network of services, such as roads, power supplies or hospitals, that support modern human life.

ingenious Something that is very clever or inventive.

innovative Something that uses original and creative ideas.

insulin A chemical made in the body to control sugar in the blood, it is also produced in labs for people with diabetes whose bodies do not make enough.

integrate To combine, or blend, different things together.

interdisciplinary The combination of different areas or fields of study.

Internet of Things (IoT) Physical devices that are connected to each other via the internet and that share information with one another.

investor Someone who puts money into a project, usually to make a profit.

latency The delay that can occur when data is sent over the internet.

logistical (adj. of logistics) Related to planning or organising.

logistics All the elements needed to organise and make a plan work, such as people and equipment.

low Earth orbit (LEO) When something, such as a satellite, moves around Earth relatively close to the surface – normally at a height of less than 2,000 kilometres.

machine learning A method by which computers learn to carry out new tasks by processing lots of data rather than by being instructed by a human.

matter The stuff that makes up the observable universe.

microgravity A very small amount of gravity that can make people or objects appear to be weightless.

muscular dystrophy A set of inherited diseases that gradually weaken the muscles.

musculoskeletal The skeleton and muscles of the body, including joints and tendons.

nanoscale A scale of measurement that is extremely small – between one and 100 nanometres (one nanometre is one-billionth of a metre).

nanotechnology The science of creating or working with things at the nanoscale.

occupational therapist Someone who is trained to improve a patient's health by arranging activities that will support their recovery.

orthopaedic Relating to medicines and doctors that treat joints and bones.

orthotist A trained professional who fits braces and splints for patients.

pharmacology The study of medicine and its effect on different people.

philosophy A type of thinking that informs how we understand the world around us.

plasma The fourth state of matter (the others are solid, liquid and gas) that is present in most stars and can be used to create nuclear energy.

portfolio A collection of work that you have created that represents you and your interests.

prosthetic An artificial body part, such as an implant or limb.

prosthetist A trained professional who fits artificial body parts, such as limbs, for patients.

prototype A model that can be used to test a design.

radiation Energy that moves from one place to another in the form of particles or electromagnetic waves – some types, such as nuclear radiation, can be very dangerous.

radioactive Something that contains dangerous energy.

regenerative medicine Medical treatments that help regrow, repair or replace damaged cells.

renewable Something that can be replaced easily – renewable energy includes wind or solar energy.

reservoir A human-made lake used as a water source.

resilient Strong – able to withstand difficulties.

sanitation Structures providing cleanliness for public health.

seismic Connected to the vibrations of Earth – linked to earthquakes.

sickle cell anaemia A disorder that causes a person's red blood cells to become curved. It can cause problems, such as blocking blood vessels.

simulation A mathematical model that is usually created on a computer and that can predict the behaviour of a real-world experiment.

single-molecule biophysics The study of the interactions between individual molecules that occur naturally in living organisms to understand how they carry out their functions.

slurry A watery mixture of solids and liquids, such as mud and animal dung.

social science The study of people, cultures and history.

software Part of a computer that is not physical – the instructions or programs.

start-up (company) A very new company that aims to create new products.

stem cell A young cell that has not yet specialised, meaning that it has the potential to be turned into whatever cell type is needed (specialised cells include hair cells and skin cells).

stereotype A simplified image or group of characteristics that people think represents a person or group of people.

subsystem A system that works within a larger one.

superconductor A material that is able to conduct electricity without resistance under certain conditions.

sustainable Something that can continue at the same level for a long period of time.

sustained Something that keeps going at a continuous level.

telecommunications The technology used to send and receive messages over long distances.

variables A set of factors or quantities that, when changed, can affect the end result of something, such as a scientific experiment.

Index

3D graphene 113
3D printing 81, 93, 133, 139, 189
5G 127, 128, 129, 131, 181

A

ABSL Space Products 118
Advanced Manufacturing Research Centre (AMRC) 135–137, 145
aerographene 112
aerographite 113
Aeropowder 109–110
Aerospace engineering 10, 17, 156–157
agricultural engineering 20–21, 87
antennas 115, 117–119
ARM 75
artificial intelligence (AI) 11, 58, 75, 79, 87, 92, 119, 125, 133, 149, 167, 175, 177, 181–193, 211
Arup 65
ATLAS detector 201–202, 203
augmented reality (AR) 127, 128, 149, 175, 178, 181
Awarri 183

B

bacteria 38–39, 45, 97, 107
BAE Systems 156, 157
battery technology 162–163
BBC 117, 121–122, 123, 191
biodegradable packaging 36, 37
biomass 38–39
bioreactor 27
biosensors 89, 90
Blue Origin 207
brains 79, 186, 187, 193
bridge construction 75, 100–101
British Association of Prosthetics and Orthotics 81
British Telecom (BT) 42
broadcasting 121–123, 130
Building Integrated Modelling (BIM) 76

C

carbon 112–113, 118
carbon dioxide (CO_2) 29, 30–31, 33, 38, 47, 67, 99, 163
carbon emissions 30, 33, 45, 61, 66, 67, 99, 162, 163

carbon nanotubes 113
cars 59, 75, 144, 151, 159–161, 163, 185
Cassini (spacecraft) 197
Central Processing Unit (CPU) 74, 75
CERN (European Organisation for Nuclear Research) 49, 65, 201–203
Chessington World of Adventures Resort 176, 177
chicken feathers 109–111
climate change 9, 15, 23, 29, 38, 39, 47, 51, 73, 107, 179
clothes washing 17–19
clothing 30, 106
CNC (computer numerical control) machines 147
coffee 146, 147
computer-aided design (CAD) software 66, 123, 135, 144, 147, 159
computer-aided manufacturing (CAM) 135
computers 73, 75, 85, 139, 144–145, 185–187
concrete 23, 64, 66, 77, 99–101
COVID-19 pandemic 9, 95, 191
CRISPR 94, 95

D

Dale Power Solutions 53, 54, 55
Department of Trade and Industry 42
diamond 112
Diamond Light Source (DLS) 202
DNA 94, 95, 106, 107
drones 9, 44–45
Dyson School of Design Engineering 111

E

earthquake-proof technologies 69–71
electric vehicles 59, 113, 162–163
electricity 18, 29, 31, 33, 34–35, 39, 51, 54, 113, 117, 133, 163, 167
Engineering Development Trust 25, 65
Engineers Without Borders 17–18, 65
Environment Agency 23, 34
escalators 154, 155

Extended reality (XR) 179

F

factories, smart 148–149
Fairbrics 31
farmers 15, 39, 44, 45
farm-free products 26–27
fashion industry 30–31, 106, 107, 169
fibre-optic cables 115, 118
Firefly Creations 175–177
flight systems 156–157
flood risk management 23–25, 64–65
food storing 20–21
fossil fuels 29, 33, 38, 39, 47, 57, 61

G

Gagosian Gallery 168, 169
Galileo (spacecraft) 199
gallium nitride (GaN) devices 125
gaming 179, 182
Ganymede (moon) 197, 198
Gateway Earth project 139–140
gene therapy 90
genetic engineering 94–95
Global Positioning Systems (GPS) 151
graphene 163
graphite 112, 113

H

H2GO Power 57, 58, 59
haptic gloves 128, 129
Headstart Scheme 65
hearing aids 127
Hinkley Point C (nuclear power station) 33, 34–35
hips, artificial 84, 87
HiRISE 204
holographic glasses 128
HS2 (High Speed 2) 76
hybrid vehicles 59, 162

hydrogen batteries 57, 58
hydrogen 50, 57, 58, 61

I

Imperial College London 37, 89, 93, 106, 107, 109, 171, 172, 173, 185, 187, 199

Industrial Revolution 133, 137, 139, 148
Industry 4.0 133, 148, 181
Institute of Biomedical Engineering (Imperial College) 89
International Space Station (ISS) 206
internet 115, 124, 127, 128, 130–131, 148–149
Internet of Skills (IoS) 127–129
Internet of Things (IoT) 127, 128, 133, 148, 167

J
Jaguar Land Rover (JLR) 57, 58, 59, 161
jet engines 143–144
Joint European Torus (JET) 50, 51, 61
JUICE (spacecraft) 197–199
Jupiter mission 197–199

K
King's College London 128
knees, artificial 84

L
Large Hadron Collider (LHC) 49, 65, 201–203
LEGO 7, 37, 71, 107, 187
Li-Fi (Light Fidelity) 131
limbs, artificial 80–81, 92

M
Maglev Trains 103
MRI machines 79, 103
magnetometer (MAG) 197, 199
Mars 204–205
meat, lab-grown 26–27
MGR Foamtex Ltd 157
Mixed Reality (MR) 178
MMC (Modern Methods of Construction) 76–77
Moon, the 178, 197, 205, 210
music technology 171–173

N
nanomedicines 90–91
NASA 119, 131
National Physical Laboratory (NPL) 190–191
National Vocational Qualifications (NVQs) 12, 81
New Small Wheels 201–202, 203
NHS 83, 84, 86
NoProbLemo (robot) 191
Notpla 36, 37

nuclear energy 49–51, 60–61
nuclear fusion reactors 60–61, 103, 105, 210
nuclear power stations 33, 34–35, 60–61

O
Ooho 36, 37
Orthopaedic Research UK 86–87
orthotics 80–81
Oxford Space Systems 117, 118

P
packaging 20–21, 36–37, 83, 84, 109–111
plasma 50–51, 60, 61
prosthetics 80–81, 87, 92–93, 188–189

Q
quantum computer 103, 104–105
quantum dots 113

R
railways 10, 11, 76, 77, 100, 153, 154, 175, 176
Reach Industries 183
regenerative medicine 89–90
reinforcement learning 185–187, 193
robotic surgery 127, 128
robotics 57, 79, 92, 133, 181–193
Rolls-Royce aerospace 143–144
Rutherford Appleton Laboratory (RAL) 202–203

S
Satellite Vu 41, 42, 43
satellites 41–43, 45, 115, 118–119, 130–131, 139–140, 151, 195, 204, 207
sensors 41, 44, 45, 75, 83, 87, 131, 149, 151, 168, 181, 188, 192
silicon computer chips 113
Sky (television channel) 121, 122, 123
smartphones 74, 75, 103, 124, 127, 129, 178
solar technology 31, 113, 163, 191, 206
space exploration 195–207
Space Innovations Ltd 118
space station 139–140
space travel 151, 206–207
SpaceX 207

SPARTA (Single Particle Automated Raman Trapping Analysis) 90–91
SpinLaunch 131
Sun, the 49, 61
superconductors 103, 104, 105
Surrey Satellite Technology Ltd 41
sustainable construction 66–67
Swell X 147
synthetic biology 106–107
systems integration 57, 58

T
televisions 113, 117, 121, 210
Tempest (fighter jet) 156, 157
theme parks 175–177
thin films 103–105
TikTok 171, 173
tokamak 60, 61, 105, 210
Transport for London (TfL) 153, 154

U
UK Atomic Energy Authority (UKAEA) 50–51
Unhindr 92, 93
University of Bristol 71
University of Sheffield 135, 137
UPS systems (uninterruptible power supplies) 53–55
UtterBerry 75

V
video games 182, 183
Virgin Galactic 207
virtual reality (VR) 175, 178

W
Washing Machine Project, The 17–19
waste management 38–39, 109, 110, 111
Waterman Group 72, 73
wave power 193
Wi-Fi 131
wireless technology 74–75, 115, 130–131
WISE (Women In Science and Engineering) 25
World Wide Web 127
Worldsensing 128, 129
WSP 176

Y
YouTube 123

Selected Sources

This book was developed through extensive research and interviews with the engineers that we have featured. It's not possible to list every source that we've used, but here are a few that might be useful.

General sources
www.thisisengineering.org.uk
www.imperial.ac.uk/engineering
www.technicians.org.uk

P. 16–19 **Navjot Sawhney**
www.thewashingmachineproject.org
www.prakti.in

P. 20–21 **Dr Natalia Falagán Sama**
www.cranfield.ac.uk/people/dr-natalia-falagan-sama-15328916

P. 22–25 **Ayo Sokale**
www.ayosokale.com
www.ice.org.uk/what-is-civil-engineering/who-are-civil-engineers/ayo-sokale

P. 26–27 **Farm-Free**
www.theguardian.com/science/2013/aug/05/world-first-synthetic-hamburger-mouth-feel

P. 30–31 **Dr Benoît Illy**
fairbrics.co

P. 32–35 **Anna Gates**
www.niauk.org/industry/people-in-nuclear/national-apprenticeship-week-2022
www.edfenergy.com/energy/nuclear-new-build-projects/hinkley-point-c

P. 36–37 **Pierre Paslier**
www.notpla.com

P. 38–39 **Dr Lynsey Melville**
www.bcu.ac.uk/engineering/about-us/our-staff/lynsey-melville
www.nrel.gov/research/re-biomass.html

P. 40–43 **Anthony Baker**
www.satellitevu.com
www.sstl.co.uk/media-hub/latest-news/2022/mwir-constellation-satvu

P. 44–45 **Drones**
www.eea.europa.eu/publications/delivery-drones-and-the-environment

P. 48–51 **Katriya Sabin**
www.gov.uk/government/organisations/uk-atomic-energy-authority
www.bbc.co.uk/news/science-environment-60312633

P. 52–55 **Samantha Magowan**
www.dalepowersolutions.com

P. 56–59 **Manjot Chana**
www.h2gopower.com

P. 60–61 **Nuclear Power**
www.world-nuclear.org/information-library/economic-aspects/economics-of-nuclear-power.aspx
www.energy.gov/science/office-science
search: 'DOE Explains…Tokamaks'

P. 64–65 **Malithi (Milly) Hennayake**
www.arup.com/our-firm/milly-hennayake

P. 66–67 **Will Arnold**
www.arup.com/our-firm/will-arnold
www.rica.rw

P. 68–71 **Professor Anastasios Sextos**
www.bristol.ac.uk/people/person/Anastasios-Sextos-f7d6d9aa-632d-45de-b2eb-3ea95fbdadf0

P. 72–73 **Georgia Lilley**
www.watermangroup.com/careers/georgia-lilley

P. 74–75 **Heba Bevan**
utterberry.com/about
www.womenoftheyear.co.uk/team/heba-bevan-obe

P. 76–77 **Building with MMC**
www.global.royalhaskoningdhv.com/digital/resources/blogs/bim-and-digital-twins
ww3.rics.org/uk/en/modus/built-environment/construction/why-2020-is-the-year-of-modular.html
www.hs2.org.uk

P. 80–81 **Alan James Proud**
www.youthemployment.org.uk/alan-prouds-engineering-apprenticeship-led-him-to-improve-the-lives-of-people-with-disabilities

P. 82–85 **Dr Samantha Micklewright**
www.neonfutures.org.uk/case-study/biomedical-engineer-samantha-micklewright

P. 86–87 **Dr Arash Angadji**
www.oruk.org

P. 88–91 **Professor Molly Stevens**
www.stevensgroup.org
www.imperial.ac.uk/people/m.stevens

P. 92–93 **Dr Uğur Tanrıverdi**
www.imperial.ac.uk/alumni/alumni-stories/ugur-tanriverdi
www.unhindr.com

P. 94–95 **Engineering Genes**
www.theguardian.com search: 'Scientists create tomatoes genetically edited to bolster vitamin D levels'
www.nationalgeographic.com/science/article/can-a-laugh-be-inherited--how-genes-define-who-we-are

P. 98–101 **Mimi Nwosu**
www.port.ac.uk/student-life/student-stories/mimi-nwosu-beng-civil-engineering
www.hs2.org.uk/building-hs2/viaducts-and-bridges/colne-valley-viaduct

P. 102–105 **Dr Clara Michelle Barker**
edu.admin.ox.ac.uk/people/dr-clara-barker
www.energy.gov/science/office-science
search: 'DOE Explains…Superconductivity'

P. 106–107 **Professor Tom Ellis**
www.imperial.ac.uk/people/t.ellis
www.genome.gov/about-genomics/policy-issues/Synthetic-Biology
www.imperial.ac.uk/news/238531/fashion-industry-collaboration-create-lab-grown

P. 108–111 **Dr Elena Dieckmann**
www.imperial.ac.uk/people/elena.dieckmann13
www.aeropowder.com/about-us

P. 112–113 **Super Carbon**
www.britannica.com/science/carbon-nanotube

P. 116–119 **Mike Lawton**
oxford.space
www.esa.int/Enabling_Support/Space_Engineering_Technology/Origami_antenna_springs_up_for_small_satellites

P. 120–123 **Jahangir Shah**
www.thisisengineering.org.uk/meet-the-engineers/jahangir

P. 124–125 **Dr Nikita Hari**
nikitahari.com

P. 126–129 **Professor Mischa Dohler**
www.worldsensing.com
mischadohler.com/about

P. 130–131 **Staying Connected**
www.spinlaunch.com
lifi.co/what-is-lifi
www.esa.int/ESA_Multimedia/Images/2020/03/Low_Earth_orbit

P. 134–137 **Bethany Cousins**
amrctraining.co.uk/news/bethany-cousins
www.youtube.com/watch?v=EefFxEGVbWo
'Machining of internal gear – Power skiving'

P. 138–141 **Dr Matjaz Vidmar**
www.eng.ed.ac.uk/about/people/dr-matjaz-vidmar
www.gatewayearth.space

P. 142–145 **Kate Todd-Davis**
amrctraining.co.uk/news/apprentice-of-the-year-2021
santapod.co.uk
www.standishengineering.co.uk/blog/what-is-the-difference-between-milling-and-turning

P. 146–147 **Neil Glover**
figmentcoffee.com/about-us/about
www.swell-x.com

P. 148–149 **Factories of the Future**
www.epicor.com/en-uk/blog/what-is-industry-4-0

P. 152–155 **Sonny Kombo**
careerfinder.ucas.com/article/interview-with-sonny-kombo-graduate-at-tfl
education.nationalgeographic.org/resource/geographic-information-system-gis

P. 156–157 **Krystina Pearson-Rampeearee**
www.britishscienceweek.org/smashing-stereotypes-krystina-pearson-rampeearee
www.baesystems.com/en/home

P. 158–161 **Todd Downs**
www.thisisengineering.org.uk/meet-the-engineers/todd
www.astonmartin.com/en-gb/models/past-models/db9
www.jaguarlandrover.com

P. 162–163 **Battery-Powered Transport**
www.tesla.com/en_gb/supercharger
www.tesla.com/en_gb/powerwall
www.reuters.com/business/autos-transportation/solid-state-ev-batteries-could-cut-carbon-emissions-further-says-climate-group-2022-07-18

P. 166–169 **Pavlina Akritas**
www.arup.com/our-firm/pavlina-akritas
gagosian.com/locations/london-grosvenor-hill

P. 170–173 **Dr David Trevelyan**
www.thisisengineering.org.uk/meet-the-engineers/david

P. 174–177 **Michelle Hicks**
www.thisisengineering.org.uk/meet-the-engineers/michelle
www.fireflycreations.uk

P. 178–179 **Extending Our Reality**
www.smithsonianmag.com/innovation/how-virtual-reality-can-help-us-feel-pain-climate-change-180960918/

P. 182–183 **Silas Adekunle**
www.lumi.systems

P. 184–187 **Professor Aldo Faisal**
faisallab.org/members/aldo-faisal
www.imperial.ac.uk/people/a.faisal

P. 188–189 **Jennifer Olsen**
www.youtube.com/watch?v=1CtKQhws94Q&t=65s
'Jenny Olsen – Biomedical Engineer'

P. 190–191 **Joshua Schofield**
www.npl.co.uk/press-media/scientists-at-npl-create-low-cost-ventilator

P. 192–193 **Machines with Brains**
www.whoi.edu/what-we-do/explore/underwater-vehicles/auvs/orpheus
www.neurotwin.eu
www.carnegiece.com/ceto-technology

P. 196–199 **Professor Michele Dougherty**
www.imperial.ac.uk/people/m.dougherty
solarsystem.nasa.gov/people/1200/michele-dougherty
sci.esa.int/web/juice/-/59905-juice-s-primary-target-ganymede
solarsystem.nasa.gov/missions/cassini/overview

P. 200–203 **Jamie Pinnell**
www.technicians.org.uk
www.exploreyouruniverse.org/scientist/jamie-pinnell
www.home.cern/science/accelerators/large-hadron-collider
www.ukri.org/about-us/stfc/locations/rutherford-appleton-laboratory

P. 204–205 **Dr Veronica Bray Durfey**
veronicabray.com
mars.nasa.gov/mro/mission/instruments/hirise
mars.nasa.gov/mro

P. 206–207 **Watch This Space**
www.spacex.com
www.blueorigin.com
www.virgingalactic.com
spacecenter.org/nasa-vaccine-research-in-microgravity
asteroidminingcorporation.co.uk

Picture Credits

The publisher would like to thank the following for permission to reproduce their photographs. While every effort has been made to credit images, the publisher apologises for any errors or omissions and will be pleased to make any necessary corrections in future editions of the book.

Key: top (**t**), bottom (**b**), left (**l**), right (**r**), centre (**c**).

P. 8 Dr Shini Somara; **P. 14** Jiraroj Praditcharoenkul/Alamy; **P. 16** The Washing Machine Project; **P. 18** John Cairns/Alamy; **P. 20** Cranfield University; **P. 22** Ayo Sokale; **P. 26** robertsre/iStockphoto; **P. 28** Fred Tanneau/AFP/Getty Images; **P. 30** Maan Al Jurdi; **P. 32** EDF; **P. 34** EDF; **P. 36 t** Ursus Productions; **b** David Lineton/Ooho; **P. 38** Peter Medlicott; **P. 40** Polly Sheldon; **P. 42 t** Google Maps; **c** Satellite Vu; **P. 43** Satellite Vu; **P. 44–45 t** Kwangmoozaa/Shutterstock; **P. 44 b** VCG/Getty Images; **P. 45 c** Zapp2Photo/Shutterstock; **P. 46** timandtim/Getty Images; **P. 48** Shauna Ward; **P. 50** CEA-IRFM/EUROfusion/ZUMA Press Wire/Shutterstock; **P. 52** Andy Towse; **P. 54** Reggie Lavoie Shutterstock; **P. 56** Peter Italiano; **P. 60–61 c** goktugg/iStockphoto; **P. 60 b** Bloomberg /Getty Images; **P. 61 t** Twin Design/Shutterstock; **P. 62** Sean Pavone/Alamy; **P. 64** This is Engineering; **P. 66** Neil Wood-Mitchell; **P. 67** Iwan Baan; **P. 68** Ursus Productions; **P. 72** Ursus Productions; **P. 74** Heba Bevan; **P. 76** Chris Gorman/Getty Images; **P. 77 t** vipman/Shutterstock; **b** Maja Hitij/Getty Images; **P 78** Callista Images/Getty Images; **P. 80** This is Engineering; **P. 82** Tom Micklewright; **P. 84** Dr Samantha Micklewright; **P. 86** Mohamad Ali Asadi; **P. 88** Jo Mieszkowsi, Imperial College London; **P. 92** Jason Alden, Imperial College London; **P. 94–95 t/b** Andy/iStockphoto; **P. 95 c** Explode/Shutterstock; **P. 96** Benjamin Schmuck; **P. 98** Mimi Nwosu; **P. 100** Copyright HS2 Ltd; **P. 102** Ursus Productions; **P. 106** Professor Tom Ellis; **P. 108** Thomas Angus, Imperial College London; **P. 112–113 t/b** Harper 3D/Shutterstock; **P. 112 b** Imaginechina Limited/Alamy; **P. 113 c** VCG/Getty Images; **P. 114** Lucian Coman/Shutterstock; **P. 116** Innovate UK; **P. 120** This is Engineering; **P. 121** Hufton+Crow-VIEW/Alamy; **P. 124** Dr Nikita Hari; **P. 126** Professor Mischa Dohler; **P. 130** NicoElNino/Shutterstock; **P. 131 t** SpinLaunch; **b** Maxiphoto/iStockphoto; **P. 132** Nataliya Hora/Shutterstock; **P. 134** Chloe West; **P. 138** Dr Matjaz Vidmar; **P. 142** Jonathan Brent; **P. 146** Neil Glover/Figment Coffee; **P. 149** AlexLMX/iStockphoto; **P. 150** Great North Air Ambulance/ Stuart Boulton; **P. 152** Rare Recruitment; **P. 156** BAE Systems; **P. 157** BAE Systems; **P. 158** Lalita Ajit; **P. 160** Jaguar Land Rover Limited; **P. 163 t** Sjo/iStockphoto; **b** jullasart somdok/iStockphoto; **P. 164** teamLab, Forest of Resonating Lamps – One Stroke © teamLab; **P. 166** This is Engineering; **P. 169** Joseph Asghar; **P. 170** Nadia Mokhlesi; **P. 174** This is Engineering; **P. 176** Copyright Firefly Creations Ltd; **P. 178** Gorodenkoff/Shutterstock; **P. 179 t** aldomurillo/iStockphoto; **c** vectorfusionart/Shutterstock; **P. 180** Wyss Institute at Harvard University; **P. 182** Silas Adekunle; **P. 184** Thomas Angus, Imperial College London; **P. 186** Thomas Angus, Imperial College London; **P. 188** Jennifer Olsen; **P. 190** Ursus Productions; **P. 193 tl** Andriy Onufriyenko/Getty Images; **tr** Carnegie Wave Energy Limited; **P. 194** NASA/KSC/Rocket Lab/Trevor Mahlmann; **P. 196** Thomas Angus, Imperial College London; **P. 198** ESA/ATG medialab, NASA/ESA/J. Nichols, NASA/JPL; **P. 200** Leonora Saunders, Courtesy of The Gatsby Foundation; **P. 203** Jamie Pinnell; **P. 204** Kenneth Sterns; **P. 205** NASA/JPL-Caltech/University of Arizona; **P. 206–207 c** Virgin Galactic; **P. 206** NASA/MSFC; **P. 207** Raymond Cassel/Shutterstock; **P. 208 tl** Kenneth Garrett/Danita Delimont/Alamy; **tr** (Telescope) Bettmann/Getty Images; **br** Prisma by Dukas/Getty Images; **P. 209 tl** Science & Society Picture Library/Getty Images; **bl** (First computer program) Science & Society Picture Library/Getty Images; **bl** (Hot-air balloon) Ann Ronan Picture Library/Heritage-Images/Alamy; **br** Science & Society Picture Library/Getty Images; **P. 210 tr** NASA; **bl** GL Archive/Alamy; **P. 211 bl** Leonid Andronov/Alamy; **br** NASA; **P. 212** For all images, please see credit on engineer's profile page.